Dawning
of the
Pagan Moon

Dawning
of the
Pagan Moon

DAVID BURNETT

OLIVER
NELSON

THOMAS NELSON PUBLISHERS
Nashville

Published in Nashville, Tennessee, by Oliver-Nelson Books, a division
of Thomas Nelson, Inc., Publishers, and distributed in Canada
by Lawson Falle, Ltd., Cambridge, Ontario.

This edition issued by special arrangement with Monarch Publications,
1 St. Anne's Road, Eastbourne, East Sussex, BN21 3UN, England.

Unless otherwise noted, the Bible version used in this publication is
THE NEW KING JAMES VERSION. Copyright © 1979, 1980,
1982, Thomas Nelson, Inc., Publishers.

Library of Congress Cataloging-in-Publication Data

Burnett, David, 1943–
    Dawning of the pagan moon / David Burnett.
       p.   cm.
    Includes index.
    ISBN 0-8407-9644-7 (pbk.)
    1. Occultism—Religious aspects—Christianity. 2. Paganism—
Controversial literature. 3. Christianity and other religions.
I. Title.
BR115.O3B87   1992
299—dc20   92–32015
                                                 CIP

Printed in the United States of America.
1 2 3 4 5 6 — 97 96 95 94 93 92

Contents

Introduction

As I hurried through the bustling crowds of the streets of London, I turned over in my mind what sort of questions the television presenter might ask me. I was new to television studios, and perhaps apprehensive of being questioned especially about witchcraft. My book on traditional religions had just been published. It was written primarily for missionaries working in the Third World. It seemed somewhat strange that British television would find it more than a passing curiosity, and yet here they were wanting to interview me alongside a practicing British witch.

I knew of the growing pagan movement in Britain, but like many I had discounted it as merely a fringe phenomenon. I was more interested in the beliefs and rituals of ethnic peoples in Africa and Asia. I had been attempting to understand their way of thinking that resulted in beliefs such as witchcraft and sorcery, and how they dealt with these evils. I knew that the people that I had sat with in the villages of Africa actually believed in their traditional religions. I felt it somewhat irksome to talk to a person who I felt was merely "playing" at paganism. However, that meeting in the television studio was to change my thinking.

"The witch," named Leonora, was not the eccentric that I had expected, but a thoughtful woman convinced of her beliefs. She expressed appreciation of my book that she had read in preparation for the interview and made a few intelligent comments. I began to realize that if Leonora was an advocate of this movement, it was one that embraced more than the few cranks or perverts that I had condemned to its ranks. Paganism in the West is becoming a significant new religious movement. In the recent past I had been concerned with the question of how people of traditional religions were being converted to major world religions such as Islam and Christianity. Now I was faced with another question. How is it that nominal Christians, Jews, Muslims, Buddhists and even atheists are becoming pagan?

I would like the reader to be aware of my aim and the development of the material in this book. Some readers like to dive straight into the heart of a book, so I have divided it into five parts that can be read almost as distinct sections. However, the text is ordered to achieve a certain goal.

An attempt to understand

This goal, at its simplest, is to attempt to understand the new pagan movement within Britain. My approach has been similar to that which I have used in studying other cultures in Africa and Asia. I have listened to what the people say and sought to understand what they have written. I have cross-checked information to try to separate the spurious from the genuine. This approach is often termed the anthropological method, but there are two major differences.

First, although I have tried to keep an anthropological detachment and objectivity, I have realized my own subjectivity concerning those claiming to be "witches," "pagans," "magicians," or "satanists." The mere words conjure up images and prejudices that I had not known when studying people such as the Karimojong of Uganda. The Karimojong were different from me in their looks, language, habitat, and thought. No matter how hard I tried, my genetic inheritance and personal history would always mark me as an outsider to the Karimojong, but this is not so among the new pagans of Britain. I am British, I am white, and I am middle-class like most within this new movement. I am also a committed Christian, and as such have drawn lines as to how far I have been involved with the movement. I have not been involved in pagan rituals nor been initiated into a coven as have some anthropologists.[1] I remain an outsider to the movement, but one who has attempted to understand the persuasions of the movement.

Second, what we are concerned with is a religious movement and not the religious beliefs of some traditional society. By definition, movements move. The neopagan movement can be likened to a fast-flowing stream forcing its way through a rocky valley. This results in turbulence and swirls, waves and sprays of cascading water. It therefore becomes an impossible task to draw up a neatly packaged description of the movement. As Chris Bray, manager of the Sorcerer's Apprentice, the country's largest occult supplier, expressed it to me: "If you manage to piece together an overall generalization it will be a synthetic one liable to contradiction when you meet the very next pagan."[2] The pagan movement is one of intense religious creativity. It is possible on the macro scale only to point out the general direction of the movement and on the micro scale to study particular features that may soon disappear with the coming of a new trend.

The word "pagan" comes from the Latin *paganus,* which means a country dweller. Similarly, "heathen" originally meant a person who lived on the heaths. The derogatory nature of the word originates from Roman times when the urban Romans used it as a term of insult for those who populated the outskirts of their empire. The word was adopted by the church and applied to those persons outside Christianity. Pagans were considered ungodly and immoral, not simply members of a different religion. Today, pagans would identify themselves as adherents of these ancient traditional religions. Margot Adler writes, "I use Pagan to mean a member of a polytheistic nature religion, such as the ancient Greek, Roman or Egyptian religions, or, in anthropological terms, a member of one of the indigenous folk and tribal religions all over the world."[3] This is essentially the definition that we shall use.

An attempt to communicate

True understanding involves meaningful communication. I am seeking to communicate both to the Christian and the new pagan. This book therefore seeks to provide an understanding of pagan vocabulary and the pagan worldview.

Part 1 deals with the historical development of the pagan movement. To understand the new pagans one must first understand the old. Who were the pagan peoples of Britain, and what did they believe? How were they converted to Christianity? How did their traditions continue with the dominance of the church? Many terms and expressions that are used by the modern pagan can only be understood by a prior comprehension of the ways of the ancient Celts and Anglo-Saxons.

Part 2 begins the study of the beliefs of the modern pagan movement. Out of the hundreds of theories and ideas that may be found, the attempt is to identify common themes that distinguish the movement both from contemporary secular society and Christian theology.

Part 3 describes the rituals practiced by those in the movement, including magic. Magic will be defined as ritual acts to achieve certain practical goals.

Part 4 considers the pagan community within Britain. What sort of people are they? In what forms of paganism do they partake? How do they express their beliefs in artistic forms?

Finally, Part 5 looks at the interaction between Christians and pagans. In it I have attempted to look at the issues of persecution and proclamation, philosophy and power.

My hope is that this book will act like a mirror. To the pagan, I trust, it will reflect his or her own position both in its strengths and weaknesses. The pagan accepts assumptions that I personally find inadequate and deficient. However, I have come to appreciate how, due to lack of a more satisfactory worldview, they may be adopted by Western people today.

To the Christian, I hope the book will help to distinguish truth from stereotype. More than this, I trust that the text will show the spiritual hunger of the pagan heart within the materialism of our secularized society. It is the challenge to the church today, as it has been in every generation, to be the people of God demonstrating a spiritual reality within contemporary culture. Many pagans criticize the church as being unspiritual. What is the Christian response?

Notes

1. Tanya Luhrmann, *Persuasions of the Witch's Craft* (Blackwell: Oxford, 1989).
2. Chris Bray, personal correspondence of September 17, 1990.
3. Margot Adler, *Drawing Down the Moon* (Beacon Press: Boston, 1986), p. 10.

Part 1

◯)

KEEP BRITAIN PAGAN

1

Celtic Britain

The very word "Celt" immediately brings to mind images of Druids and Bards, warriors and princes, harps and swords, stone crosses and rocky coasts. Theirs was a civilization that was overtaken by the passage of time and the coming of the Romans, the Saxons, and the modern industrial world. Yet this has only cloaked the Celts in further mystery and magic. They are like the lone piper in the forest glade whose wistful tune stirs the heart of the passing listener.

Through all the imagery rises a surprisingly simple question: Who were the Celts? The Celts wrote down nothing of themselves; they had no literary classics such as those of Greece and Rome. They were the first prehistoric civilization to arise from obscurity in northern Europe. The Celtic language had many variations, but all of them stemmed from a common Indo-European root that they shared with Sanskrit of India. The Greeks called them "Keltoi," and the Romans called them "Galli" (Gauls).

The Celtic people

Archaeological evidence suggests the development of a Celtic civilization as early as 1200 B.C. in the area of what is modern France and southern Germany. This "Urnfield" culture, as it is called, is named after the particular burial customs employed. Archaeologists have identified the ensuing period as being from the seventh to the sixth century B.C. and named it after the burial grounds near Hallstatt in northern Austria. These burial grounds comprise chamber graves containing many beautiful examples of Celtic art: splendidly adorned four-wheeled wagons, gold decorations, jewels, and pottery.

The Celts came to the zenith of their power in the fifth to the first centuries B.C. with what is called "La Tène" culture. This period epitomizes the essential vision of the Celtic people and the assertion of their presence within Europe.[1] The Celts struck terror into the civilizations centered around the Mediterranean Sea. Siculus, a first-century B.C. historian from Sicily, writes of them:

> On their heads they wear bronze helmets which possess large projecting figures lending the appearance of enormous stature to the wearer; in some cases horns form one piece with the helmet, while in other cases it is relief figures of foreparts of birds or quadrupeds. Their trumpets again are of a peculiar barbaric kind; they blow into them and produce a harsh sound which suits the tumult of war. Some have iron breastplates of chain mail while others fight naked, and for them the breastplate given by nature suffices.[2]

During the Hallstatt period, the Celts expanded through France into the Iberian Peninsula and across to the British Isles. A second migration in the fourth century B.C. took some eastward into Bulgaria and even into Turkey where they settled and became known as "Galatians," the very people to whom the apostle Paul was to write some 300 years later (see figure 1:1).

By the first century B.C., the Celts were divided into many tribes. The Helvetii lived in present-day Switzerland, the Galli in central France, the Aquitani and Veneti along the Atlantic coast of France, and the Belgae in the north crossing over into the British Isles. Each tribe had its chief who was chosen from among the nearest relatives of the previous chief. The tribes themselves were largely independent of one another, though related tribes often cooperated in times of war when common interests were involved.

The basic economy of the Celts was mixed farming. Various grains were grown with several kinds of vegetables. Cattle and sheep were also important. They were hospitable people, fond

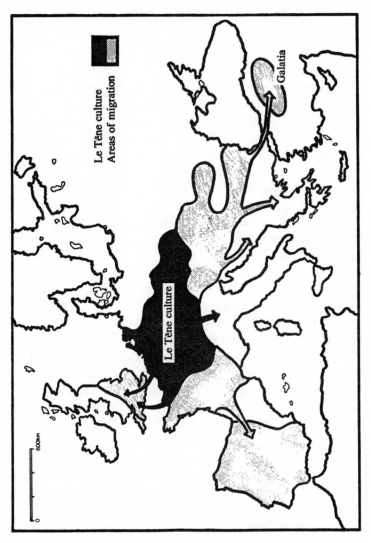

Figure 1:1 Geographical expansion of the Celtic peoples by 200 B.C.

of feasting and drinking, and the bards would sing the praises of those who were present. The Celts prized music and all forms of oral communication. They were proud people with a rich culture.

In the middle of the first century B.C., the Celts were caught between two developing forces: the Roman Empire in the south and the Germanic (Teutonic) tribes from Scandinavia. The advance of the Germanic people caused the Celts to move westward and southward, which the Romans considered a threat to their stability. Julius Caesar, in 58 B.C., deliberately sought a conflict with the Aedui tribe, which he quickly defeated. As Caesar's legions moved north, the Belgae gathered an army of 300,000 but it fell apart in the face of the disciplined Roman army. The final conflict came in 52 B.C., at the battle of Alesia in central France. In the face of defeat, King Vercingetoix and his countrymen chose to surrender. In true Celtic style, he put on his finest robe and rode to Caesar's tent to lay down his sword at Caesar's feet. On Caesar's return to Rome, Vercingetoix was paraded through the streets of Rome and finally strangled.

Before the Roman conquest, the British Celts consisted of several Celtic tribes similar to the Celts of the continent resulting from the steady migrations over several centuries. The main settlements were those of the Belgae along the south coast. Despite Caesar's major thrust in 54 B.C., the British Celts remained substantially independent. Boadicea's rebellion broke out in A.D. 60, and she and her warriors sacked Colchester, the old Celtic center that the Romans had made their capital. However, like Vercingetoix a century before, the disciplined Roman army was to quell the uprising. According to Tacitus, Queen Boadicea—rather than surrender—took poison and died.

Roman influence and culture spread through the Celtic people of mainland England. Boadicea's rebellion was the last breath of a culture about to submerge beneath the colonization of Rome. The immigrant Roman officials eventually worked alongside the native Romanized Celts in governing the country. The rich Celtic culture did not entirely disappear but remained part of the folk culture of the Roman Celts. At the fringe of the *Pax Romana*—in Scotland, Wales, Cornwall and Ireland—Celtic culture continued, little influenced by the might of Rome.

Celtic religion

Celtic religion and mythology is difficult, if not impossible, for modern man to reconstruct completely. What remains are stone carvings, burial mounds, writings of Roman conquerors, and wondrous myths passed on by word of mouth to younger generations. The Celts lived in a mysterious world that supported life itself. Nature itself was considered alive, and it was watched over by the gods who were rightly owed reverence. These gods were believed to inhabit rivers and mountain peaks.

The Celtic gods

It is difficult to construct the pantheon of the Celts. Julius Caesar in his *Gallic War* distinguishes only five deities, and the poet Lucan later supplies the names of three more gods.[3] Sculptures and inscriptions have revealed the names and images of other Celtic divinities. The oral mythology passed on from generation to generation has given an identity to these gods.

The great god of the Celts was called Mercury by Caesar, but among the Irish he was Lugh of the Long Arm. He was a god of many talents: a scholar, a magician, a musician, a warrior. His exploits were famous, especially that of killing the one-eyed giant Balor by driving a stake through his eye. Lugh gives his name to one of the great Celtic festivals, Lughnassah, celebrated on August 1.

Taranis was the Celtic sky-god, whose name derives from the Celtic word "taran" meaning thunder. Taranis holds a lightning bolt in his hand, and a wheel, the solar symbol, at his side. As with many Celtic deities, these two gods were merged with the Roman deities. Taranis was identified with the Roman sky-god, Jupiter.

Cernunnos, the horned god, is of ancient origin. As with images of all the major Celtic deities, he is pictured sitting in a lotus posture. He is depicted on the Gundestrup Cauldron with the horn of a stag and surrounded by animals. In his right hand he holds a torque as a symbol of authority, and in his other hand he holds a serpent with the head of a ram (see figure 6:1).[4] The Celts saw Cernunnos as an earth god of fertility and plenty;[5] the serpent being the symbol of the powers of regeneration, a theme that often occurs in Celtic religion.

The most popular of the Celtic deities appears to have been the earth-mother goddess. Although many images of her have been found, a Celtic name has never been given. The fact that mother goddesses were held in great reverence by the Celts is shown not only by the large number of surviving sculptures and inscriptions but also from the highly formal way in which they were portrayed. No matter how crude the carvings, the goddess is portrayed in a position of power with commanding authority. She appears to have been the only Celtic divinity actually honored in Rome and simply was referred to as Matres of Matronae. This deity was normally pictured as a triad, frequently carrying infants and baskets of fruit.

There can be little doubt that certain animals were sacred to the Celts. Some animals may have been regarded as totems or at least as symbolic of certain clans or families. This is suggested by the use of animal symbols on military equipment, and the taboos among many Britons against eating hares, fowl, and geese, mentioned by Caesar.

The Druids

The Druids remain one of the most fascinating but controversial aspects of Celtic religion. Nora Chadwick writes of them,

> Despite the very considerable body of literature devoted to their study published since the Renaissance, the Druids remain obscure.

This is understandable for they apparently, in common with many early priesthoods, attempted to keep secret all things concerned with their activities.[6]

The word "Druid" is generally regarded as deriving from the Celtic word *drus* used for "oak tree," and *wid* meaning "to know." In other words, a Druid is one who has "wisdom of the oak tree" that could refer to some druidic ritual. The pages that Julius Caesar devotes to the Druids in *De Bello Galico,* Book VI, provide us with one of the most important sources concerning Celtic religion.

> The Druids officiate at the worship of the gods, regulate public and private sacrifices, and give rulings on all religious questions. Large numbers of young men flock to them for instruction, and they are held in great honour by the people. They act as judges in practically all disputes, whether between tribes or between individuals. . . . The Druids are exempt from military service and do not pay taxes like other citizens. These important privileges are naturally attractive: many present themselves of their own accord to become students of Druidism, and others are sent by parents or relatives.[7]

Like the Brahmans of India, the Druids were the priestly class who performed sacrifices to appease the gods. In an early period, human sacrifices were probably offered. Certainly the Romans recorded severed heads that had been dried, and archaeology has found shrines with skulls embedded in the lintels of the doors. The Celts held the head in reverence. They saw it not only as the essence of the person, but also the "soul-stuff" that made the head a symbol of spiritual power. The taking of an enemy transferred his fighting qualities to the victor. Caesar states that an important part of Druidic teaching was that the soul did not die but passed into another body.

Not only were the Druids priests, but they were the chief teachers of the young people and advisors of the chiefs. The Druids rejected writing in preference to learning the oral tradition by heart. That which was taught was the esoteric wisdom kept secret to all but the initiated. This, in part, explains our ignorance of Celtic beliefs. If the Druids committed anything to writing they used Greek.

The Druids have frequently been linked with Stonehenge, but this is an unlikely connection. The earliest Celtic groups to migrate to the British Isles are believed to have come in about the fifth century B.C. It would have been as part of that migration that the Druids came and eventually established themselves as the most influential priestly cult in the land. In contrast, the construction of Stonehenge is generally dated as somewhere between 2000–1500 B.C.[8]

The Emperors Augustus, Tiberius, and Claudius all sought to suppress the Druids in order to curb Celtic nationalism. Yet in the third century, when Roman pressure lessened, there was a renaissance of Celtic religion as the Druids regained their authority.

Festivals

The Celtic year was divided into four periods of three months marked by four great festivals. The great festival of Samhain, on November 1, commenced the new year. The Celts believed that on the eve of Samhain all the spirits emerged from their dwellings in the hills, lakes, and burial mounds. It is this festival that became Halloween. The second festival was Imbolc held on February 1. The great Celtic May Day festival of Beltane is associated with the god Belenus, and the name means "Bel's fire." The midsummer festival of Lughnassah on August 1 was in reverence of the god Lugh whose name means "light." It was a time of great assemblies lasting a month, usually starting in mid-July with much feasting and mock fighting.[9] We shall consider the nature of these festivals and their relevance to the modern neopagan movement in chapter 9.

As far as we know, the Celts had little by way of temples before the coming of the Romans, and they performed their ceremonies in forest glades. Lucan tells of a sacred wood that Caesar felled near Marseilles.

A grove there was, untouched by men's hands from ancient times whose interlacing boughs enclosed a space of darkness and cold shade, and banished the sunlight from above. No rural Pan dwelt there, nor Silvanus, ruler of the woods, no Nymphs; but gods were worshipped there with savage rites, the altars were heaped with hideous offerings and every tree was sprinkled with human gore.[10]

(The Roman writer must be allowed some poetic license.)

Contact with Roman civilization had many influences on the Celts, and one appears to have been the constructing of temple buildings, many of which have been discovered by archaeologists. The main form of a Romano-Celtic temple consisted of a square "cella" in which stood the cult statue. Surrounding the cella was a low wall carrying a row of columns, and the whole structure stood on a raised podium with a flight of steps up to the main door of the shrine. An altar stood in front of the temple, where the people could offer their animals for the priests to perform the ritual slaughter.

A different category of sacred places were the healing spas, where the sick could come to commune with the ritual deity. In Britain the most important was the hot springs at Bath. The ceremony probably consisted of purification in the waters, a ritual meal in the presence of the deity, followed by a "holy sleep" during which the god was believed to heal the patient, if he or she so wished.

History, however, is written by the victor. The Roman advance overcame the bold but reckless Celtic warriors. With them died much of the Celtic culture, overcome by the civilization of the Mediterranean peoples. Their religion became blended with that of pagan Rome, leaving us only with a vague understanding of what the old Celtic religion was really like. However, a new and more dominant religion was to come to Britain in the wake of the *Pax Romana*—Christianity.

The conversion of the Celts

The Romans ruled much of England for the period A.D. 55–407. It must have been early in that period that Christianity was introduced into the British Isles, because we know that there were three British bishops at the Synod of Arles in A.D. 314. The Venerable Bede writes that in A.D. 156 the British king, named Lucius, wrote to Pope Eleutherus asking to be made a Christian. "This pious request was quickly granted, and the Britons received the Faith and held it peacefully in all its purity and fullness until the time of the Emperor Diocletian."[11]

It has been frequently suggested that Christianity was introduced to Britain by the Roman army of occupation, but the evidence seems against this. F. F. Bruce proposed that it is far more likely that Christianity was carried to Britain by ordinary people trading between Britain and Gaul.[12] The *Pax Romana* made a huge trading network stretching from Carlisle to Babylon, and along these trade routes spread the religions of the world. Trade even existed between the Celts of Ireland and those of Roman Britain and nearby Gaul.

One ancient myth concerning the coming of Christianity to Britain focuses on the town of Glastonbury.[13] Legend tells that in about A.D. 63, St. Philip sent twelve missionaries from Rome, led by Joseph of Arimathea, to bring the gospel to Britain. They landed in Wales to a hostile reception and continued east till they came to the territory of King Arviragus of Wessex. He gave them twelve hides of land at Glastonbury, where they built the first church of St. Mary on the site of the future Abbey. On the slopes of the Tor, Joseph of Arimathea was believed to have buried the chalice used at the Last Supper, the "holy grail" of the Arthurian legends.

By the end of the fourth century, the Roman territories of Britain were subject to frequent invasion by the Picts from Scotland and the Scotii from Ireland. In A.D. 407, in order to meet serious threats nearer home, the Romans withdrew their last soldier from the British Isles.

Patrick, apostle to Ireland

While there seems little doubt that there were Christians among the Irish Celts in the fourth century, traditions point to St. Patrick as the one who established Christianity in that country. Like so much of Celtic history, fact and myth blend in the story of Patrick. Patrick begins his "Confessions":

> I, Patrick, a most untutored sinner and the lowest of all the faithful and the most despicable in the eyes of many, am the son of Calpurnius, a deacon who was the son of Potitus a priest, from the village of Bannaventa Berniae, who had an estate near it, where I was taken prisoner. At that time I was about sixteen years of age, I had no knowledge of the true God and I was borne away into captivity with thousands of people.[14]

Patrick's own writings tell us that he was taken captive from his home (now generally considered to have been near Dumbarton in Scotland) to work as a slave in what is now Ireland. Six years after his abduction, he turned wholeheartedly to the Christian God worshiped by his father. He managed to escape from his master and make his way to a seaport where, after some difficulty, he persuaded the pagan crew to take him on board. The rest of the account is difficult to untangle chronologically, but some time later he had a vision in which he saw a man from Ireland bringing him many letters and urging him to return to the land of his captivity.

In order to prepare himself for his vocation, Patrick went to the Abbey of Lerins (France) to study the Christian faith. Before long he was ordained deacon by Amator, the bishop of Auxerre. In about A.D. 432, some twenty years after his escape from Ireland, he was finally consecrated bishop and returned to the island. Although the power of Rome was waning, its civilization still carried great prestige. Christianity was now the religion of the Romans. Thus, the coming of Patrick, a Roman bishop, marked a new stage in the growth of the church among the Celts.

Patrick landed on the east coast of Ireland and sought to contact Christians already in the country. After doing this he traveled north to Ulster where the story is told that he was welcomed by the local chief whose fortress was at Downpatrick. It has been suggested that the chief's wife was a daughter of Patrick's former master. The chief listened to Patrick, accepted his message, and was baptized with his family.

In North Antrim was the territory of Dalriada, populated by people called the Scots. It was from this region that the Scots first went by sea to the land to which they were later to give their name. The area of Scotland in which they first settled was Argyll which also shared the name Dalriada. This Scottish Dalriada was in time to prove important as its royal house gradually extended its influence over all Scotland.

Patrick understood the tribal society of the Celts and adapted his missionary strategy accordingly. The Irish were divided into several small tribal areas, each ruled by a king. Some of these kings maintained a degree of authority over the neighboring kings so that Ireland was divided into five provinces. In turn, these five provincial kings held a measure of allegiance to the ruler of Meath, who reigned at Tara and was known as the "high king" of Ireland.[15] Patrick sought to win over the kings with the aim that their people would follow them into the Christian faith. In one place in his "Confession" he writes: "On occasions I used to give presents to the kings, besides the hire that I gave their sons who accompanied me."[16] Patrick successfully converted many kings, and they were baptized with many of their family and tribe.

It is interesting that many Druids converted to the Christian faith.[17] This did not mean that the Druids welcomed the new religion, but they saw Patrick as one who worked greater miracles than anything they knew. The new religion did not destroy everything of the old but substituted a new office to fulfill similar functions to the old. In place of the schools of the Druids there now came into existence the monasteries with a peculiarly Celtic character. Instead of the standing stones with images of animals, high crosses were constructed as a testament to the new religion (see figure 1:2).

This illustrates the way in which Christianity was adapted to the Celtic culture and became an integral part of it.

> Patrick engrafted Christianity on the pagan superstitions with so much skill that he won the people over to the Christian religion before they understood the exact difference between the two systems of belief; and much of this half-pagan, half-Christian religion will be found, not only in the Irish stories of the Middle Ages, but in the superstitions of the peasantry of the present day.[18]

Perhaps it was the emphasis on the study of the Christian scriptures that stopped this syncretistic tendency perverting the basic Christian message.

Figure 1:2 Celtic Cross.

Celtic missionaries

With the retreat of the Romans and the expansion of the Germanic peoples across Europe, the Celtic church became separated from that of Rome and developed its own traditions. A central feature of Celtic Christianity in Ireland was the monasteries. These were centers of scholarship in which Latin was studied extensively for the study of the Holy Scriptures. These monasteries observed three principles: poverty, chastity, and obedience. However, each monastery developed its own rule of conduct. It was from these monasteries that one of the greatest missionary movements in Europe was to spring. While Europe was entering its Dark Ages, the Celtic church began to send out its most adventurous as missionaries.

One of the first was Ninian (c. 360–432), the son of a converted chieftain of Cumbria. He went to Rome as a young man, where he was instructed in the faith and consecrated bishop. He returned home to work for the conversion of his own people. Later Ninian and his monks worked to convert the Scots.

During these years there arose a great Celtic Christian scholar called Pelagius who was active in Rome. "Pelagius was typical of the British Church at that time: rigorously moral, highly scholarly and, if not a missionary, certainly a man with a message. . . . What troubled Pelagius was the shocking morality of the times, as the ancient Roman Empire was crumbling to ruins."[19] History has classed him as a heretic, but he reveals the moral strength and intellectual caliber of the Celtic church that challenged the domination of Roman Christianity.

Perhaps the most famous Celtic missionary was Columban, born about A.D. 540, in the southeast of Ireland. He appears to have been a full-blooded, handsome youth, but he along with others heard the call to the monastic life. He joined the monastery in Bangor, and after a few years he led a band of twelve monks across the sea to Britanny. He traveled on into the Frankish kingdom where, stirred on by the nominality of the Christian population, he preached a more earnest Christian life. By the time of his death in A.D. 615, Columban had made a deep impression upon the nominal Frankish Christians. Numerous monasteries were established, and from his example many others went as missionaries to tribes that were still pagan.

Another important Celtic missionary was Columba, born in

Donegal in A.D. 521. His parents were of the royal family, and from youth he was brought up in the Christian faith. It seemed that it became the custom of the royal families of Ireland to send one of their sons to be brought up as a monk. In due time, Columba was ordained deacon and then priest, but he was never made a bishop. In A.D. 563, he, like Columban, led a group of twelve men across the seas, but in his case it was northward to Scotland. He made his headquarters on the Isle of Iona.

Three years before Columba arrived in Iona, the Dalriada, who had been encroaching on the territory of the Picts in central Scotland, had been decisively defeated by them under the leadership of Brude. Columba, in true Celtic missionary style, sought first to convert the king. Initially, Brude was not willing to see Columba, probably because of his close contact with the Dalriada. However, Columba made many journeys into Scotland from Iona and is credited with converting the Picts who dwelt north of the Grampians. Stories are told of the contests that he had with the Druids who were his bitterest enemies.[20] He is said to have met their magic with miracles and healings that illustrated the power of the Christian God.

The Celtic missionary movement is one that is often forgotten, but it undoubtedly made a major impact on the people of northern Europe. With the collapse of the Western Roman Empire and the advance of the Germanic peoples, it was the once pagan Celts who were a major Christian force. They were, however, to face a new situation with the expansion of the pagan Angles and Saxons into England, who in turn were followed by the fierce Norsemen.

Notes

1. Nora Chadwick, *The Celts* (Penguin Books: Harmondsworth, 1970), pp. 33–41.
2. Frank Delaney, *The Celts* (Guild Publication: London, 1986), p. 31.
3. Mircea Eliade, *A History of Religious Ideas,* Vol. 2 (University of Chicago Press: Chicago, 1984), p. 145.
4. Delaney, op. cit., p. 166.
5. Graham Webster, *The British Celts and Their Gods under Rome* (Batsford: London, 1986), p. 56.
6. Chadwick, op. cit., p. 149.
7. Delaney, op. cit., p. 94.
8. Gerald S. Hawkins, *Stonehenge Decoded* (Fontana Books: London, 1967), p. 63.
9. Webster, op. cit., pp. 31–33.
10. Chadwick, op. cit., p. 146.
11. Bede, *A History of the English Church and People* (Penguin Classics: Harmondsworth, 1968), p. 42.
12. F. F. Bruce, *The Spreading Flame* (Paternoster Press: Exeter, 1966), p. 354.
13. Information leaflets produced by the Tourist Information Centre, Glastonbury, Somerset.
14. Delaney, op. cit., p. 50.
15. Bruce, op. cit., p. 375.
16. Harold R. Cook, *Historic Patterns of Church Growth* (Moody Press: Chicago, 1971), p. 45.
17. Ibid., p. 43.
18. Ibid., p. 46.
19. James Atkinson, "The Celtic Way," *Christian History,* Vol. V, No. 1, p. 19.
20. K. S. Latourette, *A History of the Expansion of Christianity,* Vol. 2 (Zondervan: Grand Rapids, 1970), p. 53.

2

Saxon Britain

Following the withdrawal of the Romans from northern Europe (c. A.D. 400), there are long periods about which we have little historical detail.[1] Into the vacuum that the Romans left behind them swept the Germanic peoples from the north. These tribes had hardly ever come in touch with Roman culture and civilization, nor even with Christianity. They came as invaders and carried out a war of extermination. From the continent of Europe, the Angles, Saxons, and Jutes began to invade the southern shores of the British Isles.

The coming of the Germanic peoples

Bede writes that the Angles and Saxons first came to Britain in A.D. 449 at the invitation of King Vortigern and were granted lands in the east on condition that they protected the country.[2] They were soon joined by a larger force of warriors who demanded grants of land from the Britons. Soon an increasing number of Angles, Saxons, and Jutes arrived, driving the Britons west. The distinctions between the Germanic tribes soon lost significance as they began to regard themselves as "English," though divided into several kingdoms.

In the middle of the sixth century, the East Angles were probably the most powerful people in southern England. They settled in the areas of Norfolk (North folk) and Suffolk (South folk). To the south lay the Saxon territories: Essex, Sussex, Middlesex, and Wessex. The Jutes settled in the area of Kent, and it was they who had the closest contacts with the Franks of the mainland.

In the north, there were two distinct Anglian kingdoms by the end of the sixth century. To the north of the River Tyne was Bernicia, and to the south Deira. In the midlands developed the kingdom of Mercia (see figure 2.1). The remaining Celtic people were pressed back into the mountainous western areas of the British Isles.

King Arthur

The British monk named Gildas, writing a little before A.D. 547, tells of the agonies of the Celtic peoples facing Saxon invasions. There was certainly resistance, but Gildas is strangely silent of a legendary Celtic hero of the time named Arthur. Nothing is said of Arthur until the ninth-century compilation of the Welsh writer Nennius. "But," as Frank Stenton writes, "it should not be allowed to remove him from the sphere of history, for Gildas was curiously reluctant to introduce personal names into his writing."[3]

Arthur was born, so far as we can tell, some time in the fifth or sixth century, either in Wales or western England. He seems not to have been a king but a war-leader who united the forces of the various kings and petty chiefs to fight the common Saxon foe. He may have been the leader of mounted cavalry whose mobility allowed them to strike deep into enemy territory. Such tactics could have been learned from the Romans. Legend records a series of great battles in which Arthur fought with his shield on which was painted the image of the Virgin Mary. He led his warriors with such effect that what began as an invasion ended as a more or less peaceful settlement.

Although little by way of historical facts are known about Arthur, he has become part of a rich mythology that has played a significant part in the neopagan movement of modern Britain.[4] The first writer consciously drawing on the largely oral sources pertaining to Arthur was a twelfth-century writer named Geoffrey of Monmouth. He wrote an extensive series of stories concerning the exploits of Arthur, his knights, and magician Merlin. Although he was criticized even by his near-

Figure 2:1 The British Isles at the time of Bede, A.D. 700.

contemporaries as a "writer of lies," the stories of the Celtic hero have caught the imagination of many over the centuries.

In general, the Celts hated the Anglo-Saxon invaders and would have no dealing with them. As James Atkinson writes, "they even refused them Christianity. The Anglo-Saxons continued their heathenism."[5]

Germanic religion

As with the Celts, we only have a fragmentary knowledge of the religion of the Germanic peoples. What we know about these old religions comes from books by Christians who opposed them. Their religion was undoubtedly similar to that of the Vikings, the stories of whose gods were told long enough for them to be written down. From this information we are able to piece together a partial understanding of their beliefs. The expansion of the Germanic peoples throughout half of Europe resulted in the development of various local expressions, but one can still detect a certain fundamental unity in their religion.[6]

When, in the fourth century, the Saxons adopted a seven-day week, they replaced the names of the Roman deities with those of their own gods. The worship of the Sun and the Moon was common to Germanic peoples, but almost nothing is known as to how they were worshiped. Tuesday is called after Tiw or Tiwaz. He was the great sky-god equivalent to the Roman Jupiter and the Greek Zeus. Later Woden became the chief god and Tiw became the god of war.

Woden seems to have been the god most widely worshiped by the Germanic peoples. In the north he was called Odin, and he was associated with the Roman god Mercury from *mercredi*, French for Wednesday. Thor was a popular deity with the Saxons who regarded him as the child of Woden (the sky-god) and Jorth (the earth). Thor was the thunder-god, and his name has been ascribed to many areas of Saxon England: Thursley in the Wey valley, Thundersfield near Reigate, and Thundersley in Essex.

Friday is named after the goddess Frig who was regarded as

the goddess of fertility and love. She was associated with the
Roman goddess Venus. Another common deity of Germanic
religion is the Green Man. He is portrayed as a mixture of man
and tree. Leaves grow out of his head and mouth. He is connected with the Greek god Bacchus and is related with spring
and new growth. It is interesting that his face is often found
carved into the decoration of early European churches, and
many public houses continue to bear his name.

The vitality of ancient Anglo-Saxon paganism is shown by
the large number of place-names indicating the location of a
temple. The Old English word *hearh* meaning a hill temple is
found today in place-names such as Harrow on the Hill, and
Harrowden in Essex. The word *weoh* was used for an idol or
shrine and was often compounded with the word *leah* meaning
a grove. Thus remain places with names such as Weedon near
Aylesbury and Willey in Surrey.[7]

The conversion of the Anglo-Saxons

As the pagan Germanic peoples moved into Britain, they displaced the Christianized Celts. Bede considered this to be a
judgment of God for the Celts' lack of religious piety. The
Celtic church was still involved in its missionary outreach but
did little towards converting the invading Germanic peoples. It
was from Rome that the Christian message was to reach them.

The story, recounted by Bede as a folk tradition, tells how
Pope Gregory saw boys of fair complexion for sale at the Roman slave market. Asking from which people they came, he
was told that they were Angles. "That is appropriate," he said,
"for they have angelic faces, and it is right that they should
become joint-heirs with the angels in heaven."[8]

A small group, under the leadership of Augustine, was commissioned by Gregory and left Rome in A.D. 596. While travel-
ing through Gaul, the group became frightened of the dangers
and sent Augustine back to Rome to ask Gregory permission to
abandon the mission. Gregory sent Augustine back with firm
orders to continue to Britain. When Augustine and his group

reached Britain it was not to the Angles that they went, but to the Jutes of Kent. This was fortunate because Kent has closest contact with mainland Europe. King Ethelbert had a Frankish wife from the mainland who was a Christian, and as a condition of their marriage he had promised to allow her to observe her religion. She worshiped at an old Roman church in Canterbury, the capital of Kent.

Augustine and his party, with interpreters provided by the Franks, landed at the Island of Thanet, on the northeastern corner of Kent. They sent a message to Ethelbert telling of their arrival and the purpose of their mission. After some days, Ethelbert went to the island to meet them.

> But he took precautions that they should not approach him in a house; for he held an ancient superstition that, if they were practisers of magical arts, they may have opportunity to deceive and master him. But the monks were endowed with power from God, not from the Devil, and approached the king carrying a silver cross as their standard and the likeness of our Lord and saviour painted on a board.[9]

Augustine presented the Christian message, and then Ethelbert allowed the group to preach to the people and win converts. The group established themselves at Canterbury. At first converts came slowly, but once Ethelbert was baptized many followed his example.[10]

In A.D. 601, Pope Gregory wrote to Augustine giving him guidance on his missionary strategy toward the pagan English.

> The temples of the idols among the people should on no account be destroyed. The idols are to be destroyed, but the temples themselves are to be aspersed with holy water, altars set up in them, and relics deposited there. For if these temples are well-built, they must be purified from the worship of demons and dedicated to the service of the true God. In this way, we hope that the people, seeing that their temples are not destroyed, may abandon their error and, flocking more readily to their accustomed resorts, may come to know and adore the true God. And since they have a custom of

sacrificing many oxen to demons, let some other solemnity be substituted in its place, such as a day of Dedication or the Festival of the holy martyrs whose relics are enshrined there. On such occasions they might well construct shelters of boughs for themselves around the churches that were once temples, and celebrate the solemnity with devout feasting. They are no longer to sacrifice beasts to the Devil, but they may kill them for food to the praise of God, and give thanks to the Giver of all gifts for the plenty they enjoy. If the people are allowed some worldly pleasures in this way, they will more readily come to desire the joys of the spirit.[11]

Later in history, the Jesuits were to develop this principle in their missionary endeavors in other parts of the world but not without strong criticism from the Franciscans.[12]

The success of the Roman missionaries was confined chiefly to the south of England. In about A.D. 605, Augustine died, and about a decade later Ethelbert, the first Christian king among the English, also died. Eadbald succeeded Ethelbert as king of Kent, but he was a pagan who rejected the Christian marriage regulations. A pagan reaction occurred. However, Eadbald finally became a Christian and gave stronger support to his new faith than Ethelbert had done. Eadbald ordered that idols were to be destroyed throughout his realm.

Edwin, the King of Northumbria, asked to marry Eadbald's sister. This was granted on the condition that he would not interfere with her Christian religion. The marriage took place in A.D. 625, and a priest named Paulinus was sent with the princess to act as her bishop. Eventually, King Edwin was converted, and with many of his nobles and many of the population was baptized at York. The powerful influence of Edwin aided the expansion of Christianity among the other Angle kingdoms. The conversion of the Anglo-Saxons took approximately a century to complete.

The American historian, Latourette, writes,

The conversion of England, it is well to note, was effected without any political pressure from abroad. Christianity did not come as the faith of a conqueror or as an agent of imperialism. Nor was much compulsion employed even by native rulers. To be sure, kings and the upper classes led the way, and the masses usually followed. . . . Here may be one reason for the zeal which the English and the Irish early displayed in propagating their faith in other lands.[13]

Celtic and Roman Christianity

The conversion of the Anglo-Saxons came from two sources. The first, as we have described, was from Rome's spreading from Kent. The other was from the Celtic missionaries primarily based on the Island of Iona slightly later than the Roman missionaries. The Roman missionaries had their main influence on the conversion of the local kings, while the Celtic missionaries appear to have had a greater influence among the ordinary people.

The Celtic and Roman forms of Christianity provided markedly different expressions, and it is not surprising that conflict arose. This centered on the form of church government, the date of Easter, the recognition of the supreme authority of the Pope, and the form of tonsure. The views of the two parties were presented at the Council of Whitby in A.D. 664, in the presence of the King of Northumbria. The Celtic party was outdebated when asked the rhetorical question, "Why should the British stand out against the whole of Christendom? Had not Peter and his successors been given the keys of heaven?"

The Council of Whitby decided to accept the Roman tradition. The Celtic monks asked but one thing—to be allowed to return to the monasteries at Iona and Lindisfarne and end their days in the ways of the Celtic tradition. With them passed a rich Christian tradition with an intellectual and spiritual greatness that has been almost forgotten with the passing of time.

St. Boniface

The Anglo-Saxons had been Christian for less than 100 years

before one of their most important missionaries was commissioned. He was St. Boniface, born in Crediton, Devon in A.D. 680.[14] In A.D. 716, he set out on his first journey with two friends. They went via London to Rome. There he much impressed the Pope who commissioned him as a missionary with the task of converting the Saxons in Germany and the Frisians in Holland.

Boniface headed north preaching to the Saxons and Thuringians. One of the well-known stories about Boniface was how he decided to challenge the pagan gods. He heard about a tree at Geismar known as "Thor's Oak." It was probably a tree that had been struck by lightning. Boniface found people worshiping there, seized an axe, and started to cut it down. Willibald wrote that when he had cut a *V* in the trunk, a strong gust of wind dashed the tree to the ground, and it split into the shape of a cross. A later German legend tells that a tiny fir sprang up among the roots, and this was to lead to the institution of the Christmas tree.

When people saw that no harm came to Boniface, they lost faith in Thor. By A.D. 731, many thousands of Thuringians had been baptized. In A.D. 754, Boniface set out on his last journey, this time to the Frisians. The small party took a boat down the Rhine and across the Zuyder Zee. After they disembarked they were attacked by armed men and the whole party was slaughtered.[15] The Christians in the rest of Frisia were so angry at the death of Boniface that they killed the murderers and destroyed the pagan shrines throughout their country.

The Vikings

The British Isles suffered small scattered raids from the Vikings as early as the end of the eighth century. During the ninth century these increased into major military expeditions as the Vikings expanded into Britain and the Frankish kingdom. Lindisfarne was sacked in A.D. 793 and Jarrow in A.D. 794. In A.D. 865, a large Danish force came to East Anglia intent on conquest. By A.D. 871 they had captured York, much of East Anglia, and had established a puppet king in Mercia.

Viking religion

Of all the traditional religions of the European peoples, we know most about the Viking religion. They were the last of the European peoples to be Christianized, and their myths were remembered and written down by Christian scholars. As mentioned before, the traditional religion of the Germanic peoples had a similarity to that of the Vikings, and they had many common deities.

Central to their cosmology was the tree Yggdrasill that symbolizes and also constitutes the universe. Its top branches reach the sky and cover the whole earth, and its roots go down to the realm of the dead. From the time of its emergence, Yggdrasill was threatened with ruin. An eagle set out to eat its foliage, its trunk began to rot, and the snake Niohogg began to gnaw its roots. At some future time, Yggdrasill will fall, and that will be the end of the world.[16]

The Viking pantheon was divided into two groups: the Aesir and the Vanir. Of the Aesir the most famous are Odin and Thor, while for the Vanir they are Njoro and Freyr.[17]

Odin is the most important of the gods, being their father and sovereign. In the poem "Havamal," the story is told of how Odin wounded himself, abstained from food and drink, and hung from the tree Yggdrasill for nine days. Yggdrasill means "the horse" (drasil) of Ygg, Ygg being one of Odin's names. The gallows is called the hanged man's "horse," and victims sacrificed to Odin were hung on trees.[18] By this act of self-sacrifice, Odin obtained the runes, symbols of occult knowledge. It seems strange that today, a plastic set of rune stones can be obtained from a major newsdealer for the divinatory use of twentieth-century Britons.

Gwyn Jones writes of Odin:

He was the god of the gallows and those who died on it, god of war and those who perished by it, god of occult knowledge and master of the dead from whom this must be won. He was no Christ who hung on the tree for others. He sought his own gain—dominion and knowledge—and his suffering has more in common with shamanism than with Christianity.[19]

Odin was no god for the ordinary person, but Thor was the most popular deity. Here was a god who was boisterous but straightforward, a huge eater and drinker. His name means "thunder" and his weapon is the hammer, the mythical image of the thunderbolt. Thor was the defender of the Aesir and their divine dwelling place. His chief enemy was the cosmic snake Niohogg who encircles the earth.

Odin and Thor were of the Aesir, but Freyr was of the Vanir. The Vanir represented an earlier religion in the north. The Aesir overcame them in battle but didn't destroy them or drive them out. They were fertility gods. Njoro, the eldest of the Vanir, married his sister and had twins by her, Freyr and Freyja. Njoro's name and function connect him by some sexual ambiguity with the Earth Mother. Freyr was a god of fruitfulness and sexuality. His statues are distinguished by an exaggerated phallus.

The old Viking religion appears to have had no vocational priest. It was a function of the local chief to act as a mediator between humans and the gods. The primary ritual was one of sacrifice in which human beings, animals, weapons, boats, and artifacts of all kinds were offered to the gods. The ceremony would include feasting, singing, dancing, and even divination with rune stones.

Pagan Viking culture was rich in myth and in material achievement. From this period derives some of the most beautiful Scandinavian traditional art. It also stimulated the Vikings to expand seaward to Britain and France, and inland towards the heart of modern Russia where they established the Kingdom of Rus.

King Alfred

In Celtic Ireland, the Viking immigrants were predominantly Norwegian, while in Teutonic England they were Danes. Northumbria came under Danish rule in A.D. 867, followed by East Anglia in A.D. 869. Finally Mercia collapsed in A.D. 874.

The Danes, under Guthrum, had been repulsed from Wessex on two previous occasions. Then, in A.D. 878, Guthrum made a midwinter attack that caught the West Saxons by surprise. Alfred was able to regroup his men and finally drive the invaders out of Wessex. The importance of Alfred's victory needs to be stressed. It prevented the Danes from becoming the masters of the whole of England and allowed him to recapture London in A.D. 886. Renewed attacks by the Danes residing in England caused widespread damage but had no lasting results. (See figure 2:2.) Alfred was the most effective opponent the Vikings had met anywhere and deserved the title "the Great."

Not only did the Danes have to settle for living within the limits of the Danelaw, but King Guthrum also accepted Christianity.[20] However, it must be recognized that the Vikings were generally tolerant in matters of religion. Many of them underwent some form of Christian baptism when overseas.

> The sign of the cross was made over them to exorcise evil spirits, they could attend mass without committing themselves to Christianity, and live in communion with Christians. This was a common custom of the time among traders and those who went on war-pay along with Christian men: for those who were prime-signed held full communion with Christian and heathens too, yet kept to the faith which was most agreeable to them. (*Egils Saga*, 50.)[21]

Conversion of the Vikings

In none of their invasions did the Vikings seek to convert their victims to their religion. They were raiders, not missionaries. They did seriously weaken the church, looting many church buildings and damaging the quality of life. Centuries before the

*Figure 2:2 Viking colonies in Britain and France. The Danes
who had tended to raid the rich lowlands of England
astonished the English in A.D. 876 by sharing out
the conquered land and beginning to farm it.*

conversion of the Vikings was accomplished, Christianity had already filtered into Scandinavia. This may well have been through the slaves which they captured and took to their homes. When it was accepted it was with a Viking perspective. One of the chief attractions was the belief in Jesus Christ who, as a mighty warrior, had hung from a tree, like ancient Odin, and had risen to life triumphant.

The mass acceptance of Christianity followed the same pattern in all three of the major Scandinavian lands—Denmark, Norway, and Sweden. The assembly of leaders debated the wisdom of becoming Christian, and a decree was made to the effect that the whole community would become Christian. This type of process has been observed among many other tribal societies by western missionaries during the last 100 years.[22]

It is King Harold Bluetooth who is claimed to have "made the Danes Christian." It is during his reign that we first hear of bishops among them (about A.D. 948). However, it was his son Knut, familiar to children as King Canute, who made Christianity an effective part of the life of the Danes. Knut made England the center of his realm which, when his brother died, also included Denmark. The death of Knut in 1035 did not halt the progress of Christianity, as illustrated by the increase in the number of bishops.

Olaf Tryggvesson (969–1000) was a typical swashbuckling Viking warrior. While raiding in the Scilly Isles he encountered a hermit who made a deep impression on him. As a result he accepted baptism before returning to Norway in A.D. 995. Shortly after his return, he was elected king of the whole country and commenced to make Christianity the religion of his people. Olaf seems to have made use of every means available to him from persuasion to sheer coercion. When the leaders' council finally realized that Olaf was intent on instituting Christianity, they all agreed to accept the new religion. Olaf Tryggvesson died in 1000, and after a battle with his enemies Olaf Haroldson (995–1030) became king in 1016. Like his predecessor, Olaf Haroldson continued the process of the Christianization of his people, but he did the work in a less violent way. He brought in bishops and priests from England to baptize and teach his people.

The Vikings not only settled in Britain but also in the north of the Frankish kingdom. These Normans also became Christians and were to invade Britain under the well-known William the Conqueror in 1066. The Normans brought with them new ideas of church building, organization, and Latin and French words. With their coming, the rich cultural heritage of the British people was completed, and all called themselves Christians.

Notes

1. Sir Frank Stenton, *Anglo-Saxon England* (Oxford University Press: Oxford, 1985), pp. 1–30.
2. Bede, *A History of the English Church and People* (Penguin Classics: Harmondsworth, 1968), pp. 55–57.
3. Stenton, op. cit., p. 3.
4. John Matthews, *The Arthurian Tradition* (Element Books: Shaftesbury, 1989).
5. James Atkinson, "The Celtic Way," *Christian History*, Vol. V, No. 1, p. 22.
6. Mircea Eliade, *A History of Religious Ideas,* Vol. 2 (University of Chicago Press: Chicago, 1984), p. 154.
7. Stenton, op. cit., p. 101.
8. Bede, op. cit., p. 100.
9. Ibid., p. 69.
10. Ibid., p. 71.
11. Ibid., p. 87.
12. Eugene A. Nida, "The Role of Cultural Anthropology in Christian Mission," in William A. Smalley, *Readings in Missionary Anthropology* (William Carey Library: Pasadena, 1974), p. 308.
13. K. S. Latourette, *A History of the Expansion of Christianity,* Vol. 2 (Zondervan: Grand Rapids, 1970), p. 78.
14. John Sladden, *Boniface of Devon* (Paternoster Press: Exeter, 1980).

15. Stephen Neil, *A History of Christian Missions* (Pelican: Harmondsworth, 1964), pp. 74–77.

16. Eliade, op. cit., p. 157.

17. Davidson, H. R. Ellis, "Scandinavian Cosmology" in C. Blacker and M. Loewe, *Ancient Cosmologies* (George Allen & Unwin: London, 1975), pp. 172–197.

18. Eliade, op. cit., p. 160.

19. Gwyn Jones, *A History of the Vikings* (Oxford University Press: Oxford, 1986), p. 320.

20. Stenton, op. cit., pp. 255–257.

21. Jones, op. cit., p. 315.

22. Donald McGavran, *The Bridges of God* (World Dominion Press: London, 1955).

3

Pagans, Witches, and Heretics

By the end of the twelfth century, Europe—from Italy to Scandinavia and France to Russia—was almost entirely Christian by profession. Only the Muslims of the south and east, and a few of the Baltic peoples remained outside the Christian orb. This expansion of Christianity did not occur without a continual confrontation between Christianity and the pagan religions of the European peoples. Even when the peoples were converted to Christianity, this did not mean that the old pagan ways totally disappeared. Often they either went underground or were reinterpreted into more acceptable forms. In this chapter we will look at the attitude of the church in Europe at that time toward pagan religions, especially witchcraft.

Traditional Roman beliefs

Prior to the conversion of Constantine in A.D. 312, the early Christians lived as a minority within a pagan society. The first century was a period of religious experimentation and syncretism. People were free to worship any deity, provided they showed loyalty to the Roman state.

The Romans worshiped many gods of markedly different kind and origin. These ranged from great deities such as Jupiter, and deified heroes such as Hercules, to nature spirits and household gods. This acceptance of a diversity of deities had arisen over the long period of historical evolution of the people of Rome. In earlier times the adoption of an alien cult was seen as a means of overcoming an enemy people. According to tradition, the Romans were unable to defeat the neighboring Etruscan city of Veii until they had special prayers to the goddess Juno and enticed her to abandon Veii and migrate to Rome.[1]

Besides the gods known by name, the Romans worshiped a number of rather vague spirits, often called "numina." These spirits were intermediaries between humans and the deities of heaven and the underworld. They tried to control the deities by means of prayers, sacrifices, and even magic. In his *Natural History* (XXVIII, 3), Pliny writes:

> Do magic words and spells have any power? . . . Individually, one by one the wisest have no faith in such things; but collectively throughout their everyday lives, they act as though they believe, without being aware of it.[2]

Roman religious observance may be divided into two main areas of activity: the offering of sacrifices to their many gods and the practice of divination. It was believed that the goodwill and assistance of the gods could be procured by sacrifices and prayers, and the will of the gods could to some measure be obtained through divination.

In Rome there were close links between religion and society that required the practice of sacrifices. It was not even necessary to believe in the gods, provided that the traditional sacrifices were offered. Some of the non-Christian scholars scoffed at the stories of the traditional gods, but they were careful to continue offering sacrifices.[3] There was no priestly class, and all the priests were elected from the governing class in the Republican period. For example, Julius Caesar was both consul and Pontifex Maximus (chief priest) in 44 B.C. This led to the growing acceptance of the divinity of the emperor.

Divination, as mentioned earlier, was the other element in traditional Roman beliefs. Divination was not a method of directly predicting future events but rather a means of ascertaining whether a proposed course of action was favorable to the gods. Several methods were practiced, such as observing the flight of birds, the sacrifice of animals, and the examination of their entrails.

Magic was practiced at all levels of society from peasant to emperor. The Emperor Nero apparently had recourse to magicians following his arranged murder of his mother. He was so tormented with guilt that he tried to call up her ghost so that he could beg her forgiveness.

For the Romans, magic and religion were closely linked although some distinctions can be made. Magical practices implied an element of compulsion if the ritual was correctly performed. Religion was more a matter of an appeal to a deity with the persuasive use of prayers and sacrifices. Many magical rites invoked the assistance of ghosts and deities of the underworld, and often made use of human remains.

The Roman law recognized a distinction between what was legal and illegal magic. The use of divination, such as the flight of birds, was quite acceptable, but antisocial rites were condemned. For example:

> Persons who celebrate, or cause to be celebrated impious or nocturnal rites, so as to enchant, bewitch, or bind anyone, shall be crucified, or thrown to wild beasts. . . . Anyone who sacrifices a man, or attempts to obtain auspices by means of his blood, or pollutes a shrine or a temple, shall be thrown to wild beasts. (Sentences of Paulus 5.23.15–18, dated about A.D. 210.)[4]

During the first and second centuries, magic became much more prevalent in Roman society than it had been until then. This may have been partly due to the introduction of magic allegedly based upon Zoroaster or Egyptian practices. With these came the mystery religions, or oriental cults, as they are sometimes called. Among them was the worship of Isis coming from Egypt, the cult of Mythras from Iran, the great Mothergoddess Cybele from Asia Minor, and Bacchus from Greece. The worship of these deities involved initiation ceremonies for their devotees that were held in secret and often involved all kinds of licentious activities.

The requirement of an initiation into the mystery cults meant that the cult was one of personal choice and conviction. The adherents of the cult cut across national and racial boundaries. The details of the rites and initiation ceremonies of the mystery religions are now rather obscure.

The worship of the goddess Isis was a popular mystery religion in the Roman world. It seems to have been powerfully influenced by ideas of syncretism and the belief that all human perceptions of deities are actually one universal god. Isis was known as the "Glory of Women" for she was believed to give women equal power with men. The cult of Isis was strongly institutionalized. The temples had a hierarchy of priests, and magnificent processions were organized in which the image of the goddess was carried, accompanied by music.

Romans and Christianity

The Roman world harbored many quite separate religious sects and systems of belief and allowed an unprecedented degree of religious tolerance. There were, however, some notable exceptions to this general principle. The Celtic Druids were permanently suppressed, and on occasions some of the mystery religions were restricted. It was the Jews and Christians who suffered some major persecutions. The causes of the persecutions of the Christians seem to have been various. Nero seems to have made them a scapegoat for the fire of Rome in A.D. 64, in order to divert suspicion from himself.

Many pagans believed that Christians were involved in harmful magical practices. A possible example of this misunderstanding of a Christian is seen in the second-century Roman novel known as *The Golden Ass,* or *Metamorphoses.* This is the only complete Roman novel that has survived, and it has as its hero a man called Lucius who becomes interested in magic and accidentally turns himself into an ass. Being unable to reverse the spell he is compelled to serve various masters, but he retains his human mind and observes many trials and situations. Finally, he is restored to human form by the intervention of the goddess Isis.[5]

While in the form of an ass, Lucius is at one point sold to a baker whose wife appears to be a Christian. She is described as worshiping only one god, of drinking unmixed wine early in the morning, and of giving her body to continual sexual license. The drinking of wine may be a misunderstanding of the daily practice of communion, and the sexual license to the practices that were believed to occur during the "love feasts." The woman was accused of rejecting polytheism and worshiping only one god.

What made Christian conversion so surprising to the Romans was the exclusive claims that it made on its followers. They were to acknowledge no other "Lord," be he pagan deity or the emperor himself. It was over this very point that many early Christians suffered martyrdom in the arenas of Rome. The Jews had provided interest and hatred because they alone had stood out for monotheism and the destruction of idols. The Christians followed their stand, regarding conversion as a radical change from one religion to the Christian faith. The church therefore took the position, from its earliest days, that there was salvation in no other religion except Christianity.

With the conversion of Constantine, Christianity became the state religion of the Roman Empire. There are two issues that the church had to deal with which, while interrelated, should not be confused. The first was the attitude toward antisocial magic, which was already considered evil within traditional Roman culture, and the second was the attitude toward pagan culture and religion.

Concerning antisocial magic, Christian emperors from Constantine onward introduced legislation against such and progressively restricted the limits of what was regarded as acceptable magic. In A.D. 321, Constantine forbade any magical rites that endangered the health of other people but permitted those used for medicinal practices. In A.D. 357, Constantinus forbade magic altogether: "Chaldeans, magicians, and others who were commonly called malefactors on account of the enormity of their crimes shall no longer practice their infamous arts."[6]

A second greater issue for the church was how it could relate

the classical traditions of learning and culture with the monotheistic dimensions of Christianity. Much of pagan Roman
culture was adopted into the new Christian society of the
Romans. For example, the great temple of the Pantheon was
transformed into a church in the seventh century. However,
they also recognized a clear break with their pagan past.
For their new churches and palaces, the popes and princes
stripped the Colosseum of its precious marble, travertine, and
metal.

A further issue was how the Christianized Romans viewed
the generally pagan peoples of the north who were raiding their
borders. It was Augustine, in the fifth century, who became the
polemic leader of his day. He lived at a time when the waves of
Germanic peoples surged into the Roman Empire, causing
public anxiety nearing that of panic. The Goths sacked
Rome in A.D. 410, and the Vandals were besieging the city
of Hippo even as Augustine, the city's bishop, lay on his deathbed.

The Germanic warriors appeared to the Roman world as the
children of the unclean spirits who wandered the wasteland
marshes. Attila the Hun appeared to be the very lord of sorcery
as he came with his magicians. Before the battle with Actius,
"Attila assembled the sorcerers. There in the great tent lit by
torches gathered together a council of magicians; the Ostro-
gothic auspice, his hands plunged into the entrails of the victim
whose palpitations he watched; the Alaric priest shaking in a
white flag his divination sticks, according to the intermingling
of which he read out their prophecies; the Hunish sorcerer
whirling round beating a drum and evoking the spirits of the
dead until, with foaming lips he rolled over exhausted and grew
rigid in catalepsies; while at the far end of the tent sat Attila on
his stool, watching these convulsions and listening to every cry
of these interpretations of hell."[7]

Although paganism was powerless in the Roman Empire, it
was never fully exterminated. Many people murmured that the
old gods would never have let Rome fall if the people had still
believed in them and offered sacrifices to them. This argument

stirred Augustine to write a great thesis about the nature of the church and humanity. It took several years for him to complete what was to become one of the most influential texts of the Christian church—*The City of God*.

With time, the invading Germanic peoples were Christianized. Like Constantine, many kings of northern Europe saw distinct personal and social advantages in becoming Christian. Not only did it help to unite their kingdoms but also allowed them to develop important trade and social links with other Christian nations. It was the Celtic missionaries who quietly moved among the ordinary peoples of northern Europe, teaching them the true nature of the Christian religion. Even so, the superstitions and myths of the earlier religions remained as folk traditions, and one of the most important of these was the belief in witchcraft.

Witchcraft

The Germanic peoples believed in witchcraft and sorcery that caused sickness and ill-fortune. These powers were especially attributed to women, and it was from this background that the stereotype of the witch as an old hag became common to European tradition. In ancient Greece and Rome, magic was often ascribed to the gods themselves, and certain goddesses, such as Diana and Selene, were particularly associated with the performance of malevolent magic that took place at night. The response of the early church was to condemn all other religions, together with antisocial magic.

In A.D. 690, Theodore, Archbishop of Canterbury, legislated against those who sacrificed to demons or used divination.[8] Witches, diviners, and adulteresses were to be driven out of the land by the laws of Edward (A.D. 901). Charlemagne condemned witchcraft as evil and passed the death penalty for those who practiced such. The position of the church was stated at the little known Council of Ancyra in the ninth century.

Some wicked women, reverting to Satan, and seduced by the illusions and phantasms of demons, believe and profess that they ride at night with Diana on certain beasts, and with an innumerable company of women, passing over immense distances, obeying her commands, as their mistress, and evoked by her on certain nights. . . . Therefore, priests everywhere should preach that they know this to be false, and that such phantasms are sent by the Evil Spirit, who deludes them in dreams. Who is there who is not led out of himself in dreams, seeing much in sleeping that he never saw waking? And who is such a fool that he believes that to happen in the body which is done only in the spirit?[9]

The Council showed sturdy skepticism as to the suggestion that witches undertook night-flying to cause harm. However, this statement of the church that night-flying is illusory did not stop the belief in such events. Folk belief in witchcraft, nocturnal gatherings, and werewolves persisted and even grew stronger in the minds of the ordinary people.

One major development was the concept of a pact with the devil. This seems to have originated from Isaiah 28:15 in the Latin Vulgate Bible, which reads: *percurrimus foedus cum morte et cum inferno fecimus pactum*[10] ("You boast, 'We have entered into a covenant with death, with the grave we have made an agreement.'") It was the word *pactum* in the Vulgate that created the notion of people making a pact with the devil. This notion was to become important in the Middle Ages. As Keith Thomas writes,

It was only in the late Middle Ages that a new element was added to the European concept of witchcraft which was to distinguish it from the witch-beliefs of other primitive peoples. This was the notion that the witch owed her powers to having made a deliberate pact with the Devil.[11]

Witch-Crazes of Europe

The Crusades directed religious fervor and personal ambition toward the Muslims. All Europe was Christianized, and so the attention of the Europeans was directed toward the world of Islam. This stretched around them as a belt from Spain, along North Africa, and northward through the Holy Land, Persia, and beyond. This contact with the Muslim world brought many changes to Europe.

First, the contact with Arabic culture introduced studies such as alchemy, and astrology produced a new interest in what has been called "natural magic." While learning was only kept alive through the monasteries of Europe, in the Arab world there were major advances in mathematics, astronomy, and chemistry. This new learning came into Europe through Muslim Spain in the twelfth century. Many ancient writings of the Greek philosophers that had been lost from Europe were translated from Arabic into Latin. New ideas were to come as a shaft of light that was ultimately to lead to the Renaissance.

Second, the Black Death, which spread across Europe from 1346–1351, killing at least a quarter of the population, led many to look for scapegoats. Jews were commonly blamed for poisoning the wells along with those branded as witches. Even though the Jews were dying in equal numbers as other people, many were killed. In Strasburg alone, some 2,000 Jews were burnt to death as a result of the panic that gripped the populace.

Third, in 1417, a strange dark-complexioned people suddenly appeared on the eastern frontier of Germany—the gypsies. They were dressed in exotic and colorful clothes and claimed to be exiles from the country they called "Little Egypt," probably northern India.[12] As these people spread throughout Europe they brought with them a variety of folk beliefs from India: fortune-telling, charms, and sorcery. E. B. Trigg argues that this probably led to a sudden revival of belief in witchcraft in the fifteenth century.[13]

The Roman church reacted to these changes by an expression of its exclusivism in the decree of the Council of Florence (1438–45). This led to the inquisition.

The Holy Roman Church firmly believes, professes and proclaims that none of those who are outside the Catholic church—not only pagans, but Jews also, heretics and schismatics—can have part in eternal life, but will go into eternal fire, "which was prepared for the devil and his angels," unless they are gathered into the Church before the end of life.[14]

It was a decree of Pope Innocent VIII in 1484 that finally opened the door to a wave of witch-crazes throughout Europe. This decree allowed two Dominican friars, Heinrich Kramer and Johann Spenger, to extirpate witchcraft in Germany, and two years later these men produced the *Malleus Maleficarum* (The Witches' Hammer).[15] This was an encyclopedia of demonology in which witches were condemned not for the harm they may cause to others, but because they were devil worshipers—the greatest of all heresies. The church, in formally recognizing witchcraft as a heresy, associated paganism, magic, and sectarianism as demonic.

It is difficult to chart the developments of the beliefs through the next four centuries. However, the pact with the devil became a central issue, and this led to the definition of a witch still held by English law today. It originates from Sir Edward Coke who defined a witch as "a person that hath conference with the Devil to consult with him or to do some act."[16] As Geoffrey Parrinder says: "In European witch trials the Devil played a prominent part, and this addition of Hebrew-Christian demonology distinguishes witchcraft in the Christian era from that of other lands, and makes its interpretation more complex."[17] The whole phenomenon of witchcraft activity became the opposite to normal, decent Christian worship as seen from the following record: "They first worship Satan, who appears to them now in the shape of a big black man and now as a goat; and to do him greater homage they offer him candles, which burn with a blue flame; then they kiss him on the shameful parts behind."[18]

The Papal Bull of 1498 did not have any influence in England until the following century. Three Acts of Parliament were passed (1542 repealed 1547; 1563 repealed 1604; 1604 repealed

1736) that made witchcraft a statutory offense. In 1542 it was made a felony "to practise witchcraft, enchantment or sorcery, in order to find treasure; waste or destroy a person's body, limbs, or goods; to provoke to unlawful love; to declare what had happened to stolen goods; or for other unlawful intent or purpose."[19] Only in the third witchcraft statute of 1604 did the full continental doctrine take effect.

Britain was saved from the worst of the persecution by the Reformation, but one of the greatest English witch-finders was Matthew Hopkins who was most influential between 1642–49. His method of ascertaining guilt was by "pricking," which meant that persons were pricked with a needle all over their bodies to find the insensitive spot produced by being touched by the devil. Accusations of night-flying, practice of the "Black Mass" at nocturnal gatherings, and sexual perversions were common. Animal familiars were another common feature of this period.

Confessions were an essential part of witch-finding. Torture was common during the witch-crazes, and people were subject to the rack, thumbscrews, and branding. Trial by ordeal was also known, as with the ducking stool. Trickery was used in which people were promised a light pilgrimage if they confessed but many were burned at the stake still confessing their innocence. At the height of such panics, people were executed at the testimony of a single person who claimed that they had been bewitched. The last execution for witchcraft in England was at Exeter in 1648, but in Scotland and in other parts of Europe the executions continued into the following century. This is one aspect of European history that tends to be forgotten. "The vast majority of those tried and convicted during the witch persecutions were innocent—which few would now dispute."[20] Evil can destroy and harm in many ways—through the accuser or the accused.

Secularism

The famous Salem witch trials of 1692 are usually regarded as the end of the period of witch-crazes among European peoples.

The discovery of trade routes to the New World and to Asia opened up new opportunities. Technological developments began to occur that were to result in the modern secular worldview. This radical change in attitude to witchcraft was due to three major factors.

1. Metaphysical

The Cartesian division of mind from matter led to the assumption that reality is that which can be observed, measured, and analyzed. It therefore raised many important questions about the whole nature of the supernatural. How could one make a scientific study of witchcraft activity or magic? It was not possible to study these phenomena in the same way as one could examine gravity or steam power. The result was that witchcraft and magic became increasingly regarded as illusionary by mainstream science. Only among a small minority did the beliefs remain.

2. Legal

The major weakness of all witch prosecutions had always been the trustworthiness or otherwise of the evidence. The extreme example was the evidence of witnesses who claimed to see beings that were invisible to the court. Another was the validity of evidence resulting from confessions often obtained by torture. Although witchcraft probably did exist, because of its illusive nature it could hardly be used as proof of itself.

3. Medical

During the medieval period, whenever there was a plague, fire, or flood, many in the church were quick to point out that it was an act of God to judge an immoral society. A sudden death, impotence, or some physical seizure was attributed to the work of the devil. However, with developments in modern medicine, and especially the availability of clean water, the plagues that broke out with frightening suddenness in the growing cities of Europe began to decline.

The development of modern psychology revealed more of the complexity of the human mind. Dreams of flying were recognized as common, and Freud showed that with the censorship of the conscious mind removed, friends and enemies alike may be attacked.

In the minds of most European peoples, witchcraft therefore became a mere superstition. The notion of the witch became a figure of fun—an old woman with a black pointed hat riding on a broomstick with her black cat. In 1951, the witchcraft act was repealed on the order of the House of Lords who were revising the statute books of the time. The witchcraft laws were seen to be antiquated and bore no bearing on contemporary society, and so were simply abrogated.

Esoteric mysticism

Before we turn to look at the rise of the neopagan movement in the twentieth century, it is necessary to consider another tradition that is to have a major influence and that is mysticism. We need to note two particular aspects: Gnosticism and Kabbala.

Gnosticism

The word "gnosticism" derives from the Greek word *gnosis*, meaning "knowledge." It is a generic term for the belief and practices of a bewildering number of syncretistic movements that flourished in the Roman Empire during the early Christian era.[21] It sought to fuse the rational traditions of the classical world with the mystery cults of pagan religions. Its secret practices ranged from extreme asceticism to extreme licentiousness.

The key concept of gnosticism was the possession of secret knowledge that would ultimately serve to unite the soul to God. It is considered generally by Christian commentators that it was against an incipient form of gnosticism that Paul wrote his letter to the Colossians.[22] The history of gnosticism is beyond the scope of this book, but its influence within the mystical tradition of the Christian church continues to emerge through the centuries.

Kabbala

Jewish mysticism claimed to have the secret knowledge of the unwritten Torah that had been communicated by God to Moses and passed on orally by Moses to Aaron and Joshua. Though observance of the Law of Moses remained the basic tenet of Judaism, Kabbala provided a means of approaching God directly. The name is said to come from the Hebrew root *kitel* which means "to receive."

The earliest form of Kabbala, called Merkava, emerged in Palestine in the first century and was mainly concerned with mystical contemplation of the divine throne or chariot of Ezekiel 1. Some time between the third and sixth centuries a speculative teaching emerged concerned with numbers. In Hebrew each letter of the alphabet also represents a number. By adding the numbers of a Hebrew word the sum was supposed to indicate a mystical connection between words.[23]

The Jewish community in Spain became a major center of Kabbalistic thought in the thirteenth to fifteenth centuries. Every word of the Torah was given a mystical explanation. Following their expulsion from Spain in 1492, the Jews were more than ever taken up with messianic hopes and eschatology, and Kabbala became popular among most Jews. Practical Kabbala involved the use of magic formulas and amulets inscribed with the sacred names of God and with the "Tree of Life."

Figure 3:1 shows the complex Kabbalistic glyph to map the descent of spirit into matter. The ten different "sephiroth" represent the different stages of the descent, and they are connected by twenty-two different paths—the Hebrew letters. Each sephiroth is associated with a particular human or divine experience, with a planet, and also a tarot card. The vertical dimensions are described as pillars, of which the middle pillar is the path of harmony and balance.

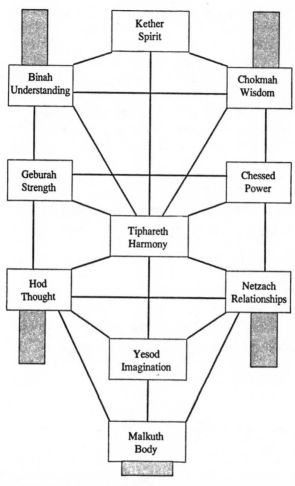

Figure 3:1 The Kabbala is complex, and the diagram only begins to map its associations. The diagram represents the descent of divinity into matter. The squares represent "sephiah," which are associated with human or divine experiences and are identified with astral bodies and tarot trumps. The vertical dimensions are described as pillars, and a student will "travel" in imagination along the paths.

Jewish mysticism exerted a continuous influence upon Christian mysticism. One of the Christian mystics deeply influenced by Kabbala was Jakob Boehme (1575–1624) and through him to a nineteenth-century group known as the Golden Dawn. In 1849, a German author by name of Johann Scheibel published a book that was claimed to be the secret magic of the Israelites and is known as *The Sixth and Seventh Books of Moses*.[24]

We are now in a position to look at the rise of the "new pagans" that has occurred during the twentieth century.

Notes

1. Margaret Lyttelton and Werner Forman, *The Romans: Their Gods and Their Beliefs* (Orbis Publications: London, 1984), p. 25.

2. Ibid., p. 30.

3. Michael Green, *Evangelism and the Early Church* (Hodder & Stoughton: London, 1970), p. 144.

4. Stephen Benko, *Pagan Rome and the Early Christians* (Batsford: London, 1984), p. 129.

5. Ibid., pp. 103–4.

6. Ibid., p. 129.

7. Charles Williams, *Witchcraft* (Meridian Books: New York, 1960), pp. 67–68.

8. Geoffrey Parrinder, *Witchcraft: European and African* (Faber & Faber: London, 1970), p. 17.

9. Ibid., p. 19.

10. Williams, op. cit., p. 56.

11. Keith Thomas, *Religion and the Decline of Magic* (Penguin Books: Harmondsworth, 1978), p. 521.

12. A. L. Basham, *The Wonder That Was India* (Sidgwick & Jackson: London, 1988), pp. 512–15.

13. E. B. Trigg, *Gypsy Demons and Divinities* (Sheldon Press: London, 1973), p. 4.

14. Kenneth Cracknell, *Towards a New Relationship* (Epworth Press: London, 1986), p. 9.

15. Heinrich Cramer and Johann Spenger, *Malleus Maleficarum* (Arrow Books: London, 1986).

16. Thomas, op. cit., pp. 523–24.

17. Parrinder, op. cit., p. 63.

18. Ibid., p. 63.

19. Thomas, op. cit., p. 525.

20. Matthew Hopkins, *The Discovery of Witches,* 1647 (pamphlet in British Museum).

21. Benjamin Walker, *Gnosticism: Its History and Influence* (Crucible: Wellingborough, 1983).

22. Donald Guthrie, *New Testament Introduction,* Vol. 2 (Tyndale Press: London, 1968), pp. 162–166.

23. Francis King, *Magic: The Western Tradition* (Book Club Associates: London, 1975), p. 108.

24. Migene Gonzalez-Wippler, *The New Revised Sixth and Seventh Books of Moses and the Magical Use of the Psalms* (Original Publications: New York, 1982).

4

The Pagan Revival

The eighteenth century was one of European expansion, with first explorers and then traders coming in contact with people who to them were both strange and exotic. Perhaps it was the voyages of Captain Cook that most gripped the imagination of the British people. China, India, and the Isles of the Pacific wove their stories for the European—a mixture of part fact and part fiction. In general, there were three ways in which the European of the eighteenth century tended to look at "savage" life.

The first was that these primitive people embodied all the savage feelings that were part of the Europeans' own makeup. The savage was seen as corrupt, crude, and primitive. This led to feelings of hatred and disgust that resulted in the cruel massacre of many peoples as seen with the conquistadors in America and the British in Tasmania.

The second view saw the "savage" as being basically innocent but lacking the advantages of Western education. It fell, therefore, as the burden of white people to bring civilization to the savage, and this would of necessity involve the presentation of the Christian religion. The Jesuits illustrated this paternalistic attitude in their work in Paraguay where the Indians were gathered into settlements to protect them from the exploitation of the European settlers.

A third view was that which has often been called "the noble savage." William Hodges was an artist who traveled with Captain Cook to Tahiti. His painting pictured the island as an earthly paradise. The people were hospitable and happy, with a freedom from sexual inhibition that fascinated the European. It appeared like a golden age, which the European in his march for progress had somehow lost. The savages appeared worthy of envy as the European viewed them through the romantic notion of ancient Greek civilization.

The glorification of the noble savage became a dominant theme in Romantic writing, especially in the works of Jean-Jacques Rousseau. His autobiography affirms his basic tenet of the innate goodness of natural man uncorrupted by civilization. However, all Romantic writing recognized that for Westerners the golden age had gone, and it could not be imitated.

In the nineteenth century, scholars began learning more about the religions and philosophies of the mysterious East. The more they studied, the more they were amazed by the intellectual perspectives of a people so different from their own. Anthropologists and folklorists began to study the culture of tribal people and to appreciate that they were not as simple or primitive as they had first thought but had an innate richness of culture and thought. Sir James Frazer's book *The Golden Bough* (1890) made a broad study of traditional religion and became a best-seller that influenced a whole generation.

As Western science and technology developed, many Victorians felt as if the mysteries of God's creation were being pushed further and further back. Some people felt attracted to the romance of ancient ways. Modern druidry was founded in 1717 by John Toland. Edward Williams, generally called "Iolo Morganwg," claimed to have rediscovered the secret poetic rules and practices of the Welsh Druids that had been passed on unchanged in his native Glamorgan. This stimulated a revival of interest among the Welsh in their language and culture. In 1792, he organized the first Gorsedd (enthronement) of a "druidic bard" on Primrose Hill in London. By the 1820s the picturesque but entirely spurious trappings of druidism were being formulated into the Welsh Eisteddfodau.[1]

Other Victorians became interested in alternative spiritual ideas and practices. Animal magnetism, mesmerism, spiritualism, and mysticism found a new popularity within the Victorian age, especially among the upper classes. John Dale, in his controversial book *The Prince and the Paranormal* makes the following claims concerning Queen Victoria:

> She accepted the existence of clairvoyance and psychic power. She possessed a willingness to experiment—with table turning, for instance. . . . With less confidence, we can say that she may have been a secret Spiritualist and that John Brown was her private medium-in-residence.[2]

Victorian magicians

Eliphas Levi (1810–75) was a French occultist whose romanticization of magic through his writings was to exert a marked influence. Levi was a pious youth, which seemed to make him a candidate for the priesthood. He never received his ordination although he did become a deacon in the Roman Catholic church. For the following twenty years, he involved himself in revolutionary activities. Finally, after a broken marriage, Levi turned to occultism.

Levi's writings draw much upon that form of Jewish medieval mysticism known as Kabbala. He had come in contact with Kabbala through meeting a Polish messianist named Hoene Wronski in 1854. Although Levi mocked Wronski in his writings, Wronski's influence was profound. It was he who showed Levi the possibility of formulating a logical philosophy based on magical mysticism and convinced him of a coming age with a new and purified magic that would fix "the absolute nature of man."[3]

The outcome of Levi's contact with Wronski was the experimentation with ceremonial magic. It is a curious fact that Levi, generally regarded as the most outstanding magician of his generation, rarely practiced magic—preferring to consider the theory of occultism. He, in fact, formulated a series of three laws that were to become the foundation of most modern magic.

The first was the law of correspondence, in which every part of man's body corresponds with some part of the cosmos. This is most readily seen in astrology. In the second law, he regarded the human will as being a real force able to achieve anything. Levi's third law concerned the assumption of a formless, invisible power that he called the Astral Light, believed to permeate the whole of nature.

The Golden Dawn

Levi intrigued many, including a young Englishman named Kenneth MacKenzie. He visited Levi in 1861, and later developed into a leading occultist. He may have been responsible for the appearance, in 1887, of a mysterious cipher manuscript. The task of deciphering the manuscript fell to a young Freemason called S. L. Mathers, who had already translated some Kabbalistic texts. The manuscripts proved to be a skeletal outline of certain initiation rituals of the Rosicrucian orders.

Mathers later added to the rituals' secret knowledge, which he claimed to have gained through a sophisticated version of the Ouija board that was a feature of Victorian seances. In 1888, Mathers was involved in establishing what was called "The Isis-Urania Temple of the Hermetic Order of the Golden Dawn." An important feature of this association was the elaborate rite of initiation.

> When the newly created Adept had passed through the rite of initiation into this degree—a magnificent ceremony, at the very lowest estimation a very good piece of dramatic construction based on the symbolic death and resurrection of the candidate—his first task was the construction of the magical "weapons" and insignia. In all there were seven pieces of such equipment: a cup for water, a dagger for air, a disc for earth, a wand for fire, a sword for the fiery energy of Mars, a lotus wand for general invocations and banishing, and a Rose Cross designed to be worn on the breast.[4]

The use of color in the Rose Cross and the other insignia resulted from the doctrine that color could be a link between the world of spirits and that of matter. An astral doorway could thus be constructed through which the initiate could enter the joys and miseries of all shared mankind.

The Order of the Golden Dawn went through some measure of disintegration in 1903, but it was to have a great influence on later practitioners of magic. It was into one of these remolded groups that Dion Fortune was initiated in 1919. In 1922 she founded a group that was to become known as the Servants of the Inner Light (SIL). Today they call themselves the "Western Mysteries."

Masons

The history of the Freemasons is clouded in myth and speculation, but a widely held belief is that they emerged from the Knights Templar.[5] When the city of Acre fell to the Saracens in 1291, it meant the end of the last bastion of the Crusaders in the Holy Land. With the loss of the Holy Land, the Knights Templar lost the very purpose for their existence, which was to protect the pilgrims on their journey to Jerusalem. They were subsequently suppressed by the Pope in 1314. A small band of escapees somehow returned to Scotland, and in the face of growing persecution, they continued to exist as a secret organization.

In the eighteenth century the craft of Freemasonry grew with great rapidity among the artisan-craftsmen and spread into Europe and America. The connection, whether real or mythical, between the Knights Templar and the Freemasons added the element of romance that many educated people were looking for in the Victorian era. The very secrecy of the Order encouraged the need for rituals of initiation and with them cult objects and rituals. One important person within this movement was a German journalist Theodor Reuss. Reuss was a man on the fringe of British Freemasonry with an interest in Tantric Yoga and the study of phallic religious practice. He was encouraged by an Austrian industrialist to establish a new "Masonic Academy" in Germany, which finally led to the formation of "The Order of the Temple of the Orient" (OTO). In

1912, Reuss met up with Aleister Crowley to whom we shall refer in more detail later.[6]

In 1904, the OTO announced its teachings in their magazine *Oriflamme*. "Our Order possesses the KEY which opens up all Masonic and Hermetic secrets, namely, the teaching of sexual magic, and this teaching explains, without exception, all the secrets of Nature, all the symbolism of FREEMASONRY and all systems of religion." The OTO is a magical order but has been linked with satanic cults, especially in the U.S.A.[7]

Theosophy

It was this movement, perhaps more than any other, that was first responsible for popularizing Eastern esoteric teaching in the West. The Theosophical Society was founded in New York in 1875 by Madame Helena Petrovna Blavatsky (1831–91), an eccentric Russian mystic.

Theosophists believe that all great religions and the teachings of the wise throughout history have a certain core body of knowledge that is referred to as theosophy. The principle doctrines are closely connected with Hindu traditions. The universe is regarded as a unity based upon certain fundamental universal laws. Mankind is part of a general evolutionary process. While the forms in which life express themselves are transient, the human spirit is eternal. Thus, when a person dies the individualized spirit continues, and the spirit will in time be reincarnated into a new body. The individuals' resulting earthly conditions are determined according to the law of karma. However, within this, individuals have the power to free themselves from all human limitations and to experience reality directly through the process of meditation.[8]

These various themes were to be drawn together in the twentieth century and synthesized into new forms (see figure 4:1).

Witchcraft reappraised

Witchcraft and ritual magic were first given a pseudoscientific

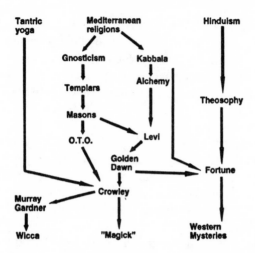

Figure 4:1 Historical development of the neopagan movement.
(OTO = Ordo Templi Oriento)

standing through the theories of the anthropologist Margaret Murray in her book *The Witch Cult in Western Europe*.[9] Her views were expressed in a more popular way in the article on "Witchcraft" in the fifteenth edition of *Encyclopedia Britannica* (1981).[10] Murray put forward the theory that the witches of western Europe were the lingering adherents of a once general pagan religion that has been displaced, though not completely, by Christianity. Margaret Murray was a recognized anthropologist and Egyptologist, but her views provoked a storm of controversy. Many of her critics pointed out that there is no record of covens as such prior to the fifteenth century, and they criticized her sources as being unreliable. She died in 1963, at the age of one hundred years but admitted before death that she was a witch herself.[11]

Margaret Murray was not the first to propose this idea. A few continental scholars had made similar suggestions. Franz Josef Mone, for example, proposed in 1839 the theory that witchcraft was an underground pagan religion.[12] Mone proposed that the Germanic tribes that had once populated the area of the Black Sea had come in contact with the cults of Hecate and Dionysus and had absorbed much of their ecstatic religious practices into their religion. This included the worship of the goat god through nocturnal gatherings and the use of magic. As this religion was practiced only by the lower strata of society, it survived with the Christianization of the tribes only as a persecuted minority.

Most scholars today regard this to be a highly imaginative theory, and it is generally discredited. However, Margaret Murray found an eager follower in the person of Gerald B. Gardner (1884–1964) who has been called everything from the "Grand Old Man of Witchcraft" by his followers to a "dirty old man" by his detractors.

Gardner was born into a well-to-do family in the north of England in 1884. In his early years he suffered from asthma, which provided the excuse for his Irish nurse, called Com, to take him abroad for winter months. This was actually a way by which Com was able to have sexual relations with young men.[13] Com finally married and settled down in Ceylon, and it was arranged that Gardner should travel there and work on a tea plantation. He was a withdrawn young man and spent much of his time with the natives studying their beliefs and rituals. In 1908 he moved to Borneo where he came to know the Dyaks, a people who had formerly been headhunters.

He returned to England in 1936 and continued to pursue his interest in folk religion. In 1955 he wrote the book *Witchcraft Today,* in which he claimed to have discovered centuries-old covens still practicing their ancient "craft" in modern Britain. In the preface to the book Murray writes,

> Dr. Gardner has shown in his book how much of the so-called "witchcraft" is descended from ancient rituals, and has nothing to do with spell-casting and other evil practices, but is the sincere expression of the feelings towards God which is expressed, perhaps more decorously though not more sincerely, by modern Christianity in church services. But the processional dances of the drunken Bacchantes, the wild prancings round the Holy Sepulchre as recorded by Maundrell at the end of the seventeenth century, the

jumping dance of the medieval "witches," the solemn zikr of the Egyptian peasant, the whirling of the dancing dervishes, all have their origin in the desire to be "Nearer, my God, to Thee," and to show by their actions that intense gratitude which the worshippers find themselves incapable of expressing in words.[14]

In later years, Gardner founded and was curator to the Museum of Witchcraft and Magic on the Isle of Man. It was, however, his ability of catching the attention of the news media that catalyzed the growth of neopaganism. To Gardner, witchcraft was a nature religion in which the witches met in covens led by a priestess. They worshiped two principal deities, the god of forests and what lies beyond, and the great Triple goddess of fertility and rebirth. The participants met in the nude in a nine-foot circle and raised power from their bodies through dancing and meditation.

Gardner's writing and the opening of the witchcraft museum led to a flood of people wanting to be initiated into covens. Gardner and his associates duly obliged, and the renaissance of witchcraft began. Today some followers of Gardner would themselves question whether Gardner had discovered an ancient coven or had made the whole thing up.[15] Alternatively, a witch who used the pseudonym of "Lugh" claimed that Gardner may have been initiated into one of George Pickingill's covens.[16]

George Pickingill was a colorful figure living in East Anglia and reputed to be the head of nine witch covens. Lugh believes that Pickingill, in an attempt to revamp his rituals, incorporated rites from earlier magical societies including the Freemasons. Pickingill retained the traditional coven structure with its three degrees of entry.

Crowley and Hitler

Another person claimed by Lugh to have been initiated into one of Pickingill's covens was Aleister Crowley (1875–1947). Crowley was an eccentric character noted for his sexual and drug-taking excesses. He was an expressionist painter whose works attracted considerable attention when exhibited in Berlin after the First World War.

Francis King identifies four major components combined by Crowley to formulate his particular brand of magic, which he called "magick," with a final *k*, to differentiate it from other forms.[17] The first component was the magic of the Golden Dawn into which Crowley was initiated in 1898. The second was Yoga with which he had become familiar in India and China. The third was the sexual magic of the Order of the Temple of the Orient (OTO), a German magic fraternity. Finally, the "Law of Thelema," a new religion of "Force and Fire" that was based on the "Book of the Law," a poem that Crowley claimed had been dictated to him in 1904 by a spirit called Aiwass. A summary of Thelemite teaching was, "Do what thou wilt shall be the whole of the law"—AL.I.40.

Extracts of Crowley's "Book of the Law" are found in one of the most influential books among Gardnerian witches, *The Book of Shadows*. Gardner claims that this book is of great antiquity, but because of the inclusion of Crowley's material and the incorporation of many rituals derived from "magick," King suggests that Crowley could well have been the author of the whole text.[18] However, Vivianne Crowley, a high priestess of Wicca, disregards this association while acknowledging the influence of Crowley.[19]

Aleister Crowley had numerous contacts with occultists in Germany, which as a country has had a long tradition of occult societies. Within the Middle Ages there were various secret esoteric orders such as the Teutonic Knights. In the nineteenth century, Freemasons, Rosicrucians, and the OTO were important. One leading occultist was von Liebenfel who edited a magazine entitled *Ostara*. (Ostara was the Teutonic moon goddess whose festival was celebrated each Spring.) Von Liebenfel proposed Darwinian evolutionary ideas, expounding the superiority of the Aryan race and Norse mythology. One of von Liebenfel's most enthusiastic readers was Hitler.

After the armistice of 1918, Hitler moved to Munich where he became a police agent spying on secret societies. Before long he had managed to infiltrate several occult-political groups. One such group was the German Workers' Party, which Hitler joined as member number seven. The leader of the group was Dietrich Eckart (1868–1923), a racist magician who, like Hitler, had been gassed in the trenches and had turned to morphine to overcome the pain. On his deathbed, Eckart appointed Hitler as the new leader, and he soon renamed the group the National Socialist German Workers' Party, Nazi for short.[20]

In recent years, German scholars have been examining the teaching and practice of the Third Reich.[21] Many of the symbols of the Third Reich were drawn directly from Norse religion. The great Nazi festivals coincided with the ancient pagan calendar rites. Some people have speculated that Hitler and his circle may have been Satanists. However, in general the Nazis sought the power that they assumed transcends the worship of gods—"the cosmic power that makes a man a god in his own right."[22]

Nigel Pennick writes,

> Among this welter of half-forgotten occult lore resurrected by the Nazis was the physical control of nations by means of the ancient science of geomancy which some call "earth magic." In ancient times, they found, a nation's most sacred place was also invariably its seat of government. Possession of this sacred place, the psychic centre of the nation, meant domination over it. . . . The Nazis pursued this idea with alacrity.[23]

Following the "flower people" of the 1960s, numerous tightknit groups emerged based around Eastern gurus. However, the style has been changing with the growth of the New Age movement. Within this new climate of religious creativity, the movement that we shall call neopaganism has become an attraction for many. Both in Europe and North America, the neopagan movement has attempted to rediscover ancient traditions and transform them into suitable forms for the contemporary scene.

Contemporary traditions

Although syncretism is part of the very nature of the neopagan movement, resulting in many crosscurrents, it is necessary to distinguish four major streams. Followers of some streams seek to distance themselves from others, while some look with disdain upon others as being theoreticians or "pop pagans." Throughout this book we shall attempt to keep the four streams distinct, while recognizing all the time the intermingling that occurs (see figure 4:2).

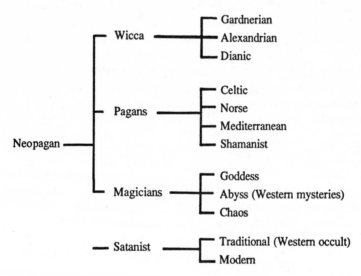

Figure 4:2 Schema of the various neopagan paths.

Wicca

In the popular press, the term *witch* has often been used to cover all neopagan groups. However, this tends merely to add to the confusion in understanding this movement. The terms *witch, witchcraft,* and *wicca* derive from the Old English *wicca,* which has to do with religion and magic. This stream has a number of overlapping traditions. The Gardnerians follow the rituals described by Gardner mentioned earlier. The Alexandrian tradition came out of a coven started by Alex Sanders in England. Sanders claims to have been initiated by his grandmother in 1933. Dianic tradition stems from the ideas of Margaret Murray that witchcraft was an ancient Dianic cult drawing upon Mediterranean religions. Nudity in ritual tends to be a characteristic of Wicca.

Paganism

The theory proposed by Margaret Murray that witchcraft was the remains of the ancient pre-Christian religion of Europe has sparked an interest in the pre-Christian religions of Europe. Ancient sites such as Stonehenge, which have always stimulated mystery and superstition, have now become the focus of ritual. The folklore of Celtic and Viking traditions are being studied afresh with the aim of reconstructing the past religion and magic of the European peoples.

Within paganism itself there are various paths. One of the most common paths is that of the Celtic tradition which can be labeled as Irish, Scots, Cornish, or Welsh traditions. *Inner Keltia,* for example, is a leading Scottish journal devoted to "reanimating virtually every aspect of Keltic-Pagan culture and spirituality."[24]

A second path is that of the Northern Tradition, which follows the pagan religion of the Teutonic and Norse peoples. Britain, it is claimed, is a land with two ancient traditions, the Celtic and the Germanic (northern).[25] Followers of the Northern Tradition have turned to a study of Scandinavian myths and legends. They may call themselves "Odinists" or "Asatru," which in the old Norse language means the belief in the gods. As we saw earlier in this chapter there was a close connection between Norse religion and the practices of the Nazis' Third Reich.

Third, there are the Mediterranean traditions drawing upon a multitude of ancient Greek and Middle Eastern legends. The Fellowship of Isis has its temple at Clonegal Castle, Eire, and draws upon ancient Egyptian religious sources. They have members in sixty-two countries, with some 4,000 in Nigeria.[26] Gnosticism, a religion that was a major problem to Christianity in the fifth century, is another stream of inspiration for the pagan movement.

A fourth pagan path is that known as Shamanism. While some North Americans have looked back to European paganism, others have turned to the ancient religions of North America, especially the anthropologically well-documented beliefs in "Shamanism." These practices have been popularized by two anthropologists, Carlos Castaneda and Professor Michael Harner.[27] More recently the shamanistic notion has been regarded as a primary religion inherent to every society including the European.

Ritual magic

Some magical groups draw on the sexual magic of Aleister Crowley for their inspiration. As we have seen earlier, Crowley drew together many occultic practices and rituals that have become the basis of many of the contemporary magical rites and "weapons."

We have already mentioned the groups drawing their inspiration from Dion Fortune, which are called "Western Mysteries." This name is used because it is seen as the continuation of the mystery traditions of the West, notably that of Egypt, Druidism, Kabbalistic magic, and that of the legendary Atlantis. In this path the universe is supposed to have evolved into a complex collection of different planes of existence of which the material is the lowest. Initiates perceive themselves as guardians over a naive humanity.

More recently, there has developed a new form of magic known as "Chaos." This owes its inspiration to ideas of A. O. Spare and Pete Carroll.

Satanism

Some people have reacted from the Christian tradition as a counterculture movement and have adopted Satanism. Many wiccans and paganists are concerned to draw a sharp distinction between themselves and Satanists. Analytically one can identify a marked difference. Paganists are drawing inspiration from pre-Christian traditional religions, while Satanists are adopting an anti-Christian position involving a perversion of Christian rites and beliefs.

"Blessed are the strong, for they shall possess the earth. If a man smite you on one cheek, *smash* him on the other!" This is the inverted gospel from Anton La Vey's Satanic Bible. La Vey and his followers invoke Satan not as a supernatural being, but as a symbol of man's self-gratifying ego, which is what they really worship. Their rituals are essentially the reverse of established Christian rituals with inverted crosses, good prayers said backwards, and nude women forming altars in the black mass.

Paganists and white witches are usually eager to stress that they do not perform any of the rites and activities that Satanists are accused of in the popular press. One white witch writes, "We do not abuse children. . . . We do not sacrifice animals (nor babies). . . . We do not have sex orgies." Within Satanism, practitioners are tending to identify two paths: traditional and modern. With regard to modern Satanism the cult focuses on the anti-Christian god, usually to the personal gain of some cult figurehead. An example is Anton La Vey of the Church of Satan.

With regard to traditional Satanism, it may be best to allow a practitioner to express his personal understanding of this path.

Traditional satanism (Shaitanism now being preferred) is entirely different. Although it is labelled as a form of Satanism, it is actually the modern-day form of the original traditional Western occultism. Granted, in its external form it appears to be usual run-of-the-mill satanism (Black Masses, anti-religious propaganda, etc.), but this is merely a cover for its more secretive, internal functions of orders with the aims of continuation of the traditional Western occultism and the reaching of godhood by individuals. There are no leaders, cult figures, etc., and orders are there as teaching orders only, with individuals working alone most of the time. One aspect of adepthood is the running of a magickal group for a period of time, leading to temporary groups such as the infamous Temple of the Sun, which hit the papers a few years ago. The Order of Nine Angels is the main teaching order for this form of occultism.[28]

The 1989 Occult Census organized by the Sorcerer's Apprentice Press reported that their respondents had the following commitments:[29]

Paganism	46%
Witchcraft	42%
Satanism	4%

Although these three groups have areas of overlap and commonality, it is necessary to distinguish between them. In the following chapters, the beliefs and rituals of those involved within the pagan movement will be considered. However, the reader is encouraged to appreciate and recognize the different strands that do exist.

This book is primarily concerned with the major traditions of paganism and wicca. We will consider some aspects of magic and Satanism, but due to the secrecy of these groups little clear, authenticated information can be obtained. Even so, much of the theoretical discussion would be relevant to all paths.

Notes

1. Charles Kightly, *The Customs and Ceremonies of Britain* (Thames and Hudson: London, 1986), pp. 107–8.
2. John Dale, *The Prince and the Paranormal* (Guild Publishing: London, 1986), p. 139.
3. Francis King, *Magic: The Western Tradition* (Book Club Associates: London, 1975), pp. 17–19.
4. Ibid., p. 25.
5. Michael Baigent and Richard Leigh, *The Temple and the Lodge* (Guild Publishing: London, 1989).
6. Peter Partner, *The Murdered Magicians* (Crucible: London, 1987), p. 170.
7. Terry Maury, *The Ultimate Evil* (Grafton: London, 1987).
8. Stephen Annett, *The Many Ways of Being* (Abacus: London, 1976), pp. 110–112.

9. Margaret Murray, *The Witch Cult in Western Europe* (Oxford University Press: Oxford, 1921).

10. Maxwell G. Marwick, "Witchcraft" in *Encyclopedia Britannica,* III (Encyclopedia Britannica: Chicago, 1981), 15th Edition, Vol. 19, p. 898.

11. Leo Louis Martello, *Witchcraft: The Old Religion* (Citadel Press: Secaucus), p. 59.

12. Vivianne Crowley, *Wicca: The Old Religion in the New Age* (Aquarian Press: Wellingborough, 1989), pp. 45–46.

13. Gerald B. Gardner, *Witchcraft Today* (Magickal Childe: New York, 1988), p. ii.

14. Ibid., p. 16.

15. Margot Adler, *Drawing Down the Moon* (Beacon Press: Boston, 1986), pp. 80–85.

16. Lugh, *The Cauldron* (Beltane, 1984).

17. King, op. cit., pp. 29–30.

18. Ibid., p. 31.

19. Crowley, op. cit., p. 50.

20. Nigel Pennick, *Hitler's Secret Sciences* (Neville Spearman: Saffron Walden, 1981), p. 18.

21. Esther Gajek, "Christmas under the Third Reich" in *Anthropology Today,* Vol. 6, No. 4 (August 1990), pp. 3–9.

22. Pennick, op. cit., p. 92.

23. Ibid., p. 3.

24. Adler, op. cit., p. 488.

25. Nigel Pennick, *Practical Magic in the Northern Tradition* (Aquarian Press: Wellingborough, 1989).

26. Personal correspondence with author.

27. Carlos Castaneda, *The Teachings of Don Juan: A Yaqui Way of Knowledge* (Pocket Books: New York, 1968).

28. Personal correspondence (June 30, 1990).

29. Eileen Barker, *New Religious Movements* (Her Majesty's Stationery Office: London, 1989), p. 198.

Part 2

◯)

BLESSED BE!

5

Gaia—The Goddess

Leonora arrived at the television studio a few minutes after me. We were both going to be interviewed by Brian Redhead on a Channel Four talk show. I was present because of the publication of my book looking at traditional religion from a Christian perspective, and Leonora as a self-confessed witch. The production crew made some of the usual comments such as: "Did you have any difficulty parking your broomstick?" Leonora took the banter with good humor. Soon we were ushered into the broadcasting studio, and for a few minutes we were both interviewed by Brian.

> Brian Redhead: Doesn't it [witchcraft] lack a core of theology which Christianity has brought to the world?
> Leonora: In fact we are working, at the moment, on actually articulating the theology.

The fact that witches and many in the pagan movement do not have a clearly defined theology comes as a surprise to many outside the movement. On the other hand, most people involved in neopaganism shrink from the very use of the word *theology,* and some practitioners felt that Leonora had fallen into Mr. Redhead's trap.[1]

Religious creativity, not dogmatic orthodoxy

A fixed, dogmatic statement of orthodox belief is contradictory to the pagan movement, which encourages freedom of belief and practice. Neopagans claim that dogmatic Christianity led to the persecution of heretics and Jews during past centuries. In general, witches and pagans are primarily concerned with practice rather than philosophy, ritual rather than theology. "Neo-pagans think of their religion as based on what one does, not on what one believes," declares Margot Adler, a practicing witch.[2] She adds, "Most neo-pagan religions have few creeds and no prophets. They are based on seasonal celebrations, the cycles of planting and harvesting, on custom and experience rather than the written word." However, Leonora's answer shows the need of some witches to state their belief in a rational way.

Why is it that such religious creativity is emerging within contemporary society? Essentially, it reflects an individual's dissatisfaction with the existing religious system and a desire for spiritual growth. This has been formulated in the following way as suggested by Geoffrey Nelson:

1 Religious innovation occurs when an individual who has strong spiritual needs
2 is unable to satisfy these needs within the context of the existing religious institutions.
3 Consequently he either withdraws from or is expelled from existing institutions
4 and retreats to develop his own methods of spiritual growth and expression
5 leading to the establishment of new religious movements.[3]

We shall return to the reasons for which people become part of the movement in chapter 12. We need first to consider what neopagans believe. This is not a question that can be readily answered. Chris Bray says,

Occultists are religious opportunists and pagans will quite rightly use any format or philosophy which appeals to their nature while linking with the overall pagan tenets. Therefore whilst there is a definite pagan philosophy underpinning the popularity of paganism, often worship and activity ends as an individual and personal blend of magical tradition drawn from various currents some of which may outwardly seem in conflict.[4]

Dan Hussey argues that no one could draft a thesis on the theology of neopaganism in a similar way to that found within Christianity. All one can produce is "half a dozen clear sentences, each proclaiming one aspect of belief . . . simple, but sufficiently broad as to embrace the many variants of the Old Religion."[5] Dan Hussey's attempt to define the essentials of pagan belief, for example, includes the following: "My faith is born of the adoration of Life; I share the World with all living things. They are my brothers and sisters; Earth is our Mother and Heaven our Father."

There are three major tenets of the pagan belief system that are universally held by neopagans. These are,

1. The Earth goddess
2. Polytheism
3. The transpersonal nature of the human psyche

The goddess and polytheism are essential themes of the belief systems of the wider neopagan movement. However, as we shall see, the rationale of these beliefs is based upon an understanding of the human psyche characterized by the teaching of Carl Jung. To the outsider, the beliefs and ideas of pagans appear to have no logical foundation, but this is because they are applying a different model of the human psyche than that held by most in Western society. This, as we shall see, is a vital key to understanding many religious movements now emerging.

Before we consider the nature of the human psyche and its repercussions, we need first to gain an understanding of the general beliefs of the movement with regard to their cosmology. We will therefore begin with an examination of the theme of the goddess. This is found not only within the pagan movement but within much of the wider New Age movement. The goddess theme is fundamental to the neopagan movement and leads to an understanding of the importance of feminism and ecology within the movement, and to some extent their attitude toward Christians.

The Lady

The expression "Mother Earth" is not merely an idiom of speech in the English language but is common to many traditional languages reflecting a deeper concept of the worship of the Earth as a female deity of fertility. In Greek mythology the goddess of the earth was called Gaia, while among the Romans Diana was the goddess of fertility. Throughout northern Europe archaeologists have discovered many images of goddesses. These deities were often associated with rivers and healing spas such as at Bath and Buxton. In ancient Egypt, the goddess Isis was worshiped, and her cult flourished in many parts of the Roman Empire before the Christian era. Kali is the major female deity within Hinduism. In the Old Testament, one reads of the Canaanite worship of Baal, the sky-god, and Ashtaroth, the earth-goddess (1 Sam. 7:3–4).

Neopaganism considers that the goddess is known by different names depending on the particular path followed. Within Wicca, many of the goddesses' names are considered sacred and must not be spoken except in a ritual context. For this reason, the words *the Lady* or *Aradia* will be used in written texts. Those following a Mediterranean path usually adopt the name Isis, while those involved in aspects of channeling have tended to adopt the name Devi from Hinduism. The actual name that is used is not considered important in itself. Whether the name is famous or merely a local deity, all are she. As one writer expresses it: "We believe that regardless of whichever Goddess' Holy Name you care to choose, she will relate to you in a personal and unique way which is tailored perfectly, in Her infinite wisdom, to suit *you*."[6]

There is one neopagan tradition that tends to give less emphasis to the goddess than others, and that is the Northern Tradition, which draws on the ancient Viking religion for its inspiration. The Norse religion puts emphasis on war, and therefore on male deities such as Odin. This in turn leads some pagans to dismiss Norse paganism as "patriarchal."[7] Even so, this path would have great respect for the Earth and the power within it.

The role of the goddess is seen as one of fertility and the subsistence of life. Thus, the sexual motif requires not only the goddess, but also a god. As Vivianne Crowley writes, "Wicca worships the divine in the way of our ancient ancestors which is as the Triple Goddess and a Dual God. These are seen as ultimately two aspects of the one divine force which is beyond male and female."[8] The god has been likened to a straight line surging forever onwards through space but achieving nothing until it is received and acted upon by a restraining influence that curves it into a vast circle. This circle is likened to the goddess who sustains and nourishes all things.

Within this pattern of fertility, the goddess manifests herself in the three phases of womanhood: virgin, great mother, and crone. She is virgin not in the sense of unsexed, but in the sense of a woman not owned by or needing man. In this form she teaches woman's independence of man. "For a man the Goddess is the anima, that all-powerful, frightening and beautiful figure who beckons him from the portals of his unconsciousness to make the heroic journey into the psyche to find the Grail, the divine essence of himself."[9] It is in this context that the priestess mediates to the man.

The second aspect of the goddess is the lover/mother. This is the woman who has known sexuality and carries the seed of the man within her womb. The goddess is here seen as having descended to the earth to bear a child. It is in the strength of her sexuality that woman retains her strength and independence. Finally, the goddess is seen as the crone, the old woman who is no longer fertile and has given over her earthly dominance to others. A parallel is often drawn with the Hindu deity Kali, who is perceived in the dual role of both the bringer of life and the destroyer. It is in the frightening aspect of destroyer that Kali is equated to the aspect of the goddess known as the crone.

These three forms are revealed in the changing seasons of

the year: spring, summer, autumn. It is the cycle of sowing, growth, and harvest. "The goddess is cyclicity and transformation, rise and fall, waxing and waning. She embodies the knowledge that out of every destruction there comes creation, and from all creation follows death."[10] As we shall see in chapter 9, these are celebrated in the various calendar rites that characterize the modern pagan movement. They are also seen in the new moon's growing to its fullness and dying away only to be reborn. For neopagans the Triple Goddess relates in a kind of symbolic experience to the totality of nature—the feeling that one is part of the divine reality that is the living world.

Not only is the goddess worshiped through the calendar rites, but a sense of awareness of the goddess in all nature is required. This may occur through quiet meditation to allow one the opportunity of attunement with her. It may be through walking in the stillness of a moonlit evening or embracing a tree, which is part of her very life.

The Earth Goddess must not be perceived as some transcendent deity living outside this world and having responsibility for planet Earth. The goddess is both transcendent and immanent. She is the very soul of nature. She is a specific deity, but also she is all and in all. Philosophically this is pantheism—the belief that all is god, and god is all. Christianity sees a dualism between God and creation. The pantheism of Hinduism, on the other hand, perceives no dualism, but a creation formed by deity from the very essence of deity. This important stream of thought common to the whole of the New Age movement has its origins with the Theosophical Society that drew much upon the great Hindu text, the Bhagavad Gita.[11]

This belief is illustrated in a strangely whimsical little poem written by a pagan mother for her child.

> "Mummy, where does the goddess live?"
> "We walk upon her in the Earth,
>   We breathe her, in the air.
>   We sail upon her in the sea
>   For she is everywhere.

> She's all around us every day
> In everything we see,
> In every stick and every stone
> In every plant and tree.
> She's there in every sparkling stream,
> In all things wild and free.
> And if you look down deep inside
> She's there, in you and me."[12]

Two issues arise from the belief in the Earth Goddess: feminism and ecology.

Feminism

Margaret Murray, writing in the 1920s, placed the emphasis upon "the god of the witches," which is the title of one of her books. It was Gerald Gardner who, in the 1950s, changed the focus of attention to the goddess as the major deity. He wrote, "The goddess of the witch cult is obviously the Great Mother, the giver of life, incarnate love. She rules spring, pleasure, feasting and all the delights. She was identified at a later time with other goddesses, and has a special affinity with the moon."[13] In drawing upon the ancient goddess theme he provided a way in which women could take on a fuller religious status and role. It was the female who becomes the priestess able to minister power to the male.

This focus upon the goddess contrasts with that of the major religions in which the popular concept of deity is male. Neopagans would especially point to the Christian idea of "God the Father," and the continual reference to deity as "He" in the Bible. Why do English-speaking people continually speak of "mankind," "brother of man," and "man" when they mean humanity? As Mary Daly expresses it so succinctly: "If God is male, then male is God."[14] Many neopagans would argue that the coming of Christianity with its male-dominated theology swamped all traditional awareness of the goddess and the status of female. Males alone could be priests able to minister to the male god. Females were excluded from the main religious cult of the European peoples. Only in the persecuted role of "the witch" could women have any role in religious practice.

One can see here a major difference between paganism in Britain and the U.S.A. In Britain, the Wiccan tradition was founded by men, and until about 1980 more men than women were involved.[15] It is generally believed that Raymond and Rosemary Buckland brought the Gardnerian tradition to the United States in the 1960s.[16]

It was at this time that the feminist movement was beginning to gain momentum, and goddess spirituality impacted with that movement. Political feminism joined with feminist spirituality as seen in the writings of Z. Budapest.[17] She and others saw Wicca as a woman's movement with the emergence of feminist covens. No wonder that Margot Adler found in her survey of American witches that feminism was the number one route by which people entered the craft.[18]

British pagans have not been unaffected by these developments. Caitlin Matthews, writing in 1989, presents a contemporary British perspective. In answer to the question of how the goddess came to the world today she writes, "She has via feminism to remind the world that women have value and potential, and that feminine symbols and images have power. The goddess has returned at the head of this movement as a meaningful symbol of women's power. The goddess has been used, among many other issues, to spearhead political reform, lesbianism, equal rights, and better social conditions."[19]

There are many attempts to reconcile the place of femininity among male practitioners. Resort is often made to Jungian psychology as we shall see later. Jung proposed that within every person there is a male and female element that he called animus and anima. A man may therefore discover the feminine element within himself. "A man can relate to a woman on a physical level, to the divine masculine on a spiritual level, and via his anima he can relate to the goddess; or he can perceive the goddess more subtly through a woman."[20] Each woman may thus act as a priestess of the goddess to a man, and in so doing cause the male to create.

As Matthews writes,

> The understanding which lies at the heart of this teaching is a hard one for some men to accept: that the goddess and her priestessly representatives are in a position of power, that the time has come to listen to the goddess' wisdom and to learn from her.[21]

Within the Gardnerian path of Wicca, the priestess is believed to incarnate the goddess at the seasonal rites. This is done through a ritual commonly known as "drawing down the moon." At these rites the priestess, standing naked in the circle, is invoked as the goddess by her male partner who is the "high priest."

Ecology

The concern for the environment has been growing ever since the Club of Rome report in 1974 extrapolated population figures, and the resulting environmental and pollution changes. However, it was the English scientist Dr. James Lovelock, while working on a project for NASA on the detection of life forms on Mars, who began to look at the topic in a totally different way. He began to appreciate that the amazing thing about the Earth, as compared with a planet such as Mars, was how suitable it was for life. It was perfectly balanced and ideally suited to the life-forms now on the planet. It was as if the Earth itself was in some way alive and able to adapt to changes.

By speaking of the Earth as alive, Lovelock used the analogy of a tree. Ninety-seven percent of a tree is dead. It is only the thin film of living cells immediately under the bark that is alive and growing. The majority of the tree is lignum—the wood. Yet, the wood has life by its very association and connection with the living tissue. Similarly, it is only the outer surface of the Earth that is alive, and the inner part only supports that life. One cannot have dogs, birds, fish, or people as living beings without reference to the very air and sea in which they live. It is the integrated whole that makes up the living planet that Lovelock named Gaia.[22]

George Seielstad, a leading New Age writer, summarized the Gaia hypothesis in these words:

> Life, acting as a collectivity and over a global basis, actively regulates and modulates the environment in just such a way as to optimise the very conditions under which that life can flourish. Earth's biosphere (life) is not independent of the atmosphere (air), hydrosphere (oceans), or lithosphere (soil). Instead, all are part of a coherent whole. In so far as that whole maintains a constant temperature and a compatible chemical composition—in short, a benign homeostasis—within a constantly changing setting, it can be considered alive.[23]

The Gaia hypothesis has some important inferences. First, such a self-regulating system cannot occur through a process of evolution. Second, even in the face of massive environmental changes Gaia will not be destroyed, but will adapt to a new environmental balance. What happens is that many species that were supported in the earlier environmental system will be destroyed. Lovelock would argue that this is exactly the danger for the human race at our present time. The population explosion will cause increased pollution, which is likely to result in a massive change in the ecological balance of Gaia. Pollution is not bad because it spoils the Earth, but because it changes the balance of the Earth, thus making human life impossible.

Although Lovelock is not a practicing neopagan, his ideas have been adopted by many. The association of the name Gaia with the ancient Greek goddess is too close to be ignored. The ancient tribal religions were recognized as having a close association with nature, their rituals being related to fertility cults and the solar equinoxes. Included in such natural religions were ideas of animism, totemism, and pantheism that drew connections between humanity and the rest of nature.

Zell, a leader of the American-based Church of All Worlds, made a distinction between what he called philosophical religions and natural religions. Philosophical religions are those taught by prophets and have formulated creeds as with the major world religions such as Christianity and Islam. The natural religions, on the other hand, never emerged with the teaching of some prophet, but are part of the fabric of life.

> Philosophical religions are like buildings: an architect (prophet) gets an inspiration (revelation) and lays down his vision in blueprints (prophecy; scripture). The contractors, carpenters, masons, etc. (disciples and followers) build the building more or less according to his specifications. It is made of non-living materials, and does not grow naturally; it is assembled. . . .
>
> A Pagan religion, on the other hand, is like a tree: it emerges alive from the Earth, grows, changes (both cyclically in seasons, and continually in upward and outward growth), bears flowers, fruit, shares its life with other living beings. It is not made or designed according to any blueprint other than genetic. And when, after many thousands of years, perhaps, it should come to an end of its time, it does not pass from the world entirely, for its own progeny have, in the interval, begun to spring up all around, again from the Earth, and again, similar yet each unique. A world of Pagan religions is like a forest.[24]

This relationship that primitive humanity is claimed to have with the environment has been fostered by many anthropologists. The story of "The Gentle Tasaday" caught the imagination of many in America and Europe. The Tasaday were claimed to be a nonviolent people living in caves in an isolated area of the Philippines. They were held up almost as ideal human beings, living at peace and harmony with nature. Recent research following the overthrow of President Marcos has shown the Tasaday to be no more than a society fabricated by the country's Minister for Indian Affairs. In practice, many traditional societies see themselves almost in a state of war with the "wild," as Dr. Jon Kirby has shown among the Anufu of Ghana.

From time immemorial, fire has been a wall of culture against the

"wild" which has been thought of as inexhaustible, evil, dangerous, unknown and useless for any socialised purpose. It [fire] has
been man's primary ally in the constant work of domesticating the
"wild."[25]

The romantic image of the primitive society is still popular
among pagan and nonpagan people. The result in pagan circles
is that most have a strong concern for "Green" issues, and advertisements for Greenpeace and ecology groups are common
in pagan magazines. Many magazines stress that they are made
from recycled paper. However, care must be taken not to confuse and classify ecological organizations with the neopagan
movement because of their similar aims.

This belief in the "living planet" means, for the neopagan,
that everything in nature has its own unique qualities that can be
recognized by those willing to find out. Nigel Pennick stresses
this fact:

> This personification of the Earth, seeing it as a sacred being rather
> than an enormous inanimate rock, is the fundamental worldview.
> As an extension of this, all aspects of the natural world should be
> revered, as should places of power within it: locations where the
> gods are present. Sacred places in the landscape are recognised by
> their special qualities as places where, by meditation, prayer, ritual
> and ceremony, one may gain access to states of enlightenment.[26]

As Nigel Pennick realized, there is a fundamental difference
between the worldview of the neopagan and the secular materialist and, one may add, the Christian, as I discussed in my book
Clash of Worlds.[27]

This power, which is attributed to different aspects of nature,
is not something that can be experienced by materialistic means
alone. It requires an integrated use of analytical and intuitive
faculties. (We will consider the nature of human understanding
further in chapter 7.) Crystals, stones, and metals all have their
own special properties. Fossils long have been considered to
have properties bringing good luck. Crystals appear as "frozen
light," and manifest the geometrical perfection that underlies

the physical world. Every tree has its own special physical and magical qualities according to neopagans. The birch is seen as a symbol of rebirth, springtime, and purification. It is the customary tree used for maypoles, and when stripped of its white bark is burned as the Yule log.

The myths of the goddess rarely speak of her in isolation from other deities. The divine feminine and the divine masculine are perceived as the symbolic emulations of pure deity that is imageless and genderless. It is considered that sexual union is one way by which humanity is able in part to experience nonduality. We therefore now turn to a study of the male divinity.

Notes

1. Dan Hussey, "The Perils of Seeking After a Pagan Theology" *The Wiccan* (August, 1989), pp. 3–4.
2. Margot Adler, *Drawing Down the Moon* (Beacon Press: Boston, 1986), p. 10.
3. Geoffrey K. Nelson, *Cults, New Religions and Religious Creativity* (Routledge and Kegan Paul: London, 1987), p. 109.
4. Chris Bray, personal correspondence (September 17, 1990).
5. Hussey, op. cit., p. 4.
6. Sirus study paper, p. 3.
7. Adler, op. cit., p. 280.
8. Vivianne Crowley, *Wicca: The Old Religion in the New Age* (Aquarian Press: Wellingborough, 1989), p. 21.
9. Ibid., p. 172.
10. Tanya Luhrmann, *Persuasions of the Witch's Craft* (Blackwell: Oxford, 1989), p. 93.
11. Ronald W. Neufeldt, "A Lesson in Allegory: Theosophical Interpretations of the Bhagavad Gita" in Minor R, *Modern Indian Interpreters of the Bhagavad Gita* (State University of New York Press: Albany, 1986), pp. 11–33.
12. Ellie, *P.A.N.*, No. 34 (April, 1990).

13. Gerald B. Gardner, *Witchcraft Today* (Magickal Childe: New York, 1988), p. 42.

14. Quoted in Adler, op. cit., p. 202.

15. Confirmed to me by three leading Wiccans, December 15, 1990.

16. Adler, op. cit., p. 92.

17. Budapest, Z., *The Feminist Book of Lights and Shadows* (Luna Publications: Venice, Cal., 1976).

18. Quoted in Adler, ibid., p. 202.

19. Caitlin Matthews, *The Goddess* (Element Books: Shaftesbury, 1989), p. 6.

20. Ibid., p. 13.

21. Ibid., p. 15.

22. James Lovelock, *Newsweek* (March 10, 1975), p. 49.

23. Quoted in Russell Chandler, *Understanding the New Age* (Wood Books: Milton Keynes, 1989), p. 121.

24. Quoted in Adler, op. cit., pp. 305–6.

25. Jon P. Kirby, "Bush Fires and the Domestication of the Wild in Northern Ghana," *Tamale Institute of Cross-cultural Studies* (Occasional Paper, April 1987), p. 19.

26. Nigel Pennick, *Practical Magic in the Northern Tradition* (Aquarian Press: Wellingborough, 1989), p. 60.

27. David Burnett, *Clash of Worlds* (Monarch: Eastbourne, 1990).

6

The Horned God and the World of the Spirits

Polytheism—the word brings to mind for many Europeans images of idols, tribal gods, lustful dance, and sacrifices. Before we can begin to examine some of the polytheistic ideas of the neopagans, we first need to appreciate how they understand the term.

Neopagan polytheism

In the nineteenth century, scholars of religion were greatly influenced by ideas of evolution as were most branches of science. It was assumed that as humanity evolved so did its religious understanding. From early ideas of animism (a spiritual life force in all material items) and belief in ghosts, the concept of spiritual beings arose as seen in a religion such as Hinduism. In time, the polytheistic beliefs gave way to monism and monotheism. For the Victorian writers it seemed beyond doubt that the highest religion was Christianity, but even this was giving way to the new religion of science.

The evolutionary model, with its assumption of development from the simple to the complex, has generally been discredited by anthropologists. Tribal peoples with a simple stone-age technology have been found to have complex religious beliefs and perceptions. Often the concept of monotheism existed alongside polytheism and pantheism. In a similar way, the idea of the goddess exists for neopagans, among pantheism and a multitude of spirits and gods known by a wide variety of names.

Anthropologists have observed that in tribal societies there is a religious tolerance of the beliefs of other peoples.[1] A society believes in certain gods and performs certain rituals because that is the tradition of their people, and anyone born into the tribe will automatically become part of the religious culture. No attempt is made to convert members of other tribes to their gods. What may happen is that one tribe adopts a foreign deity to be worshiped alongside their own because they have come to realize its special power. Missionary activity is generally a phenomenon found only among the major world religions.

This idea of diversity and tolerance is very much part of the neopagan movement. Individual practitioners have their particular concept of deity and would venerate such by various rituals and by using their own specific names. Even so, each person would claim to be willing to accept the ideas of others that may not only be different but conflicting. The whole movement has a dynamic for experimentation with new deities, names, and rituals. Some would claim to be polytheist/pantheists, others monotheists, and yet others would see themselves as monotheists at one time and polytheists at another. To the outsider, the beliefs of the movement are like some overgrown garden with a wild profusion of plant life.

The polytheism of the neopagans is in no way naive or simple. The idea of life in all things, as expressed in the Gaia teaching, shows itself in a multitude of forms that are recognized as divine in themselves. As a neopagan correspondent wrote to me:

> My perception of what Totemism/Animism means, in its anthropomorphised form, is that each member of a class of beings (animal, vegetable or mineral) has a "spirit being" associated with it, and in addition contributes to a more general "spirit being" relating to the whole class of beings, and thence on until eventually a single overall "Nature Spirit" is reached encompassing all the lesser forms. Pantheism falls out of this naturally.[2]

The theoretical basis for the defense of polytheism comes from Jungian psychology, which will be considered in more detail in the following chapter. It is necessary here only to say that according to Jung, within the human psyche are certain foundational symbols, known as archetypes, which express themselves as myths and legends concerning deities and heroes. The task is to unite the potential of these archetypes into a symphonic whole. Polytheism, it is claimed, is the rediscovery of gods and goddesses as archetypal forces in our lives.

This wide variety of beliefs tends to cause a continual process of emergence and division of neopagan groups. Ellwood, in his study of religious groups in the United States, says that polytheism can never provide social cohesion for a group.[3] One cannot totally agree with Ellwood because there have been ancient civilizations based on polytheism, but within such there has always been the emergence of new cults that have caused some fragmentation within the society. In many countries, one finds new magazines appearing and closing as specific interests wax and wane. However, some neopagans would say that this dynamic is the very strength of the movement itself as it allows a tolerance of beliefs and rituals.

In contrast, monotheistic religions, such as Islam and Christianity, are seen as being intolerant and restrictive. They dominate people's ideas, demanding that they accept a fixed pattern of beliefs. Anyone disagreeing with the established orthodox position is regarded as a heretic and liable to be persecuted or excommunicated. Such restrictive practices are recognized as allowing the growth of large monolithic empires but at the expense of religious creativity. As expressed by one of my correspondents: "I perceive that sophisticated religions arise from the continuous overlaying of stratas of rationalisation onto the base of one or more primitive religions, with elements of Darwinian evolution deciding which religions will survive."

In recognizing the great variety of beliefs among neopagans, it is difficult to analyze their beliefs. To do so would be to oversimplify the actual situation, but to avoid it would be to ignore an important dimension of the movement. We must discuss two major aspects of the polytheistic system: the "horned god" and "earth spirits."

The Horned God

> Paganism's concept of god is as a supreme, life-giving force which is present in all things from the entire universe down to the tiniest atom of existence. This ultimate deity is manifested into two complementary influences—positive and negative, simply referred to as God and Goddess.[4]

Although today many neopagan paths emphasize "the goddess," this has not always been so. In her writings in the 1920s, Dr. Margaret Murray does not even refer to the goddess, but concentrates on the "horned god." Dr. Murray's thesis stated that modern witchcraft was a relic of ancient paganism that was dominated and submerged by Christianity. The worship of the horned god, she would argue, existed from humanity's earliest times and has been found as far afield as Egypt, Greece, India, and Scandinavia.[5] Christianity has not been able to eradicate the worship completely; it has remained among the peasant class, particularly the women. As a new religion enters and eventually dominates a society, the gods of the old religion become the devils of the new. The Christian image of the devil with horns merely developed from the idea of the horned god of traditional religion. Witches are therefore only worshiping their god as they have done for countless generations.

Murray continues by asserting that the view of the devil as evil was far from the belief of witches themselves:

> To them this so-called Devil was God, manifest and incarnate; they adored him on their knees; they addressed their prayers to him, they offered thanks to him as the giver of food and the necessities of life, they dedicated their children to him, and there are indications that, like many another god, he was sacrificed for the good of his people.[6]

This horned god of traditional religion, according to Murray, was often represented by the chief personage of the cult. Thus Gerald Gardner writes: "Who and what is called the Devil? Though members of the cult never used and, indeed, disliked the term, they knew what I meant and said: 'You know him, the leader. He is the high priestess's husband.'" Gardner continues to speculate. "In the times when the People of the Heaths held their meetings, the high priest was a man of great learning in the cult, probably a tribal chief, or possibly a Druid, and most likely everyone would know who he was. He was the horned god. . . . The Church called him the 'devil' and he became known as such."[7]

Gardner supposes that as the population became Christianized, and especially with the coming of the Normans, the "devil" would wear a mask to hide his identity.[8] This would explain why in many confessions the "devil" was said to come in various disguises to meet his followers—as a dog, a cat, or a goat.

Dr. Murray's theory has been discounted by most modern scholars for various reasons.[9] First, it seems unlikely that people should have used such an emotive name as the devil for their spiritual leader, unless the title was suggested to them by their inquisitors under torture. There appears to have been no evidence of more honorable titles being used. Second, it is surprising that there are no names of ancient European gods given to devils and deities in the many confessions. All the names that are given to the personages recorded are biblical, ecclesiastical, or merely fanciful: Devil, Satan, Lucifer, Beelzebub, Serpent, Tibb, Pretty. One does not find the names of the old pagan gods such as: Thor, Woden, Loki. Third, the names of the witches themselves are nearly all biblical names. Out of 700 names of convicted witches, Murray could not find one with a Saxon name.

Thinking neopagans recognize the fallacy of the theory and acknowledge that there is no historical proof to substantiate the view that witchcraft is the continuity of the ancient religion. However, what is important to see is the impetus that this theory has given to religious speculation. The academic theory has become a myth in its own right, stimulating the growth of the religious and magical cults. As one neopagan has expressed it:

> However, Murray's fault lies in her development of her theory to a definite assertion, supported by selective quotations, that there is actual evidence for the continuing formal worship of the Horned

God into the 20th century. Let us by all means keep the folk tales of the Craft alive; such fables are the life-blood of our religion and should be told and re-told; however, we should be clear about the distinction between myth and history. Historical evidence is always open to conjecture and interpretation but looked at dispassionately and in its widest context is both useful and interesting. Myth, while open to interpretation, does not rely on "facts" for veracity, so its use and benefit are of a different order to the purely historical. There seems to be a disconcerting tendency within modern Wiccan (and Occult) movements to confuse myth with history and to suspend belief when confronted with any claims, no matter how spurious, that would be received with scepticism, if not outright disbelief, in any other field.[10]

Generally, those entering Wicca are attracted by its emphasis on the feminine and on the goddess, but the very fertility of the goddess depends on her relationship with a male deity. This therefore is part of the whole annual cycle of nature in which the solar deity mates with the goddess to bring the harvest, before he dies in the winter months. This subject will be considered further when we look at calendar rites in chapter 9. It also expresses itself in the so-called "great rite" in which the female and male practitioners unite in sexual relations.

The horned god is called Cernunnos within Gardnerian tradition and Karnayna in the Alexandrian. Within the Celtic tradition he is often named Kernunnos or Hern the Hunter. The Gundestrop Cauldron, generally regarded as one of the finest pieces of Celtic art, was found in Denmark and dated to 100 B.C.[11] On the cauldron is a powerful figure of the horned god. He holds a torque in one hand, wears another around his neck, and in the other he holds the Earth serpent depicted with a ram's head (see figure 6:1). Within the Celtic path, the horned god is regarded as the lord of animals and therefore master of the totem animals known to the shaman.

The myth of the "horned god" has stimulated much reli-

Figure 6:1 Image of the deity Cernunnos taken from the Gundestrop Cauldron, Denmark, 2nd–1st century B.C.

gious and magical speculation developed in modern art forms. Levi's drawing of the Sabbatic Goat appearing in the 1896 edition of his book *Transcendental Magic,* has the head of a goat with massive horns and a pentagram on its forehead. The body is that of a man sitting cross-legged but having the breasts of a woman. Similarly, the writings of Dennis Wheatley portray an ambiguous leader of the cult.

Earth spirits

Brownies, dryads, elves, fairies, gnomes, hobgoblins, leprechauns, oakmen, pixies, sprites, and trolls are just a few of the names for earth spirits that are used by the various neopagan traditions. The most important spirits are regarded as those concerned with the land and magical places in the landscape.

Tree spirits

Sacred groves are a common concept among tribal societies and are also part of the neopagan system. Trees are regarded as having their own life forces or spirits (Dryads). Perhaps it is the gnarled feature on the trunk that often gives the impression of a face and makes the trees look as though they do indeed have a living spirit.

As Dusty Miller writes,

Another somewhat confusing factor about trees and Dryads is the fact that they don't have a one to one relationship. Each tree doesn't have its own personal Dryad. In fact, a tree doesn't have a Dryad, any more than we have a soul, or higher self. It's the other way round; in exactly the same way as our higher self has a physical body, so a Dryad has a group of one, or more, trees forming its physical body. Being a group entity, it is quite normal for a Dryad to have a grove, (or even a wood) of trees as the multiple parts of its physical body. This means, that in a wood, of say, a couple of thousand trees, there may be only a small number of Tree Dryads. There will be one for each of the Tree-tribes in the wood (i.e. Beech, Ash, Yew, Oak, Hazel etc.) plus one each for any other trees that have been transplanted to the wood by mankind, or brought in as seeds by birds or animals.[12]

Many neopagan groups are buying a small woodland area as a center for their rituals. The flora is allowed to grow wild. Through the rituals these places become sacred.

Serpent spirits

Many Celtic stone carvings carry the image of the serpent, depicted sometimes as a lightning flash and at other times as two serpents intertwined. We have no archaeological evidence for the actual meaning of the serpent symbol, but a mythological meaning has developed within the Celtic path.

The stylised serpent type is usually depicted snaking in one direction with a zig-zag motive on its back. It reminded me of nothing so much as a River Spirit, especially as we crossed many powerful rivers with Serpent names: Wye, Wyle, Esk, Adur, Exe, Axe, on our journey through Britain. They could be seen in their huge valleys zig-zagging across the landscape.[13]

Water, the source of life, is often regarded as having its own deities and spirits. In traditional European religions, every river or stream of any size was regarded as having its own water spirit, which was often considered the causal effect in drowning. A widespread traditional way of honoring wells is to "dress" or decorate their exterior. The practice of well-dressing continues mainly in Derbyshire and has now come under the auspices of the Church.

> Great care is taken, however, to divorce the current observances from any taint of paganism: for they are invariably declared to be "symbols of Thanksgiving to the Almighty for the precious gift of drinking water," and the subjects of the elaborate dressings are nearly always biblical scenes.[14]

The idea of the serpent spirit has also been associated with the teachings of Kundalini yoga. The serpent power is raised from the base of the spine up through the various chakras. As Nicholas Mann writes, "The horned god is sexually potent but no phallus is ever shown. Here lies the key to the raising of the serpent power, the energy turns within, not out. The phallic powers of the god are contained within the double rhythm of the body."[15]

The serpent powers are also linked with the coming of Christianity and the legends of serpent slaying.

> St. Patrick was credited for removing the snakes entirely from Ireland which has to be understood metaphysically and not literally as there are still snakes in Ireland. And while dragon-killing was realised for a while to be a stage in the Mystery of the Cycle of Fertility, St. Michael and St. George assuming the roles of the dragon killer, the flourishing of Christianity saw the serpent rapidly relegated to a baser role.[16]

Ley lines

In recent years the term *ley lines* has become common knowledge, even when people are not sure what is precisely meant. The term *ley* was adopted and popularized by Alfred Watkins (1855–1935), a Hereford antiquarian who had noticed how many ancient sites were located in straight lines with one another.[17] Ancient mounds, standing stone circles, hill forts, and even ancient churches fell along a line. Watkins discovered that the churches he found on leys had been built on former sites of stones and earthworks. He always insisted that the leys were ancient trackways.

Others showed that Stonehenge and other stone circles lined up with the rising and setting positions of the sun and moon, and sometimes these lines extended through the countryside marked by standing stones or earthworks. It was proposed that these were energy lines, or "fairy paths," as Irish tradition would call them. Spirits would travel along them at certain times of the year, and there were prohibitions against building houses or other structures on them. Nigel Pennick explains their significance:

> Places where trackways, fairy paths or roads meet, pass over sacred ground or cross one another are considered especially powerful, being equivalent to shrines in their own right. They are usually ruled by a specific local power, sprite, genius or deity, either in its own right or as an aspect of the universal deity.[18]

According to Nigel Pennick, Hitler and the Nazi occultists considered special mountains to be energy centers that collect cosmic forces from space and channel them into the earth through the ley lines.[19] By controlling these peaks and special sites it was thought that one may gain control over the whole land. Some neopagans would say that this is what happened with the coming of Christianity to northern Europe. As they took over the traditional pagan sites and built churches in their place, the domination of Christianity was established over the land and paganism defeated.

In conclusion

Within the neopagan movement there is a rich mythology of gods, spirits, kings, and heroes. The inspiration for these comes from a wide variety of historic traditions. For the outsider first coming to such a complex mythology, the question asked is, "Are they true?" To ask the question is to miss the central point. The historical credibility is not important. What is critical is the discovery of a personal myth from the riches of primitive mythology. The problem of today's people is that they have lost a myth by which they can live. To understand the reason for this we must now turn to Jungian psychology and its influence on the new pagans.

Notes

1. David Burnett, *Unearthly Powers* (Marc: Bromley, 1988).
2. Personal correspondence.
3. Robert Ellwood, *Religious and Spiritual Groups in Modern America* (Prentice-Hall: Englewood, 1973).
4. Iain Steele, *Dalriada* (Autumn, 1989), p. 9.
5. Margaret Murray, *The God of the Witches* (OUP: New York, 1931).
6. Margaret Murray, *The Witch-cult in Western Europe* (Oxford University Press; Oxford, 1921), p. 28.
7. Gerald Gardner, *Witchcraft Today* (Magickal Childe: New York, 1988), p. 131.
8. Ibid., p. 131.
9. Geoffrey Parrinder, *Witchcraft: European and African* (Faber and Faber: London, 1963), p. 65.
10. Julia Phillips, *The Cauldron* (Spring, 1990, No. 56), p. 7.
11. Frank Delaney, *The Celts* (Guild Publishing: London, 1986), pp. 165–7.
12. Dusty Miller, *Moonshine* (Spring, 1990), p. 23.
13. Nicholas R. Mann, *The Keltic Power Symbols* (Triskele, Glastonbury, 1987), p. 30.
14. Charles Kightly, *The Customs and Ceremonies of Britain* (Thames and Hudson: London, 1986), p. 231.
15. Mann, op. cit., pp. 34–35.
16. Ibid., p. 34.
17. Nigel Pennick and Paul Devereux, *Lines on the Landscape* (Robert Hale: London, 1989), p. 17.
18. Ibid., p. 94.
19. Nigel Pennick, *Hitler's Secret Sciences* (Neville Spearman: Saffron Walden, 1981), p. 57.

7

The Nature of the Human

On the walls of the Temple of Delphi, built by Phoebus Appollo on Mount Parnassus, was inscribed the most famous of all Greek precepts—"Know thyself!"

Look in a mirror. What do you see? I am not speaking of the physical form reflected back at you, but the deeper element that is you. What is the real you? This question has attracted the attention not only of philosophers, but at some time or another, perhaps every person who has ever lived. What is it that constitutes a human person beyond the observable features of the physical body? What is it that constitutes that which Christian theologians have called the "soul"? When you look at the body of someone who a few moments ago was breathing, talking, perhaps even smiling, but now is dead, what has departed? Who am I?

The answer one gives to this question has radical repercussions as to how one understands the whole of life. The answer given provides one of the fundamental assumptions that every society makes and is an important part of what anthropologists call worldview.[1] In general, Western society has been affected by the Platonic notion that held that reality consists of two substances. These two substances were the material (rocks, animals, human bodies, etc.) and the immaterial (gods, spirits, souls, minds, etc.). To Plato, the soul was entombed in the body. This dualism between mind and matter, body and soul has become an integral part of Western philosophical thought. This concept came to blossom in the teaching of René Descartes (1596–1650) with the "Cartesian dualism"—the distinction of matter and mind. Matter is that which can be examined and analyzed in a scientific manner, while the mind is that outside such study and is left for the speculation of theologians and philosophers.

With the birth of psychology, people began to report experiences that could not be verified by the scientific process. For example, how can the phenomenon of love be studied objectively? One American psychologist, John Watson (1878–1958), argued that one can only study those aspects of the human personality that can be seen and measured. Thus, instead of trying to study love feelings, Watson and his followers began to study the social aspects of dating or sexual behavior. This approach, known as behaviorism, left people with a deep personal dissatisfaction because it tended to characterize human beings as no more than machines.

The reaction against the behaviorist position began in the 1950s with humanistic psychology. This approach required a study of the whole person: body, behavior and, most importantly, feelings. The proponents of humanistic psychology emphasized two factors: first, the basic goodness and worth of human beings, and second, the validity of their internal experiences and feelings. This has led to what has become known as "transpersonal psychology." The term *transpersonal* refers to the move to go beyond a person's present, personal experience to some ultimate experience.

Of all scholars, it was Carl Jung who opened a totally new approach to the question "What is man?" The reverberations have been immense, and as we shall see, have given a philosophical rationale to magic, dreams, and out-of-body experiences. It is here that we approach the key to the understanding of the belief systems outlined in the previous two chapters. However, the reader should not assume that all neopagans are well read in Jungian psychology, although many are, but all have been influenced by a major shift in their basic assumptions about the nature of reality. This movement has been away from the secular materialism of earlier generations and toward seeking an understanding of the significance of one's own inner feelings and awareness. It is only by understanding Jungian psychology that the outsider will gain any appreciation of the rationale of the neopagan movement. Without it, the movement will appear a collection of exotic ideas and practices.

Jung's structure of the psyche

To try to make an outline of Jungian psychology in one chapter is to invite the criticism of oversimplification. Jungian psychology is complex and abstruse, and perhaps this is why Jung's original ideas have been expressed by others in many different ways.

Ego and Consciousness

In speaking of mind and mental activity, Jung chose to use the terms *psyche* and *psychic* because they cover both the conscious and unconscious. The psyche has many levels, the first of which is the conscious mind (see figure 7:1). "The conscious aspect of the psyche might be compared to an island rising from the sea—we only see the part above the water, but a much vaster unknown realm spreads below, and this could be likened to the unconscious. . . . The island is the ego, the knowing, willing 'I,' the centre of the consciousness."[2] Between the ego and the outside world, the person develops a mask behind which he or she lives. Jung used the term *persona,* the name given to the masks once used by actors to signify the role that they played. The mask will change as we grow from teenager to adulthood, and as we move from one role to another. At one time a person may be the strong businessperson, at the next the warm lover, and then the caring parent.

There are four psychological functions attributed by Jung to the consciousness: thinking, intuition, feeling, and sensation (see figure 7:2). Thinking is the function that seeks to apprehend the world and adjust to it by way of thought or cognition. The function of feeling, on the other hand, apprehends the world through the evaluation based on the feelings of what is pleasant or unpleasant. Both these functions are called rational

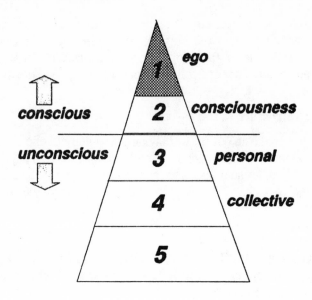

Figure 7:1 The Jungian concept of the human psyche, after Jacobi, 1973.

1. *The ego*
2. *Consciousness*
3. *The personal unconscious*
4. *The collective unconscious*
5. *The part of the collective unconscious that can never be made conscious*

because both work with evaluations and judgments. Jung calls the other two functions sensation and intuition. These are the irrational functions because they operate not with judgments, but with perceptions that are not evaluated.[3]

Personal unconsciousness and the shadow
The ego may be thought of as lying behind the persona. The ego is what we think we are really like. What belongs to con-

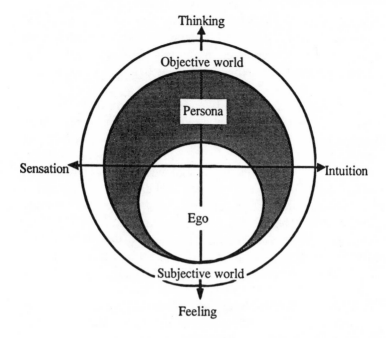

Figure 7:2 The Ego and Persona, with the four function types, after Jacobi, 1973.

sciousness and what I know about myself and the world is not fully conscious all the time. I forget things or repress what I do not like or find shameful. I have sense-perceptions that fail to reach my consciousness. They are like the little boy sitting in front of the television who seems to have suddenly gone deaf to his mother's voice. These forgotten memories and partly registered perceptions make a kind of "shadow land" stretching between the ego and the unconscious. They should be part of the ego but are in some way lost. To use the metaphor of the island, the "shadow" is land that is not always covered by the sea and can be reclaimed. Jung calls this shadow land the "personal unconsciousness" because it belongs to the individual formed from the person's repressed infantile impulses and wishes, and countless forgotten experiences that belong to that person alone.

The shadow is not entirely under the control of the will and may return when repression is reduced as during sleep. It may appear somewhat disguised in dreams and fantasies, and may be exposed by psychoanalysis. "The shadow personifies everything that the subject refuses to acknowledge about himself and yet is always thrusting itself upon him directly or indirectly—for instance inferior traits of character and other incompatible tendencies."[4] The shadow is like the Mr. Hyde to our Dr. Jekyll. Because of the negative nature of the shadow, it is both difficult for one to accept and difficult for one to look into. As Vivianne Crowley explains, "The shadow is what we encounter when we first look into the personal unconsciousness, and this is why many people are afraid to look; but we must confront ourselves and own these characteristics if we are to start the journey to our inner Godhead."[5]

Collective unconsciousness

The collective unconsciousness is a deeper stratum of the unconscious than the personal unconsciousness. It is the unknown material from which our consciousness emerges, and we can perceive its existence in part from instinctive behavior. The discovery of the collective unconscious is regarded by Jungian psychologists as "Jung's most basic and far-reaching discovery."[6] The collective unconsciousness can be accessed through dreams and its content represented in myth. As the collective unconsciousness is common to all humanity, the myths of different cultures reveal similar patterns that Jung has called archetypes.

Archetypes

Archetypes are unconscious and can therefore only be postulated. We become aware of them through certain images that recur in the psyche. Jung recognized that one could only hazard a guess at the archetypal images that formed during the thousands of years of human evolution. However, as human beings have evolved they have become increasingly distanced from primordial archetypes. This is postulated as the reason people today feel a sense of lostness.

In order to understand the nature of archetypes further, Jung sought to study the myths of various societies. He visited the Elgonian people of East Africa and the Pueblo of North America. Myths often seem like attempts to explain natural events such as the coming of spring and new life, but for Jung they are far more than this—they are the very expression of how humans experience these things.

> The rising of the sun then becomes the birth of the God-hero from the sea. He drives his chariot across the sky, and in the west the great mother dragon waits to devour him in the evening. In the belly of the dragon he travels the depths of the sea, and after a frightful combat with the serpent of the night he is reborn again in the morning. . . . The myth therefore is an expression of what is happening in them as the sun rises, travels across the sky, and is lost to sight at nightfall, as well as the reflection and explanation of these events.[7]

The most important archetypes according to Jung are called "anima" and "animus," or male and female elements. At first it seems paradoxical to suggest that man is not totally man nor woman wholly woman, yet Jung argued that it is common to find masculine and feminine traits in the same person. The most macho male can exhibit great tenderness to a small child and surprising intuition concerning a situation. The image only becomes conscious and tangible through the actual contacts with women that a man has during his life. The first and most important experience is with his mother. This shapes the whole of his life. Later the image is projected onto the various women to whom the man is attached during his life.

The image of woman, animus, because it is an archetype, has attributes that appear in every society at any age. She is often connected with the earth and is endowed with great power. She has two aspects, a light and a dark side. On the one hand she is pure and good represented as the goddess or virgin, while on the other, she is the prostitute or witch. The animus in women is the counterpart of the anima in men. It is the father figure that plays an important role within the animus. The animus can give to the woman needed courage and stimulate her to search for knowledge and truth.

After the anima and animus, the two archetypes that are likely to become influential in a person's life are those of the "old wise man" and "the great mother." Jung sometimes calls the "old wise man" the archetype of meaning, and he appears as the king, the hero, medicine-man, or savior. This archetype can be a serious danger because when it is awakened, a man may easily come to believe that he possesses the power. Jung calls this possession by the archetype inflation and is illustrated by the insane man who may think of himself as the king or as the savior. If, however, the man can quietly listen to the voice of the unconscious and understand that the power works through him, and he himself is not in control, then he is able to experience genuine personality development. The archetype of the great mother acts in a similar way on a woman.

Self

If the ego can relinquish some of the belief in its own omnipotence, a new center of personality can emerge that Jung called "the self." The ego, he says, can only be regarded as the center of the conscious, and if it tries to add some of the content of the unconscious to itself it may break under the overload of stress. The self, on the other hand, can include both the conscious and the unconscious elements. It acts like a magnet, able to attract anima and animus, conscious and unconscious, good and bad; and transmute them into something new.

Jung argues that this state cannot be reached by Westerners without suffering and considerable struggle. Unlike the Eastern mind, Westerners do not like contradictions and paradoxes.

The Chinese are able to accept the concept of Yin and Yang with the interplay of light and dark.[8]

> Jung makes it clear that his concept of the self is not that of a kind of universal consciousness, which is really only another name for the unconscious. It consists rather in the awareness on the one hand of our unique natures, and on the other of our intimate relationship with all life, not only human, but animal and plant, and even that of inorganic matter and the cosmos itself. It brings a feeling of "oneness" and of reconciliation with life, which can now be accepted as it is, not as it ought to be.[9]

Religion

The study of archetypes led Jung to some interesting conclusions. One of these was that people possess what he called "a natural religious function," and that their psychic health depended on the proper expression of this. Primitive people were concerned with the expression of this function, while modern men and women have defamed religion in place of a political creed. Jung argued that each person needs to experience the god-image within himself or herself.

> Not the individual alone but the sum total of individual lives in a people proves the truth of this contention. The great events of the world as planned and executed by man do not breathe the spirit of Christianity but rather of unadorned paganism. These things originate in a psychic condition that has remained archaic and has not been even remotely touched by Christianity. The Church assumes, not altogether without reason, that the fact of semel credidissa (having once believed) leaves certain traces behind it; but of these traces nothing is to be seen in the march of events. Christian civilisation has proved hollow to a terrifying degree: it is all veneer, but the inner man has remained untouched and therefore unchanged. His soul is out of key with his external beliefs; in his soul the Christian has not kept pace with external developments. Yes, everything is to be found outside—in image and in word, in Church and Bible—but never inside. Inside reign the archaic gods, supreme as of old; that is to say the inner correspondence with the outer God-image is undeveloped for lack of psychological culture

and has therefore got stuck in heathenism. Christian education has done all that is humanly possible, but it has not been enough. Too few people have experienced the divine image as the innermost possession of their own souls. Christ only meets them from without, never from within the soul; that is why dark paganism still reigns there, a paganism which, now in a form so blatant that it can no longer be denied, and now in all too threadbare disguise, is swamping the world of so-called Christian culture.[10]

It was Mircea Eliade who was to develop Jungian ideas in the realm of religion. Eliade (1907–1986) was born in Bucharest, Romania, and spent four years studying yoga in Calcutta (1928–32). From 1957 until his death, Eliade was the Professor of the History of Religions at the University of Chicago. As such he has had an immense influence on current thinking about religion. Eliade was not only concerned about the facts of human religion but more fundamentally the meaning of man's story.

In *The Myth of the Eternal Return,* he lays out his basic argument that humanity is divided into two polar types: archaic and modern (or historical). Modern man has become conditioned by the secular approach such that the symbolism of the archetypes has lost all significance. Archaic man, on the other hand, is the person who rejects the straitjacket of history and reaches out to the permanent that is beyond change.

Eliade represents an attempt to rediscover the meaning of religion in a postreligious age. He sees the suppression of the religious aspect of consciousness primarily in terms of the rejection of archaic mentality. The return to religion is then a return to archaic religion with its myths, symbols, and rituals. The return is not considered as one to Christianity. Christianity is seen as the religion of modern man, historical man. "In this respect, Christianity incontestibly proves to be the religion of 'fallen man': and this to the extent to which modern man is irremediably identified with history and progress, and to which history and progress are a fall, both implying the final abandonment of the paradise of archetypes and repetition."[11]

Jung and the neopagans

The first English translation of Jung's writings occurred in the 1920s and stirred much public interest. His general teaching has become widely accepted by neopagans, although there has been some reinterpretation. Figure 7:3 is a copy of a diagram in Vivianne Crowley's book on Wicca. The general model of Jungian psychology is clearly recognized together with the accepted terminology.

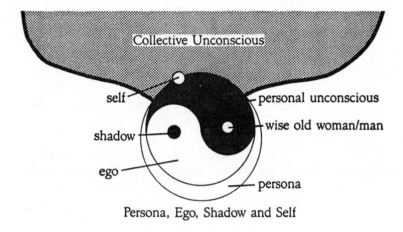

Persona, Ego, Shadow and Self

Figure 7:3 Persona, Ego, Shadow, and Self; after Crowley, 1989.

What is the importance of Jungian psychology for the neo-pagan movement?

1. The concept of the unconscious
Jung drew a limit to the comprehension of the rational conscious mind and in so doing proposed that beyond those limits were further realities to be explored. Magic and religion did not therefore need to have a rational foundation. This has allowed practitioners to claim that this new consciousness obeyed alien and irrational laws which cannot be understood by the rational functions of the psyche.

2. The collective unconscious
The enigmatic concept of the collective unconscious was interpreted by neopagans as almost another reality—a place to experience. Like the fantasy world of Tolkien's *Lord of the Rings*, the collective unconscious was a world of strange powers and magic. It was a world to be explored by the brave.

This understanding of the collective unconscious is a major development of Jungian psychology that goes beyond that which was understood by Jung himself. For Jung, collective unconsciousness was not a place, but a function of the psyche. He writes that the contents of the collective unconscious result "from the inherited possibility of psychological functioning in general, namely from the inherited brain structure."[12]

3. The Shadow
Access to our unconscious is through facing up to ourselves. As Vivianne Crowley writes about the diagram reproduced in figure 7:3,

> If you can imagine that this is not a flat two-coloured disc but a sphere, you will realise that the dark spot in the white leads like a tunnel into the centre of the ball and through to the darkness on the other side. This dark spot is the rabbit hole through which Alice fell and found herself in Wonderland and this too is the entrance to

our unconscious. . . . The light spot in the dark of the yin/yang symbol is the archetype of the Wise Old Woman or the Wise Old Man, and this is the entrance to the other tunnel, the tunnel to the Self. The Self has been symbolised in fairy tales as a golden ball which must be rescued from the bottom of a deep well guarded by a fearsome ogre and the Wise Old Woman or Man appears to help the hero or heroine in the attempt. . . . In Wicca we have to lose our fear of the dark and go down the tunnel into Wonderland.[13]

4. Archetypes

The idea of the myths, symbols, and dreams as archetypes in the unconscious provides a way of understanding the workings of magic and ritual. The manipulation of an archetypal symbol by its association with the archetype has an effect within the collective unconscious and so within human experience. Luhrmann writing of magical groups says, "They talk about 'dropping' a symbol into the collective unconsciousness by performing rituals in which certain symbols become emotionally fraught for them personally."[14]

Throughout neopagan literature, the reader encounters myths and symbols. They are regarded as the focus of meditation and become the subject of long and complex articles concerning their meaning. The exponents become skilled in seeing complex symbolic patterns, and using them to express experiences that are of significant importance to them. The archetypes may be worked out as rituals. Ultimately, they may become means of therapy not only for the individual but for the whole of society.

Archetypal re-enactment for personal, group and planetary transformation can quite likely become a tool with incredibly far reaching effects. The quality of depth of experience not only crosses the personal here and now boundaries, but reaches into the transpersonal realm of the past, and has the potential to heal the ravages encoded in the whole human experience. We can all become the priests and priestesses of the lost civilisations and continents of the Earth, the Realms of the subconscious.[15]

5. Religion

Not only did Jung express the value of religious experience, but he directed interest back to myths and symbols of early man. It was the primitive societies within the world that were closer to the archaic archetypes that modern man had almost lost. Similarly in religious studies, Mircea Eliade has pointed back to archaic religion and to a "unity of the spiritual history of humanity."[16]

The result is that there has been a great interest in the anthropology of tribal societies. This in turn has stimulated the acceptance and practice of tribal ritual and beliefs. Linda Jencson, writing an article entitled "Neopaganism and the great mother goddess," has given it the significant subtitle "Anthropology as midwife to a new religion,"[17] showing the direction of the recent thinking.

6. Race

The collective nature of the unconsciousness resulted, according to Jung, from our common humanity. *Fortune Magazine* as early as 1935 described the racial concept of the collective unconsciousness in terms of a lagoon-theory (see figure 7:4).[18]

> A man's soul is like a lagoon connected with the sea by a submerged channel; although to all outward seeming it is landlocked, nevertheless its water level rises and falls with the tides of the sea because of the hidden connection. So it is with human consciousness, there is a subconscious connection between each individual soul and the World-soul deep hidden in the most primitive depths of subconsciousness.[19]

The inherited nature of the collective unconsciousness means that each race, to some extent, has a common core of archetypes. It is therefore implied that a person will find greatest meaning if they seek the archetypes of their own racial roots. Thus, people with a Celtic origin are seeking back into their ancient religions before the coming of Christianity, and similarly with Germanic people. Frieda Fordham, a foremost

Jungian psychologist, notes how in Nazi Germany "'a religious spirit' expressed almost openly as the worship of Wotan, with all its pagan accompaniments, supplied some of the dynamic energy that permeated the Nazi movement."[20]

Nicholas Mann, an exponent of the Celtic tradition, writes,

> It is probably fair to say that each individual and culture works with the archetypes of their own race history and evolution. Cross fertilising does occur, look for example at the rise of Hindu archetypes in the Western consciousness after the experiences of colonialism. And thus as the Karmic inheritance of the race, culture and group form the archetypal conditioning of the individual, it would be most appropriate if the Gods and Goddess, folk lore and myth, images and tales of one's own land were to be most deeply worked with, although cross-cultural comparison is helpful.[21]

In other words, the current interpretation of Jungian thought encourages the modern pagan to return to his or her own tribal and cultural roots before the coming of Christianity.

7. Chthonic inheritance

Jungian psychology assumes that at the deepest level of the psyche lies the unfathomable ("chthonic") central energy out of which the individual psyche has been differentiated (see figure 7:4). Above this lowest stratum lies the deposit of the experience of our animal ancestors. Of this Nicholas Mann writes,

> Ultimately there is a chthonic inheritance, literally a springing up from out of the ground itself, whereby the archetypes of a collective race mind, the Little People, and the Giants of myth and legend, inhabit a living landscape, and there is no separation between the human, animal, plant and mineral realms.[22]

The significance of this will be shown further when we consider the role of the shaman in chapter 11.

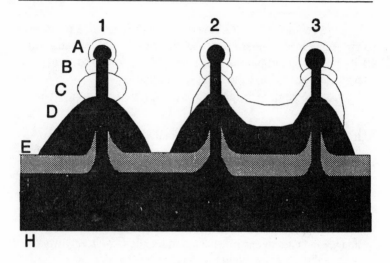

Figure 7:4 The Jungian "psychic family tree," after Jacobi, 1973.

1.   *Isolated nations*
2. & 3. *Groups of nations, e.g., Europe*

A *Individual*
B *Family*
C *Tribe*
D *Nation*
E *Ethnic group*
F *Primitive human ancestors*
G *Animal ancestors*
H *Central energy (Chthonic inheritance)*

8. Ethics

Jung gave to the notion of the development of the Self and exploration of archetypes a positive dimension with the establishment of a healthy psyche. "The archetypes of the Gods serve a dual role as archetypes of the divine forces which move in the outer universe, but at the same time they are archetypes of our own inner divinity, the Self. When we invoke the God or Goddess we attune ourselves to the divine spark within us."[23]

From the time of the behaviorists, the assumption has been held of the intrinsic value and goodness of humanity. This has been an inherent assumption of Jungian psychology. It is reflected in the views of most neopagans. Margot Adler, "Like most Neo-pagans, Odinists do not believe in sin and regard guilt as a destructive rather than useful concept."[24] Hussey, "My creed has no room for judgment and damnation."[25] Neopaganism assumes a moral relativism that allows the practitioner to explore any path.

Summary

The outsider first approaching the modern pagan movement may be surprised at the role of Jungian psychology within it. Carl Jung was the son of a Swiss Protestant pastor and mother and had six brothers all of whom were clergymen. He perhaps would be surprised at the way his analysis has been applied in recent years within the neopagan movement.

The great problem of Jung's analysis is that it is based on circular reasoning. The individual's experiences create his presuppositions, and he uses these presuppositions to interpret his experiences. However one assesses the work of Carl Jung, he was a man who saw the weaknesses of the secular worldview and the perplexity of "modern man in search of a soul."[26]

Notes

1. David Burnett, *Clash of Worlds* (Monarch: Eastbourne, 1990).
2. Frieda Fordham, *An Introduction to Jung's Psychology* (Penguin Books: Harmondsworth, 1966), p. 21.
3. Jolande Jacobi, *The Psychology of C. G. Jung* (Yale University Press: New Haven, 1973), pp. 10–18.
4. Carl Jung, *Archetypes of the Collective Unconsciousness*, pp. 284–85, para. 513.
5. Vivianne Crowley, *Wicca: The Old Religion in the New Age* (Aquarian Press: Wellingborough, 1989), p. 149.

6. Edward F. Edinger, *Ego and Archetype* (Penguin Books: Harmondsworth, 1974), p. 3.

7. Fordham, op. cit., pp. 26–27.

8. Burnett, op. cit., p. 96.

9. Fordham, op. cit., p. 63.

10. Carl Jung, *Psychology and Alchemy,* para. 12, quoted in Fordham, op. cit., p. 75.

11. Mircea Eliade, *The Myth of the Eternal Return* (Routledge and Kegan Paul: London, 1955), p. 162.

12. Jacobi, op. cit., p. 8.

13. Crowley, op. cit., pp. 150–1.

14. Tanya Luhrmann, *Persuasions of the Witch's Craft* (Basil Blackwell: Oxford, 1989), p. 281.

15. Nicholas R. Mann, *The Keltic Power Symbols* (Triskele: Glastonbury, 1987), p. 48.

16. Mircea Eliade, *A History of Religious Ideas,* Vol. I (University of Chicago Press: Chicago, 1978), p. xvi.

17. Linda Jencson, "Neopaganism and the great mother goddess," *Anthropology Today,* Vol. 5, No. 2 (April, 1989), pp. 2–4.

18. Jacobi, op. cit., p. 34.

19. Luhrmann, op. cit., p. 281.

20. Fordham, op. cit., p. 69.

21. Mann, op. cit., p. 48.

22. Mann, op. cit., p. 48.

23. Crowley, op. cit., p. 151.

24. Margot Adler, *Drawing Down the Moon* (Beacon Press: Boston, 1986), p. 280.

25. Dan Hussey, *The Wiccan* (August, 1989), p. 4.

26. C. G. Jung, *Modern Man in Search of a Soul* (Routledge: London, 1933).

Part 3

◯)

INVOKING
THE
POWERS

8

The Making of Magic

What are the differences between magic, science, and religion? At first the question sounds like a riddle, but on further reflection its significance can be recognized. Most people initially think that they can easily draw a differentiation between magic and religion. Likewise, anthropologists, following Frazer's example, have sought to clarify the distinction. Malinowski, for example, tended to consider religion as the use of nonphysical means to nonpractical ends, magic as the use of nonphysical means to practical ends, and science as the use of physical means to practical ends.[1]

In practice the distinction is not altogether clear. For example, is a Catholic priest saying a mass for rain during a drought performing magic or religion? As Sir Raymond Firth writes,

> In so far as a distinction can be drawn on broad lines it is in describing certain acts, and the situations in which they take place, as primarily magical at one end of the scale, and primarily religious at the other. In between lies a sphere in which the elements are so closely combined that the institutions may be termed magico-religious or religio-magical. In practice such intermediate types are commonly found.[2]

Within the neopagan movement both the terms *magic* and *religion* are used, and such rituals can be recognized. For example, Marian Green, the author of *Magic for the Aquarian Age,* has written, "We are not a 'religion' nor New Age."[3] Because such distinctions are made it is necessary to recognize them within the movement. Certain rule-of-thumb criteria, as follows, can be used to make the distinction between magical and religious ritual.

1. Magic is primarily concerned with manipulating powers while religious rituals are primarily concerned with supplication of spiritual beings.

2. Magic is primarily concerned with individual or group interests in comparison to religious rituals, which have a wider social function.

3. Magical powers are morally neutral but may be used for good or evil depending upon the intentions of the practitioners. Religion is regarded as being only good from the social point of view of the particular society. Thus, one may speak of "black magic" (left-hand path) and "white magic" (right-hand path) but never "black religion" in this context.

4. Religious rituals are usually related to a particular deity or pantheon and are demonstrated as calendar rites. Magical rituals are not necessarily associated with regular events although certain days may be regarded as more auspicious.

5. Religious rituals are particularly important at times of transitions in life, such as birth, marriage and death.

In the study of the neopagan movement it is helpful to recognize these distinctions between magic and religion. A practitioner of magic may be called a magician, one who operates in the areas of the occult and esoteric magic. Religion, on the other hand, is better applied to pagans following the Celtic or Northern traditions.

What is the difference, then, between magic and science? If we assume the conclusions of Malinowski's concepts that both have practical goals, the answer must lay in whether the technique used is physical or nonphysical. Both require a particular body of knowledge, the application of which it is believed will produce results. "Where is the difference then between 'magic' and 'science'?" asks Isaac Bonewits, an American magician and founder of one of the largest neopagan Druid organizations in the world.

Only this: The science and art of magic deals with a body of knowledge that, for one reason or another, has not yet been fully investigated or confirmed by the other arts and sciences. If the contents of magic and other parts of occultism are not now fully recognised sciences, they will be some day. Occultists need not fear that their realm will ever totally disappear, for by the Law of Infinite Data there will always be a few facts left to discover.[4]

In this way, Bonewits seeks to provide an academic credence for Real Magic.

This chapter is primarily concerned with magic rituals and the following two chapters with religious rituals that may include magic. Before looking at the techniques of the modern magician we must first examine the way in which the modern magician seeks to rationalize the practice of magic in today's world.

Logic of magic

Carl Jung tells the following story:

A young woman I was treating had at a critical moment, a dream in which she was given a golden scarab. While she was telling me this dream I sat with my back to the closed window. Suddenly I heard a noise behind me, like a gentle tapping. I turned round and saw a flying insect knocking against the window pane from outside. I opened the window and caught the creature in the air as it flew in. It was the nearest analogy to a golden scarab that one finds in our latitudes, a scarabaeid beetle, the common rose-chafer (Cetonia aurata), which contrary to its usual habits had evidently felt an urge to get into a dark room at that particular moment.[5]

Synchronicity is a term coined by Carl Jung for "a meaningful coincidence." For example, have you suddenly thought of someone you have not seen for a long time, and then you unexpectedly met the person in the street? Many such coincidences occur in dreams, as in the case previously described. A materialist would discount such events as being merely coincidence, but Jung sought to explain them in terms of archetypes. He said that these synchronistic events occur when we come in contact with the archetypes in the collective unconsciousness.

This concept has been accepted by many in the neopagan movement as a key in understanding the working of ritual magic. Synchronicity is a term used by neopagans for two events that happen more or less at the same time, which have no direct causal connection but arise from some underlying cause. As Vivianne Crowley explains it:

> These archetypes are activated by Wiccan initiations and when we first enter Wicca we are likely to find ourselves surrounded by synchronistic events; so much so that we cease to notice them and start to take it for granted that helpful meaningful coincidences will occur. . . . The principle of synchronicity is the principle by which divinatory symbol systems such as I Ching and the tarot work.[6]

It therefore follows that if one thinks (dreams, wishes, concentrates) in terms of archetypal forms it will have an effect in the material world without the need for any physical intervention on the part of the thinker. This dynamic interconnectedness between mind and matter completely rejects the Cartesian Dualism with its absolute dichotomy between subjective and objective. The distinction between the physical world and that of imagination is considered to be only an illusion by neopagans. There is an interconnectedness between all things, and so the exertion of the will has a distinct physical effect.

Starhawk writes of "the world view that sees things not as fixed objects, but as swirls of energy. The physical world is formed by that energy as stalagtites [sic] are formed by dripping water. If we cause a change in the energy patterns, they in turn will cause a change in the physical world—just as, if we change the course of an underground river, new stalagtites will be formed in new veins of rock."[7]

This leads to a common definition of magic, such as that given by Aleister Crowley as "the art of causing change in conformity with the will of the magician," or Dion Fortune, as "the art of causing changes in consciousness in conformity with will."[8] Magicians also believe in forces beyond those spoken of by science. These psychic powers are considered to pervade the universe and can be generated or directed by those with knowledge. This power is both part of the cosmos and yet in some ways different from physical forces such as gravity. It is accessible by human effort and can be directed for the person's use. "A ritual is a pattern which acts out in cosmic terms a code conveying your meaning to those Powers of the Universe who may bring your working to fulfillment."[9]

The importance of the archetypes means that the magician makes great use of symbols. Color, shape, motion, name, and association are all important aspects of ritual. These symbols are considered to be physical reminders to help concentrate the will, but they also link the invoked power with that in the magician.

> A spell is a symbolic act done in an altered state of consciousness, in order to cause a desired change. To cast a spell is to project energy through a symbol. But the symbols are too often mistaken for the spell. "Burn a green candle to attract money" we are told. The candle itself, however, does nothing—it is merely a lens, an object of focus, a mnemonic device, the "thing" that embodies our idea. Props may be useful, but it is the mind that works magic.[10]

Magicians use the props and other techniques in order to achieve the altered state of consciousness. Magic is possible when strong emotions are directed to desired goals in an altered state of mind. Magical practice is the attempt to train the mind through intense concentration and directed by a vivid imagination. This is achieved by an initial faith in the efficacy of magical ritual. However, it needs to be said that some people make their first magical experiments without believing in magic, but purely in the "let's see if something happens" frame of mind.

Ritual is putting into practice the ideas (myths) that are accepted. As Marian Green noted in 1970, not all occultists are willing to move from the intricacies of esoteric thought to that of practical application.

> "To know, to Dare, to Will and to keep Silent" has been over-looked. They "know" alright, but the Dare, the actual raising of the hand in a ritual gesture, the speaking of the word with intent, this is not there. It seems to me like taking lessons in carpentry or painting and mastering the theory, yet never taking saw or brush in hand to make the first practical stroke.[11]

Into chaos

A theme that dominates much of modern magic is that power is acquired by plunging into the terror of the abyss, the dark, the irrational. To enter the chaos is to empower oneself. This is a romantic concept of evil in which chaos is seen as the radical opposite of good. "The three ways (at least) to understand this chaotic darkness reflect three different sorts of magical practice, but they are intermingled and entwined."[12]

The first sees the darkness as an aspect of the goddess who is an interpretation of natural process. As we saw in chapter 5, the goddess is never perceived in the singular, but as virgin, mother, and crone. As the crone she is the old woman who has passed menopause, and her womb is lifeless. The goddess as crone represents old age, decay, and death. The path of the goddess is often said to be the one in which women may be truly themselves. The fluctuating hormones cause changes of moods and emotions that cannot be ignored, but need to be faced. The pagan view is that by accepting one's own negative impulses one can acknowledge and reject them and so cease to project them onto others. When these impulses are hidden in the darkness of the unconscious one cannot do this. It is by facing one's fears that one discovers the fear is illusory.

Kabbalism provides the second way of understanding the darkness in terms of the Abyss. The Western mystery groups teach that within all the ancient mystery religions one finds the same account of descent, struggle, and rebirth. One must go down to go up.

The third version of this dissolution is Chaos magic, which is a version gaining an increasing following. It is essentially a solitary path, but even in 1987 Bray estimated that there were between six and ten thousand Chaos magicians in the country.[13] The main themes of magic are dissolution, control, and power. These ancient themes are especially clear within Chaos magic, but this form of magic is relatively new and owes much to a new form of mathematics known as nonlinear.

In the 1970s, James York, a young mathematician, is accredited with giving nonlinear mathematics the name chaos. York believed that physicists and mathematicians were so concerned with looking for order that they completely disregarded disorder. It was not until the development of the modern computer in the 1980s that scientists were able to begin to probe the horrendous calculation involved. Professor Mandelbrot used the IBM research computers to generate a computer image of the probable answer for a simple equation containing a complex number. For example, take the equation $z \rightarrow z^2 + c$, where z begins at zero and c is the complex number corresponding to the point being tested. One starts with $z = 0$, multiplies it by itself, and adds the starting number, c. The result is then multiplied by itself and again c added. The process is repeated 1,000 times, or even more. The program must repeat this process for each of thousands of points on a grid. Each point is colored depending upon the frequency of the repetition. The result was an exquisitely intricate geometrical pattern (see figure 8:1).[14]

In the past decade Chaos mathematics has been debated among scientists. Even so, it has proved useful in describing such nonlinear mathematics as found in fluid dynamics, weather modeling, and even the large red spot on the planet Jupiter. This fascinating ordering within chaos has caught the imagination of many students in recent years. It has also left the question as to why this unexpected order and beauty emerges from chaos. Is there some inherent power within chaos if one is bold enough to enter it?

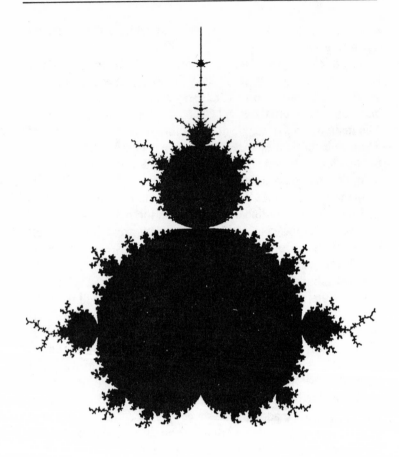

Figure 8:1 The Mandelbrot Set. By focusing on the fringe of the shape, it leads to a voyage through finer and finer scales showing the increasing complexity of the set.

One magician has identified six principles within Chaos magic.[15] The first is that there is a world of gods and spirits within each person. Second, "fake it till you make it. Life is a role playing fantasy game, though few punters seem aware of this. . . . Magic is the art of deliberately believing and pretending very hard and finding that it works." Third, do everything possible in the ordinary domain to improve your chances by mundane means, then throw in the spell to improve the probability. The amount of magic used raises the probability of the desired event's occurring. Fourth, "nothing is true." All truths are no more than statistical approximations. Fifth, everything is permitted. "If it can be imagined it can be realised; that is the exhilaration and the terror of it, for the consequences of any act are both unlimited and partly determinate." Finally, the universe is conceived as essentially a magical structure. It should be said that many neopagans would reject these ideas as they violate pagan ethics of "And it harm none" (which includes oneself).

The repercussions of this logic can lead to bizarre and degrading practices. In fact, the most stringent regulations, when violated, should result in the greatest magical power. Tanya Luhrmann writes that from her observations, "the romantic brutality of the chaos magician takes place largely in his head. I met at least one group engaged in this sort of practice in London. They reminded me of boys boasting of wild sexual exploits; far too well behaved and nervous to kiss a girl they claimed they should have raped."[16]

Preparing for magic

The most-surprising feature of modern magic, to the outsider, is the number of books and even study courses that are available on magical techniques. One of the most popular is that by Marian Green, *Magic for the Aquarian Age: A contemporary textbook of practical magical techniques,* and described as "exercises and methods to unwrap the secret, inner you and overcome the stress of twentieth-century life."[17] The two central techniques of these procedures are meditation and visualization.

Meditation

"Meditation is an altered state of consciousness in which you cease to be concerned with the time and place in which you are sitting and enter a world of information affecting various senses" (Marian Green).[18]

Meditation is a word used of various relaxation techniques that involve mental concentration. Concentration techniques are common in many cultures and religious traditions. There is little doubt that meditation does produce physiological effects such as a lower metabolic rate and a decrease in heart and respiratory rate. However, it is not clear whether this differs from the general physiological effects of relaxation.

The mind tends to be unruly and jump around many topics. The aim of meditation is to fix one's attention and not to be distracted by the multiple of external stimuli. This is similar to what many Christians, for example, may experience when praying. The discipline of the mind is not easy. The magical courses give advice as to the best posture to assume in a similar way to Yoga. They may give advice on breathing techniques and even provide music or verbal images on which to meditate. Those who succeed in their quest for such skills claim profound mystical experiences where the body loses all sensory perception.

For the magician, meditation is not merely a training technique to relax, but a part of his or her basic equipment. It is the method by which the altered state of consciousness is achieved. However, those who follow the path of magic tend to be more aware of the physical world than are the mystics, and they tend to have a somewhat ambivalent attitude about meditation. They differentiate themselves from those who are on the mystic quest and consider meditation only as a tool to serve their particular ends.

Visualization

Meditation is both a passive state and a perceiving state in which feelings can be recognized, and images can appear. Visualization, on the other hand, is the method of directing these images. From the fragments of one's mind a new condition or situation is formed. Visualization is an essential tool for the magician, and whole books have been written on the subject.

The person first must have learned to meditate before he or she can effectively develop the skill of visualization.

> Once you are still and relaxed, you should imagine that part of you can see through your closed eyelids. Try to picture or sense (not everyone gets actual pictures) some object in the room with you: a vase, a book, the cover of a magazine or the pattern on the curtains—it doesn't matter what. See it in colour, sense its texture, focus on the detail—is it real, is it solid, does it stay there for you to examine? Usually not, to begin with. Objects become vague, colours and patterns shift, detail blurs. Open your eyes and look at it. How does the actual thing differ from your impression of it? Examine it, and then try again.[19]

The ultimate exercise for visualization is "pathworking." It is called pathworking after an exercise concerning the Tree of Life used by students of the Jewish mystical system of Kabbala (see figure 3:1). What happens is that a journey is described by one person, and the others in the group try to visualize the scenes and images as clearly as they can. Sometimes people take turns continuing the story, or others may add details as the visualization is continued.

Have you ever watched a little boy playing soccer? He may be kicking the ball against the garden wall, but he is engrossed in his imagination. There he is playing in the World Cup in the main stadium in Rome. In his ears ring the shouts of the multitudes as he races towards the goal passing one player and then another. He shoots . . . it's a goal! His heart leaps within him. What is reality? As Marian Green says, "A vivid imagination, directed by magical training, is the most effective tool we have for changing the world, and it is something which has often lain dormant since childhood."[20]

The pathway exercise stimulates the imagination to construct another land in another age, just like C. S. Lewis's land of Narnia or Tolkien's *Lord of the Rings*. This is the context of the Dungeons and Dragons game. A popular pathway is that of the Arthurian tradition with its romantic stories about King Arthur and his beautiful Queen Guinevere, Merlin the magician, Sirs Lancelot and Galahad.[21] Although we recognize the stories more as myth than truth, the very names of these heroes cause the heart to rise. Practitioners of magic would say that myths are timeless and cannot be pigeonholed to suit individual inclinations. They would say that they have a meaning for me, for you, and for everyone.

In the introduction to his book on the Arthurian tradition, John Matthews writes,

> Thus the Arthurian tradition too is for everyone who cares to explore it. Nor should their involvement stop short with a mere reading of the text—rewarding though that can be. Deeper, more experiential levels can be reached by working with the Arthurian archetypes in an imaginative way. . . . Those who attempt these exercises are assured of a wholly new and developing dimension in their lives, for within these stories lies a heritage for the future of all who seek it.[22]

The rituals of magic

In popular thought, stimulated by writers of fiction, magic is the art of commanding spirits to do one's bidding or to change base metal into gold. For the secular anthropologist, a ritual is a formalized, stereotyped pattern of speech and action. The neopagan practitioner, on the other hand, regards magic as the highest form of trained imagination and will.

The general practice of this form of magic is as follows:

1. Be convinced that magic works and know what you aim to achieve. Most magicians warn of the danger of the frivolous use of magical rites.

2. Find a place where you will not be disturbed physically or mentally, and ritually seal the area. Great care is taken to

create a separate space and time that is perceived as being between the various spheres of reality. All rituals take place in a
physical circle which is drawn on the ground. Gerald Gardner
makes an interesting distinction in the meaning of the circle to
the magician and the witch.

> It is necessary to distinguish this clearly from the work of the ma-
> gician or sorcerer, who draws a circle on the ground and fortifies it
> with mighty words of power and summons (or attempts to sum-
> mon) spirits and demons to do his bidding, the circle being to pre-
> vent them from doing him harm, and he dare not leave it. The
> Witches' circle, on the other hand, is to keep in the power which
> they believe they can raise from their own bodies and to prevent it
> from being dissipated before they can mould it to their own will.[23]

3. Gather the equipment you need. The common dress of
the magician has become that of a floor-length robe often with a
hood. Marian Green recognizes that a magician must have four
elements:

Weapon	*Element*
Pentacle	Earth
Cup	Water
Sword	Fire
Wand	Air[24]

Usually these four weapons and four elements are placed on the
altar. Most rituals also involve the use of incense.

4. Following a time of meditation and visualization, the magician states aloud the purpose for which you have gathered.

5. Calls on the name of a particular power or spirit to work.

6. Waits for the power to work. A sign may be given to show
the working of the power.

7. Thanks is then given to all who have helped, both visible
and invisible.

8. The area is then ritually closed and made safe.

Black magic—white magic

Most magicians regard magic as a science rather than a religion. Like science it is perceived in itself to be neutral. This is similar to the concept of spiritual power (mana) found in many tribal societies, and which is considered to be amoral.[25]

> Morals and magic do not mix. Magic is a science and an art, and as such has nothing to do with morals or ethics. Morals and ethics come in only when we decide to apply the results of our research and training. Magic is about as moral as electricity.[26]

What is important therefore is the purpose for which the power is used. "Many teachers of magic warn their pupils never to carry out a magical working frivolously or for purely selfish motives or dire consequences will follow."[27] Frater Libra, the writer of these words, goes on to point out the issues related to the outworking of magic.

> Suppose you work a spell to enable you to win half a million pounds on the football pools and you win it, would that really make you happy? There are many winners of big money who claim that they wished they'd never won it—and many more who seem quite happy. . . . Supposing you work a spell to bring ruin to your worst enemy and, at the very moment you cast it, your worst enemy's house catches fire and he and all his family are burned to death. Would that really make you feel good? And how would you feel about it in a year's time? Or five years'? Or ten years'? You'll have to live with it for the rest of your life and your future lives as well.

It can be seen that the writer resorts to two arguments with regard to the right use of magic. The first is that of careful consideration of the implications that it has for yourself. This is a major problem as no one could make such an objective analysis or think through all the possible repercussions. The second restraint mentioned is that of one's future life, which is believed by many neopagans to be directed by a concept of karma similar to that found in Hinduism. A third reason that I was given by a practicing witch was that if she sought to cast a spell on an innocent person it would rebound on her threefold. This is closely parallel to the Bible verse, "Like a flitting sparrow, like a flying swallow, so a curse without cause shall not alight" (Prov. 26:2, NKJV).

In the light of these issues it is no wonder that one magician concludes, "magic should only be used as a last resort to solve mundane problems but if all else fails why not use it? If your intentions are true you may find your problems resolved one way or another."[28]

Does magic work?

By this point, those outside the neopagan movement may be wondering if magic actually has any inherent effectiveness or is merely ritual. The question as to whether magic is effective has been considered by many anthropologists from their studies of tribal peoples.[29] Various answers have been given as to why people believe in the power of magic.

First, some of the results aimed at by the magician actually do occur for some reason or another. It is impossible to speculate whether the same thing would have occurred with or without the magical rite. The materialist would regard this as a coincidence that had a certain probability of occurring, or the ritual is actually operating on some scientific principle that is as yet unknown. The Jungian scholar, on the other hand, may regard it as an example of synchronicity.

Second, positive examples tend to count more than negative ones. Frequently, we ignore those things that run counter to the theories in which we believe. Thus, the magician points to the positive examples of magic, while the nonmagician would indicate the apparent failures. What appears to be important is the belief of the magician and the society as a whole in the effectiveness of the concept of magic.

Third, there is the placebo effect. *Placebo* comes from the same Latin verb as the English word *please*. Most people are familiar with the idea of medical doctors' possibly making use of sugar pills. Because the patient believes in the efficacy of the drug, it can often have a positive effect on the health of the patient. In tribal societies, anthropologists have shown cases of people who have died from magic, but in all cases the person was aware of the fact that he was the subject of a curse. A friend or enemy may tell the person that he has been cursed, or a sickness could be so diagnosed by a healer.

Bonewits, a modern magician, admits to making use of what he calls "placebo spells." "I have often had people come up to me for a spell to help them. . . . Often I decide that they don't really need a spell at all or that the situation is far too complicated for me to tackle. In such cases, I may use a *placebo spell;* that is, *I tell them I will cast a spell but I actually don't.* . . . The strange thing is that *such placebo spells usually work!*"[30]

Fourth, the belief in magic implies the belief in countermagic. If a magic rite fails to produce its objective it can always be argued that there was a powerful countermagic in action. The same can be seen with regards to a white magician's concern with the moral use of magic. Tanya Luhrmann makes two interesting observations. First, the very fact of considering the responsibility of the magician reinforces the belief in the reality and power of magic itself. "If black magic is prohibited, it must be because it has an effect. . . . The negative sanction implies a positive power."[31] Second, the concern about morality may provide a worthy reason in the face of possible failure. If a situation appears to require the use of magic, this could be denied on the grounds that the person imagines himself or herself to be a moral magician. His or her good intentions may reinforce the belief that he or she has in his or her efficacy.

Finally, one must add the possibility of magic's having a supernatural cause. This raises the question as to whether magic is really neutral, or whether it has a negative and evil aspect. If it is evil, the magician must ask whether he or she can actually control this power, or whether it will end in controlling him or her. The magician will not be the master but the fool in a satanic trap.

Notes

1. Bronislaw Malinowski, *Magic, Science and Religion* (Doubleday Anchor Books: New York, 1954), pp. 85–90.
2. Sir Raymond Firth, *Human Types* (Abacus: London, 1975), p. 142.
3. Personal correspondence, 1990.
4. Isaac Bonewits, *Real Magic* (Samuel Weiser: Maine, 1989), p. 33.
5. Carl G. Jung, *Synchronicity: An Acausal Connecting Principle* (Ark Paperbacks: London, 1987), p. 31.
6. Vivianne Crowley, *Wicca: The Old Religion in the New Age* (Aquarian Press: Wellingborough, 1989), p. 130.
7. Starhawk, *The Spiral Dance* (Harper and Row: San Francisco, 1989), p. 11.
8. Marian Green, *Magic for the Aquarian Age* (Aquarian Press: Wellingborough, 1983), p. 20.
9. Leonas, "The Rite Way for Beginners," *Quest,* No. 8 (December, 1971).
10. Starhawk, op. cit., p. 110.
11. Marian Green, "Magic Is Working. . . ," *Quest,* No. 4 (December, 1970).
12. Tanya Luhrmann, *Persuasions of the Witch's Craft* (Blackwell: Oxford, 1989), p. 92.
13. Ibid., p. 97.
14. James Gleick, *Chaos* (Penguin: Harmondsworth, 1987), p. 114.
15. Pete Carroll, "Principia Chaotica," *Chaos International,* No. 8 (1990), p. 15.
16. Luhrmann, op. cit., p. 97.
17. Green, op. cit.
18. Ibid., p. 37.
19. Ibid., p. 38.
20. Ibid., p. 44.

21. John Matthews, *The Arthurian Tradition* (Element Books: Shaftesbury, 1989).

22. John Matthews, *The Elements of the Arthurian Tradition* (Element Books: Shaftesbury, 1989), pp. xiii–xiv.

23. Gerald B. Gardner, *Witchcraft Today* (Magickal Childe: New York, 1988), p. 26.

24. Green, op. cit., pp. 93–99.

25. David Burnett, *Unearthly Powers* (MARC: Eastbourne, 1988).

26. Bonewits, op. cit., p. 116.

27. Frater Libra, "If You Believe in Magic," *Quest,* No. 79 (September, 1989), p. 23.

28. Ibid., p. 25.

29. Claude Levi-Strauss, *Structural Anthropology* (Penguin Books: Harmondsworth, 1986), pp. 167–185.

30. Bonewits, op. cit., p. 129.

31. Luhrmann, op. cit., p. 81.

9

The Cycle of the Year

Winter, Spring, Summer, Autumn—birth, growth, fading, death—
the Wheel turns, on and on. Ideas are born; projects are consum-
mated; plans prove impractical and die. We fall in love; we suffer
loss; we consummate relations; we give birth; we grow old; we
decay.[1]

All societies divide the cycle of the year into distinct periods
marked by festivals and rituals. These are generally known by
anthropologists as Calendar Rites.[2] These festivals are not
merely for the pleasure of the local people but are a practical
expression of their religious beliefs and mythology. This is especially so where there is a strong belief in gods of the earth
and sky, and nature spirits. It is not surprising, therefore, that
within the neopagan movement, calendar rituals are widely
practiced. The belief in the living Earth and the deity of nature
leads to a deep appreciation of the changes of the seasons in
terms of its divinity.

The year can be divided in various ways: by solar phenomena, the seasons, or as at present, numerically fixed into days
and months. The beginning of the year has been set at various
points. The Celts calculated the beginning of their year from
the festival of Samhain (November 1). Medieval Christians began calculating on Lady Day (March 25), and this was the offi-
cial day until 1752. However, the most common date was
January 1 as set by the Julian calendar.

Before the Roman conquest of the Celtic peoples, there

appear to have been several calendars in use. One calendar found in France, dated about 50 B.C., had twelve months of alternating twenty-nine and thirty days' duration, with an additional thirteenth month to bring it in line with the solar year. The Teutonic peoples counted nights and from the grouping of fourteen days, the expression "a fortnight" is derived. However, after the conquest of the majority of the Celts by Julius Caesar, it was the Roman calendar set up in 45 B.C. that was to form the basis of the European calendar. This Julian calendar allowed an additional day every four years (Leap Year), but even so it was too long by 11 minutes, 10.3 seconds.

By 1582, the accumulated error had grown to become ten days. The spring equinox (vernal), instead of falling on March 21 occurred on March 10. To correct this discrepancy, Pope Gregory XIII decreed that October 4, 1582, should be followed by October 15, 1582. Roman Catholic countries adopted the new calendar immediately, and it became known as the Gregorian calendar. Protestant Britain did not make the change until 1752 when September 2 was followed by September 14. Many people rioted in the streets of London claiming that the government had stolen eleven days of their lives.

The eight festivals

Within the neopagan movement, the ancient calendar festivals essentially have been reconstructed. These consist of eight festivals, being a combination of the equinoxes and solstices of the solar year, and the four so-called "fire festivals." The term *fire festival* claims to have come from a tenth-century Christian Archbishop of Cashel, Ireland, who stated that in his time, four great fires were lit on the four great festivals of the Druids. "The four quarters of the May Year are marked according to Druidic custom where the declination of the sun is 16 degrees 20 minutes north or south of the equinoctial line, viewed from the Druidic omphalos four times in the yearly cycle. This makes the four dates of the festivals February 4, May 6, August 8, and November 8."[3] In actual practice the dates of the celebrations appear to have been slightly different from this, being at the beginning of the respective months, and these are the dates that are used today (see figure 9:1).

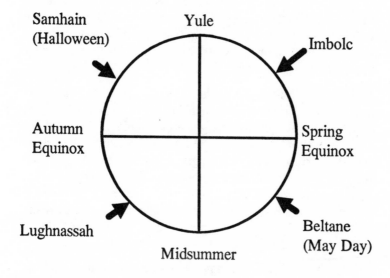

Figure 9:1 The traditional north European calendar rites.

The four fire festivals
First we will describe the fire festivals according to the Celtic tradition before looking at the celebrations practiced by other peoples.

Samhain: "Summerend" (Halloween). The Celtic new year began with the festival of Samhain. As with other festivals, this one began at sunset on the previous day and was celebrated on November 1. The Celts believed that on the eve of Samhain, all the spirits and ghosts emerged from their dwellings in hills, springs, lakes, and rivers.[4] Because of the close proximity of the spirits, this was regarded as an auspicious time for divination. The herds were gathered in from the hillside in preparation for winter. Many older and weaker animals were killed off and eaten at a great feast.

Imbolc: The festival of Imbolc began on sunset of January 31 and continued until sunset on February 1. It was the day in which daylight appeared to get appreciably longer, and the weather was at its coldest. The festival was also called Brigantia or Brigit, after the virgin bride whose festival was celebrated by the Celts with bonfires and burning torches. Brigantia was widely known among the Celts as the goddess of fertility and healing. Little is known about the actual rituals, presumably as it was mainly practiced by the women and carried out in secret.

Beltane: Bel, Balor or Belenus is the solar-fire god, and his festival of Beltane (Bel's fire) announces the arrival of the summer half of the year. The festival began at sunset on April 30 and led on to the May Day festivities. In early times, all the fires in the village were extinguished on May eve and then relit from the local Beltane fire made from the wood of nine types of tree. May Day was a day of rejoicing, dancing, and feasting. The maypole was the center of the dances and allowed mixing of young men and women.

Lughnassah: Held on August 1, this festival was the beginning of the season of autumn. It is named after the Celtic god of wisdom and illumination, Lugh, the equivalent of the Norse god Odin. Lugh was also responsible for the ripening of the crops. The festival celebrated the cutting of the first corn harvest and the baking of the first loaf from the new year's crop.

Equinox and solstice festivals

Less understood than the four fire festivals are the ancient rituals relating to the equinox and solstice. They seem to have been more important to the Germanic peoples. They are recognized and practiced by neopagans today.

Yule: The Celts apparently did not have any festival for the winter solstice, but the Germanic people held one called Yule. The name Yule comes from the Anglo-Saxon *Geola* meaning yoke. It is the point where the sun is at its lowest ebb, and daylight is the shortest. It is the time when the power of the sun seems almost extinguished, but even so it contains the promise of a new year. The festival began after sunset on December 20 and was a time sacred to Odin. The major event of the Yule festival was the feast in which food and drink was taken in great abundance.

The Romans held their great festival of Saturnalia on December 17, and it gradually extended until December 25 (the Roman winter solstice). It was a time when people exchanged presents, played gambling games in public, allowed sexual license, and reversed social roles so that masters waited on servants.[5] The festival was in honor of the god Saturn, but the mythology of the celebration is obscure. It appears to be the birthday of the Unconquered Sun. The celebration of Saturnalia appears to have been adopted by the Romanized Celts, and later this became associated with the Yule festivities of the Germanic peoples.

Ostrara: The vernal equinox is the transition between the dark and light halves of the year, giving exactly twelve hours of daylight. It occurs about March 22. At this time the light begins to overcome the dark. Nigel Pennick states, "The Asatru festival of the vernal equinox is Summer Finding, sacred to Thor, with a liturgical colour of red. Freyr and Freyja are also honoured here."[6]

Litha: The midsummer solstice was called *Litha* in Anglo-Saxon. It is the longest day of the year, when the sun reaches its highest. In Germanic tradition it was sacred to the god Balder and traditionally a great time for fairs and festivals.

Mabon: The autumn equinox occurs around September 21 and is the time of the second harvest. It is the transition time between the light half and dark half of the year.

The survival of the seasonal festivals

The ancient festivals were deeply ingrained into the fabric of Celtic and Saxon society. During the period of the Roman occupation of Britain, a mixing of Roman and Celtic festivals must have occurred as was mentioned with the adoption of the festival of Saturnalia. With the coming of Christianity, many of these festivals were adapted and became part of the church calendar, while others remained as local festivals or superstitions.

Christmas: The festival of Saturnalia, with its celebration of the rebirth of the sun god, became ideally suited for Christians to celebrate Christ's birth. The celebration of Christmas by Christians does not seem to have occurred officially until the fourth century when Christianity was adopted as the state religion of the Roman Empire.

Among the Germanic peoples Christmas acquired many more customs from the traditional feast of Yule. By the mid-eleventh century, the Roman and Germanic elements were deeply synthesized into a recognizable "Christ's Mass" in Britain. During the Reformation many pagan elements were condemned by the Protestants, and in Calvinist Scotland the public celebration of Christmas was suppressed altogether. The celebration of the secular New Year became its substitute.

It was in the 1840s that Prince Albert, together with the writings of Charles Dickens, spearheaded an upsurge of sentimentality that was to lead to the prototype of the modern Christmas festival. Christmas decorations became popular, especially the use of holly, ivy, and mistletoe that in pre-Christian times were considered magical plants powerful against witches.

The Christmas tree was introduced from Germany in 1840, whereupon it immediately became the symbol of the Victorian family Christmas.

Easter:

> Easter, being the festival of the Resurrection, had to be dependent on the dating of the Crucifixion, which occurred three days earlier and just before the Jewish Passover. The Passover was celebrated on the 14th day of Nisan, the first month in the Jewish religious year—that is, the vernal equinox. The Christian churches in the eastern Mediterranean area celebrated Easter on the 14th of Nisan on whatever day of the week it might fall, but the rest of Christendom adopted a more elaborate reckoning to ensure that it was celebrated on a Sunday in the Passover week.[7]

Celebration of the spring equinox had long been the celebration of new life among the northern peoples. The eighth-century British writer, Bede, mentions that the name for Easter itself is derived from a pagan festival of the goddess Eostra. She was an obscure spring and dawn deity whose name means East (German *Ost*). Many pagan practices were given a Christian gloss. One such practice is the ascending of some hill before dawn on Easter Sunday in order to witness the rising sun. Another is the Easter bunny, the hare being sacred to Eostra.

The survival of the fire festivals

The four Celtic fire festivals have also been adopted into the Christian calendar in a variety of ways (see figure 9:2).

Samhain: In an attempt to Christianize this festival, or perhaps protect Christians, November 1 became All Saints' Day and November 2 became All Souls' Day when prayers are made for the departed. Samhain has therefore been called Halloween.

Samhain celebrations used to last for a few days and have connections with the observance of Guy Fawke's Night. The Celtic royal new year used to begin at Samhain, and the state opening of Parliament was arranged to begin at the end of the festivities. The attempt on the life of King James I was timed to take place at the state opening of Parliament—November 5 of that year. This calendar rite is an interesting example of the merging of religious, political, and social activities.[8]

Date	Celtic/Teutonic rite	Christian form
November 1	Samhain	All Saints' (Halloween)
Midwinter	Yule	Christmas
February 2	Imbolc	Candlemas
Spring Equinox	Ostrara	Easter
May 1	Beltane	May Day
Midsummer	Litha	St. John's Day
August 1	Lughnassah	Lammas
Autumn Equinox	Mabon	Michaelmas

Figure 9:2 Christianization of north European calendar rituals.

Halloween has traditionally been celebrated by groups of children that roam the streets with flashlights, knocking on doors and asking for sweets or money. In recent years, they sometimes threaten with "trick or treat," an American custom that has developed in Britain.[9] Most neopagans regret the way in which the festival of Samhain has been debased but recognize that "the trappings of plastic and witches' hats are a continuation of a solemn festival of remembrance of death and the departed."[10]

Imbolc: This celebration was absorbed into the Christian year to become the festival of the purification of the Virgin Mary forty days after the birth of Jesus (February 2). Luke 2 tells of Mary's meeting Simeon during her visit to the temple. Simeon says of Jesus that He will be a light to the nations. For this reason, candles have often been lit at this church festival that became named "Candlemas."

In Ireland, the veneration of the Virgin is manifested as St. Bride's Day, celebrating St. Brigid.

St. Brigid, who was born in what is now the County Louth,

towards the middle of the fifth century, was of noble Christian parents. (That is, at least on her father's side. Her mother may have been originally a slave. One or both of them must have been among the earliest Irish converts, not impossibly at the hands of St. Patrick himself.)[11]

It could well have been that she was born on February 1 and so was given the name of the pagan goddess Brigid as were many other women born on that day. She founded the convent at Kildare where she died about A.D. 525.

It is said that she converted a man on his deathbed by explaining the Redemption to him with a cross which she had plaited from rushes that covered the floor, as was then usual in well-kept households.[12]

The plaiting of rushes had magical overtones among the Celts, and it seems as though she used this culturally relevant practice to communicate the Christian message.

Beltane: In Celtic Britain, May 1 was Beltane, the time when the flocks of animals were turned onto their summer grazing and the gods invoked for their protection until Halloween. Apparently two fires were lit and the cattle driven between them as a safeguard against the diseases of the year.[13]

Unlike some of the other traditional festivals, this festival has had an uneasy relationship with Christianity, probably in part resulting from an erroneous connection between the Celtic god Bel and the Canaanite god Baal. It could also have been that the festival involved considerable sexual license, which was unacceptable to Christians. With the Protestant reformation it was actually banned, only to be revived in a modified form under Victorian romanticism for "Merrie England."

Lughnassah: The festival of the beginning of the harvest in celebration of the god Lugh became the rather obscure Christian festival called Lammas (Anglo Saxon: *hlafmasse:* "loaf mass"). Newly cut corn, or bread from it, was offered in churches to the Christian God.

Ancient religions and rituals never really die. They may be converted into another religious tradition or fade away to become a superstition or some novel folk custom. People may even practice those superstitions not knowing their origin, but they remain as part of the local culture. The church should not regard this as a threat to its integrity but as a challenge to discover cultural substitutes that are relevant to and communicate to the contemporary situation.

Neopagan rituals

As we have already noted, calendar rituals and religious mythology combine, the ritual illustrating some aspect of the beliefs of the people. The connection is seen within the neopagan movement today with its attempt to return to the ancient beliefs and practices of the traditions of the people of northern Europe. In order to understand the rituals, many neopagans have made great efforts to study ancient cultures and religions. In the last decade or so, after years of neglect, there has been an explosion of books on Celtic and Viking culture and religion.

It must not be assumed that the new pagans are merely trying to copy the ancient rituals of the Celts and Germanic peoples. The lack of archaeological information would make this an impossible task. The aim is to rework the pagan concepts so that they are applicable and relevant for the twenty-first century. It is the old religion applied to the contemporary world. As the London-based Odinshof, a Norse path constituted in 1987, write in their literature:

> We do *not* follow the religion of the Danes of 1200 years ago, the Anglo-Saxons of 1500 years ago, nor the Celts of 2500 years ago. We follow the religion as their children of today. The spiritual essence that they worshipped was a timeless one, tied to these lands. The essence is still within the land, the trees, the air, only masked by concrete and motorways.[14]

Why do neopagans perform rituals? Margot Adler records the answer given by one witch that summarizes many features of modern ritual:

> The purpose of ritual is to change the mind of the human being. It's a sacred drama in which you are the audience as well as the participant, and the purpose of it is to activate parts of the mind that are not activated by everyday activity. . . . As for why ritual, I think that human beings have a need for art and art is ritual. I think that when we become sapient, we become capable of artistic expression. It is simply a human need.[15]

Neopagans are therefore formulating rituals based on ancient symbolism to produce a sacred drama that illustrates spiritual reality as they comprehend it. The primary mythology of Wicca is the mating of the male god with the Earth goddess. Yule is the birth of the sun god as a child of promise. The spring equinox celebrates him as the lord of the greenwood and lover of the goddess. Beltane is the marriage of the goddess and the god, with the sun king's assuming responsibility for the land. Lughnassah is harvest that celebrates the sacrifice of the god that fertilizes the land and allows him to conquer the underworld. Autumn equinox is when the god returns from the underworld to reclaim his queen and take her to his underworld kingdom. At Yule, the cycle repeats.[16]

The different paths within the movement therefore have developed their own particular rituals based on the ancient Celtic and Germanic rituals. Different groups or covens will perform calendar rituals in very different ways, but this only illustrates the acceptance of religious diversity and innovation. Many books and study manuals give "scripts meant to be changed, reworked, improved on, or used as they are."[17]

Starhawk, in her influential book *The Spiral Dance,* gives the following suggestions to those of a wiccan path for the festival of Brigid (Candlemas).

The central cauldron is filled with earth. Unlit candles—one for each covener and guest—are piled beside it. One candle stands upright in the centre.

The circle gathers and does the breathing meditation. The Priestess says, "This is the feast of the waxing light. What was born at the solstice begins to manifest, and we who were midwives to the infant year now see the Child Sun grow strong as the days grow visibly longer. This is the time of individuation: within the measures of the spiral, we each light our own light, and become uniquely ourselves. It is the time of initiation, of beginning, when seeds that will later sprout and grow begin to stir from their dark sleep. We meet to share the light of inspiration, which will grow with the growing year."[18]

Starhawk suggests that the priestess should invoke the goddess and god with a chant. The central candle should be lit and the spiral dance begins. "The Spiral Dance: All face out. The leader begins moving counter-clockwise, with a simple grapevine step. As the circle unwinds, she whips around, facing the person next to her, and leads the spiral inward, clockwise. As coveners pass, face to face, they kiss." When the dance unwinds back into a circle, drummers begin a stronger beat. One by one each member of the coven lights a candle from the center, and focusing on the flame visualizes what they wish for the coming season. The candles are then placed in the cauldron of earth.

Time is then allowed for trance, following which the members share their creative work—songs, stories, art work, crafts. The goddess is thanked for her inspiration. The circle is then opened, and the participants take some earth to sprinkle on their garden or to keep in their own altar.

These eight calendar rites are known as "Sabbats" in Wicca, and every member is expected to attend if possible. Besides these festivals there are thirteen regular meetings of the coven each year when magic is done, and initiates incorporated and trained. These meetings occur at the full moon and are called "Esbats."

As the various "paths" have developed, there has been a

gradual formalization of the rituals. Some items become a standard part of the particular calendar rite, and with time they will probably become more embellished and part of the established practice of the particular cult.

Festivals

In North America a new element of the neopagan movement that emerged within the 1980s is the pagan festivals. These festivals bring together an extraordinary number of different pagan paths and also many solitary practitioners. Although only a small fraction of pagans actually attend festivals, they come into contact with new ideas. The various vendors offer a whole collection of various ritual and occult items. The "purists" may scoff at these trivia, but their application has spread through much of the neopagan community and the wider society. As Margot Adler observed of the American scene: "Festivals have created a national Pagan community, a body of nationally shared chants, dances, stories, and ritual techniques."[19]

A second factor in the festivals is that they provide the easiest route into a coven or magical group. Those who have some vague interest in the movement are able to attend and participate in some group rituals before becoming involved in a particular path. As Haragano says,

> Pagan festivals are the meeting of the tribes. You come from different parts of the country, from different trainings, and traditions. You may have read some of the same books. You meet people from all spiritual backgrounds and all levels of spiritual growth. You see the whole spectrum of our belief and practice in a few days. Gardnerians and Dianics, Druids and Faeries, all acting like neighbours.[20]

The great midsummer festival at Glastonbury claims to have attracted 150,000 people in 1990. At the present time Glastonbury is still primarily a pop festival, but it is approaching the American pattern.

The significance of calendar rituals is more important than most people appreciate, and they have a marked influence upon a society. The only times many British people attend church are at the great Christian festivals of Christmas and Easter. The secular calendar continues to be marked by these festivals as major holidays.

The Third Reich in Nazi Germany recognized the need to establish their own system of calendar rites. This not only satisfied the cultural needs of the population but provided a means by which the political philosophy was reinforced.

Day of National Socialist Assumption of Power	January 30
Hitler's Birthday	April 20
National Festival of the German People	May 1
German Summer Solstice	June 21
German Harvest Festival	August 1
Remembrance Day, those who died for the Movement	November 9
German Winter Solstice	December 25

The declared object of the rituals was the substitution of the Christian calendar by one that was National Socialist. Many rituals included symbolism characteristic of the ancient Norse tradition as reinterpreted under the Nazis. As Esther Gajek writes,

Under the Third Reich, Party officials, in particular, were concerned to appropriate all important festivals in the course of the year and of life for National Socialism. This necessitated a reinterpretation of their nature and the creation of new customs, in which folklorists played an important role.[21]

The Christmas festival was transformed into a celebration of the Third Reich. The result was a strange syncretism of Norse mythology, Nazi emblems and Christian overtones (see figure 9:3).

*Figure 9:3 The reinterpretation of the symbols
of Christmas (Yule) by the Third Reich.*

Notes

1. Starhawk, *The Spiral Dance* (Harper and Row: San Francisco, 1989), p. 181.
2. David Burnett, *Unearthly Powers* (MARC: Eastbourne, 1988).
3. Nigel Pennick, *Practical Magic of the Northern Tradition* (Aquarian Press: Wellingborough, 1989), p. 34.
4. Graham Webster, *The British Celts and their Gods under Rome* (Batsford: London, 1986), p. 31.
5. Margaret Lyttleton and Werner Forman, *The Romans: Their Gods and Their Beliefs* (Orbis Publishing: London, 1984), p. 51.
6. Pennick, op. cit., p. 37.
7. "Calendar," *The New Encyclopedia Britannica,* Vol. 3 (Encyclopedia Britannica Inc: Chicago, 1981), p. 602.
8. Burnett, op. cit., p. 95.
9. Charles Kightly, *The Customs and Ceremonies of Britain* (Thames and Hudson: London, 1986), p. 132.
10. Pennick, op. cit., p. 40.
11. Constantine FitzGibbon, *The Irish in Ireland* (David and Charles Publishers: Newton Abbot, 1983), p. 72.
12. Ibid., p. 72.
13. Sir James G. Frazer, *The Golden Bough* (MacMillan Press: London, 1978), p. 814.
14. Odinshof information sheet (1989).
15. Margot Adler, *Drawing Down the Moon* (Beacon Press: Boston, 1986), p. 141.
16. Vivianne Crowley, *Wicca: The Old Religion in the New Age* (Aquarian Press: Wellingborough, 1989), pp. 189–190.
17. Starhawk, op. cit., p. 178.
18. Ibid., p. 186.
19. Adler, op. cit., p. 422.
20. Adler, op. cit., p. 430.
21. Esther Gajek, "Christmas under the Third Reich," *Anthropology Today,* Vol. 6, No. 4 (1990), p. 9.

10

The Cycle of Life

I —, in the Presence of the Mighty Ones, do of my own free will and accord most solemnly swear that I will ever keep secret and never reveal the secrets of the Art. . . . And may my weapons turn against me if I break this solemn oath. (Witches' initiation oath.)

In the previous chapter we considered those rituals that divide the calendar year as far as the neopagan community is concerned. As we have seen, such rituals are common to all societies, as are those that divide the cycle of an individual's life. This second class of rituals has been called "rites of passage" following the ideas of the Belgian anthropologist, Arnold van Gennep.

> Transitions from group to group and from one social situation to the next are looked on as implicit in the very fact of existence, so that a man's life comes to be made up of a succession of stages with similar ends and beginnings: birth, social puberty, marriage, fatherhood, advancement to a higher class, occupational specialisation, and death. For every one of these events there are ceremonies whose essential purpose is to enable the individual to pass from one defined position to another which is equally well defined.[1]

Calendar rites usually aim to ensure success and prosperity for the future. Their effect is to break up the flow of time into regular periods, and this is clearly seen with the eight calendar festivals within the neopagan movement. Similarly, rites of passage divide up the flow of an individual's life into a series of social statuses. These are usually:

Rite	New status
Birth	Childhood
Initiation	Adulthood
Marriage	Parenthood
Death	Ancestorhood

The individual moves from one social status to another in a series of discontinuous jumps: child to adult, unmarried to married, living to dead. The transition across the social boundary is facilitated by means of a ritual that includes many meaningful symbols. For example, a Christian wedding ceremony signifies the socially accepted transition from an unmarried to a married status. The white wedding dress worn by the bride symbolizes sexual purity. A common procedure in a wedding is for the groom's family to sit on one side of the church and the bride's family on the other. At the reception the two families mix together, the bride's father often being photographed with the groom's mother, and vice versa. This illustrates that marriage was formerly considered to be more than a union of two individuals; it was a joining of two families.

The concept of initiation from childhood to adulthood, often called a maturity ritual, has its parallels in the process of initiation of a person into an exclusive association. Here a person moves from the status of being a nonmember to that of a member. If a person joins a club he is required to obey the rules of the association and sign a form to express his willingness to do such. The person may have to undergo a period of training before he is accepted as a member, as in the case of the trade guilds. All but the smallest of societies have such associations, and the fraternities of the neopagan movement can be understood as such associations.

Before we examine the actual rites of passage common to the neopagan movement, we must first consider the process of initiation by which a member becomes associated with a particular path.

Initiation

The term *secret society* may sound unduly dramatic, but it does allow us to class together a wide variety of associations that are comparable in that they claim to have some esoteric (hidden) knowledge. Some neopagan groups do not have initiation but are study groups interested in Earth mysteries, UFOs, and ecology. They have little by way of ritual apart from a general gathering at some public place to welcome in the spring. The majority of neopagan groups, however, do have initiation. Most of their meetings are therefore exclusive to initiated members, although they may allow some uninitiated members to attend some activities. Fran Skinner in her booklet that describes to nonwitches some of the beliefs and practices of witches writes,

> Who can attend a coven meeting? Usually it is initiated members only for the religious meetings, and mainly non-initiated for the training circle. . . . On very rare occasions, a non-initiated visitor may be invited to be part of a meeting or an outer circle meeting for a special purpose. (Healing, Wedding, a special discussion, etc.)[2]

Purpose

The primary purpose of any initiation rite is to join the initiate to the particular society. The initiate must first commit himself or herself to the group before there is a sharing of the esoteric wisdom. The common experience of the rituals of initiation and the bond that occurs leads to a great sense of group solidarity. This attachment of the initiate may be explained in various ways. Among many neopagans the Jungian concept of the collective unconsciousness, in the terms of a group mind, is often quoted. For example, Vivianne Crowley writes,

> Each coven has its own group mind and the initiation ceremony is designed to link the new initiate with this. Many covens will therefore ask already-initiated witches who are joining their coven, per-

haps because they have moved to a different area, to undergo a coven initiation ceremony.[3]

Second, initiation is often seen as a doorway to a new life potential with magical powers. "An initiation is a symbolic death and rebirth, a rite of passage that transforms each person who experiences it."[4] It is a death to one's former ordinary life and an entrance onto a path of exploration of a new level of consciousness. The very drama of the ritual of initiation itself heightens the sense of expectation. The ritual produces the feelings of the exotic, the strange, and even the weird in comparison to the ordinariness of everyday life.

Third, the crossing of a boundary at initiation draws a distinction between members and nonmembers. It emphasizes in dramatic form the social distance across which the initiate must pass to become a member of the exclusive gathering. It requires a commitment marked by an oath, a bond, a pact. The anthropologist Jean La Fontaine in her book on secret societies remarks,

> An oath is always administered: that is, the person who swears is led through the oath by a superior. . . . The oath is thus not, as is usually imagined, the point at which the candidate freely pledges himself to the society, it is a point which tests the candidate's acceptance of the authority over him.[5]

In recent years some leaders of Wicca, such as Janet and Stewart Farrar, have suggested that people who were unable to contact a Wicca group could practice self-initiation. Although most would consider this to be a possibility, it is often likened to a patient's trying to remove his own appendix.[6] It is possible but dangerous. The illustration stresses the need for someone to guide the initiate through the dangers of the social boundary into the new life.

Preparation
Most neopagan groups stress the need for the initiates to prepare themselves before the ritual and to be convinced that they

desire that particular path. Intellectually, this preparation involves becoming familiar with the gods of the particular tradition. If the path is that of the Norse tradition, this would involve reading books about the Vikings and the god Odin. Meditation is often considered important to help calm the inner soul. In a nature religion with a veneration of Gaia, an affinity with all living things is considered important. Quiet walking in the countryside is therefore considered essential.

Starhawk, in her training manual, recommends three things by way of preparation. First, regular physical exercise. Second, daily meditation and visualization. Third, the practice of keeping a magical diary, a sort of recipe book of rituals and spells.[7]

Ceremony

Van Gennep showed that the rites of passage can be analyzed in three stages. The first phase is a stripping away of the initial state, in this case the status of a nonmember. The second is a transitional stage that van Gennep called "liminal" (from the Latin *limen* meaning a threshold), where the person is neither in nor out. This stage is characterized by danger and ambiguity. The final stage is when the person is integrated into the particular status or group (see figure 10:1).[8]

We will use the initiation into a Gardnerian Wicca coven as an example. It needs to be stressed that the words used and ritual instruments vary among the various paths, but the aims are the same. The initiation ceremony in Wicca is performed naked ("sky-clad") which, it is claimed, comes from the Celtic view that nudity was supposed to offer supernatural protection. It was for this reason that the Celts would often go into war naked apart from war paint and tattoos. The magical and northern traditions, on the other hand, prefer to use ritual robes, generally of a uniform design and color. In either case, nudity or robes act as a symbol separating the initiates from their previous life. This discarding of everyday clothing is typical of the first stage of initiation rites around the world. In maturity rites, the young people discard their children's clothing in preparation for putting on the clothes of an adult. The act of removing

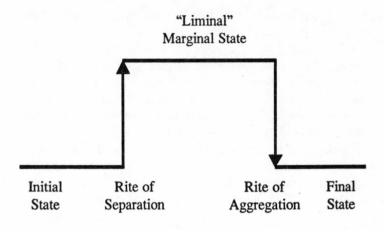

"Liminal"
Marginal State

| Initial | Rite of | Rite of | Final |
| State | Separation | Aggregation | State |

*Figure 10:1 The general three-stage schema characteristic
of most rites of passage.*

one's familiar clothing makes the initiate feel vulnerable, and so requires a willingness on behalf of the person to be placed into the hands of the new association. This is often highlighted by the initiate's being blindfolded, as with the Freemasons and many Wicca covens.

Some Wicca groups not only blindfold the person but also bind them with cords. This supposedly symbolizes the person's bondage to the world of matter and to the ego.

> By seeking initiation we have taken the first step on the path of our spiritual journey and our feet are already almost free. At the end of the initiation we are freed from the cords and can throw away the fetters which hold us back from our spiritual destiny.[9]

The initiate is therefore in the "liminal" state, neither mundane nor entirely nonmundane but an uneasy mixture of the two. Time seems to flow at a different rate in the liminal. Standing naked, bound and blindfolded, for example, will cause the initiate to feel that time has almost come to a halt. It provides an opportunity for reflection, as many wiccans mention, but primarily it makes the participant feel part of another, very different and mysterious world. Once the initiate has been prepared, she or he waits at the edge of the circle before being drawn into the center where the ritual of initiation takes place. The sponsor may give the final push that brings the initiate over the threshold into the circle to be received by the high priestess. "The world which the initiate has entered is the world of the circle."[10]

Within the circle the rites vary from coven to coven. A recitation from *The Book of Shadows* is common. The initiate is asked to swear the oath, following which he or she is untied. Some groups have a ceremonial light scourging with forty lashes (forty being the sacred number in Wicca). The Alexandrian path has the pricking of the thumb so that blood flows. Wiccans are strong to state that sex does not play a part at this level of initiation. Fran Skinner writes, "There is no ritual 'deflowering' of virgins by High Priests as Dennis Wheatley, etc., would have us believe. Neither is sex part of the initiation ceremonies, as claimed by the media."[11]

The final stage of the initiation begins with the blindfold being removed. The initiate is now being united into the group and in Wicca is often welcomed by a kiss. The "working tools" of the witch are then presented to the new member who entered the circle in weakness but will leave in power. In general, there are eight "weapons" following the general pattern of Aleister Crowley, but covens vary in which ones they use.

Weapon	Name	Meaning
Sword		Rulers of the circle
Black-handled dagger	Athame	Male element
White-handled dagger		For use in the circle
Wand	Stang	Symbol of the phallic god
Cauldron		Symbol of the womb
Pentacle		
Censer of incense		
Scourge		

The initiates are now given the first instruction: The origin of the power of witches comes from within us, and there is no part of us which is not divine. We are also told that the Wiccan Rede or Law is "Harm none and do as you will."[12] In other words, witches must decide for themselves what is right and wrong, bearing in mind that one should not cause harm to another. The ceremony is concluded with a feast.

Stages of initiation

Maturity initiation, as a rite of passage, consists of only one event, but secret societies often have a hierarchy of stages. The initiation into the society is only the first of a series leading up the social hierarchy and into deeper esoteric teaching. This is also found within the neopagan movement. The Odinshof is an example of the Norse tradition and follows the teaching and philosophy of Odin.

> The Hof shall have two grades of membership:
> (a) a novice or lower grade named "Odal," and
> (b) a higher grade named "Oak". . . .
> Members of the Odal grade must serve at least 13 full moons in that grade before being eligible for advancement to Oak grade and must satisfy the Witan Assembly that they are worthy and experienced enough to progress to the higher grade.[13]

Within the Wiccan tradition there are three degrees of initiation following the practice of Gardner. The second and third degrees are taken together in Alexandrian covens and separately in the Gardnerian. A year and a day must pass between the first and the second degree initiations, and a witch must be capable of running a circle and raising the cone of power.

The second degree initiation according to Gardnerian tradition contains many similarities to the first, but the initiate is not blindfolded. Only second- and third-degree initiates are allowed to be present, but first-degree witches are allowed to attend a mystery play that is part of the ritual. The legend is one in which the goddess descends into the underworld where she meets the god as the dark lord.

In the third-degree initiation, the goddess and the god come together in union and become one. This is known in the popular press as the "Great Rite" in which the god and goddess enter into sexual union. Vivianne Crowley says,

> Today in Wicca, sexual union with the goddess or god takes place only privately between couples. . . . The third degree initiation is usually given to a couple who are initiated together. How this is done varies between covens. In our rite, the High Priest gives the third degree to the female initiate in token and she then gives the third degree to her partner in true. Most working partnerships are likely to be spouses or lovers and will want to consummate the rite but if not, or if an initiate is to receive the initiation without a partner, then the whole of the rite can be performed in token with the initiator.[14]

The third degree entitles the witch to set up her or his own coven and to initiate others into the first, second, and third degrees.

Coven

The association within Wicca is called "the coven," in Norse tradition it is "hof," and in the magical path "the circle." These groups are regarded as being more than social entities, and reference is frequently made to Jungian psychology and the concept of the collective unconsciousness.

Within the coven the barriers between the individuals' psyches are reduced and a fusion of part of the consciousness is supposed to occur with the formation of a "group mind." The group mind of the coven exists, as it were, on the borders of the personal and the collective unconsciousness. This tends to create telepathic bonds among members, which is why new members must be initiated into a coven. Group magic requires the exercise of the group mind.

The anthropologist Victor Turner has shown the great social significance of rites of transition within societies as they facilitate the flow between social categories.[15] Initiation rites are similar to plays in that they are artificial experiences created by the participants. Use is made of theatrical performance to create lasting impressions on the new member. The Wiccan initiate experiences confusion, vulnerability and a sense of helplessness. There are dramatic moments such as when the initiate is pushed or lifted into the circle. The full meaning of a ritual, like that of a play, requires a common set of assumptions that may be difficult for the outsider to understand. Symbols may depict a variety of meanings as propounded by Jungian psychology, but they also heighten the excitement of things exotic.

Although ritual and drama have similarities, they also have marked differences. Indeed, many of the rituals are secret so that the potential audience is excluded. Ritual, unlike a play, has a purpose and is a means of achieving a practical aim. Secrecy creates a bond among the group transcending that of their loyalty to one another. The ritual confers on the initiate knowledge and rights that increase his or her status, whether publicly acknowledged or not. Tanya Luhrmann, in her study of the magical tradition, concludes, "The techniques of the liminal can be used to make the that-which-is-not seem persuasively more realistic."[16]

Rites of passage

Any new association of whatever nature must initially grow by the conversion of members of the wider society. As the association "ages," an increasing percentage of its members come as a result of being born into families who practice that religion. The same phenomenon is being seen within the neopagan movement. Although a relatively new movement, the "cycle of life" is not formalized as in older religions.

The most common sets of "rites of passage" are birth, maturation, marriage, and death.[17] One can see already the development of these, even though the main concern of contemporary neopagan writers is with initiation.

Birth

How do pagan parents, or the parent in a one-parent family, celebrate the birth of their child? This is an issue that many pagans are facing, and a "Pagan Parenting Network" has been established to help answer these questions.

> Birth is a sacred event and should be celebrated as such. Our culture makes no space for such celebration, which is probably why women crowd round a newborn and its mother in the streets and shops crying "Aah" adoringly. They instinctively feel the sacredness of the newborn and long to share in it.[18]

The emphasis on ritual that is so common to neopaganism produces a desire for birth rituals, and the inherent religious creativity within the movement is producing such rituals. One pagan family formed a circle with some friends and spoke a liturgy they had drafted to name their child. The child was presented to the god and goddess, and their blessing and guidance requested. Skinner remarks, "The parents then try to give their children as wide a view of world religions as possible, and every help along the way to wisdom."[19]

Some pagan families are involving their children in the creating of the circle as a special space into which to welcome the goddess. They have their own robes and chalices given to them as naming gifts. They write,

> Much of the time what we are doing is no different from what other parents are doing with their children. . . . Perhaps the main difference for our Pagan children is that these experiences are enriched and made meaningful through the family seasonal festivals and perhaps most importantly, connected with the goddess and her consort, which is of course what gives them their relevance and their deep resonance.[20]

The involvement of children tends to be within the family of solo practitioners, and it seems to be rare that children are involved within the coven. Skinner comments,

It used to be that children were brought into the Coven by their parents. However, because of the current antagonism against the Craft by the Church, in most covens no one under 18 may attend coven meetings, or be initiated without their parents being present, or written parental consent obtained.[21]

Puberty

Within many primal societies there is a great sense of awe concerning menstrual blood. Menstruation is frequently regarded as being connected with the lunar cycle, and rituals are developing within Wicca to celebrate the event. Menstrual blood is even being used by a few as a sacred offering.

The first menstruation is therefore of great importance, but even so it may come as a surprise to nonpagans when they come across the following advertisement, published in a British paper:

> FIRST MENSTRUATION—Celebrate with individual, handcrafted card. Ideal for daughters, grand-daughters, nieces etc. Recycled material only. Send £1.50 to. . . .

Marriage

Most pagan couples marry in a government civil office for the legal ceremony, followed by a Wiccan "Handfasting." This may take place in the couple's home. The couple may vow to stay together "for as long as love shall last," as opposed to the Christian vow, "until death do us part." The common pagan belief in reincarnation would make the traditional marriage vow nonsense when it comes to future lives.

Death

Due to the common belief in reincarnation, death is viewed as the passage to a resting place before rebirth. Grief will, of course, be felt by loved ones, but there is a sense of joy that they have moved a little closer to union with the goddess. Pagan funeral rites are being drafted as with birth rites. In general, neopagans prefer to be cremated.

Rituals mark the neopagan life more than can be appreciated

by the outsider. They mark not only the change of the year but also the stages of life. Secular life appears void of the excitement and symbolism of ritual. There is none of the theatrical color that is so attractive to many of the new pagans. The Roman Catholic Church has been characterized by such ritual, but most neopagans consider it as devoid of meaning and the participation limited to a few initiated into a male-dominated hierarchy that has negated sexuality, which is a central dynamic to the process of nature. Perhaps it is not surprising that a majority of neopagans involved in the highly ritualistic cults have come from a Roman Catholic background.

In my book on traditional religions, I distinguished three main classes of rituals: Calendar Rites, Rites of Passage, and Rites of Crises.[22] In this and the previous chapter we have considered the first two classes. We are now in a position to consider rites of crises, especially those relating to healing. This introduces the role of the shaman-healer common to many tribal areas of the world. He or she achieves healing by means of entering an altered state of consciousness. The shamanistic path is one of growing importance within the whole neopagan movement.

Notes

1. Arnold Van Gennep, *The Rites of Passage* (Routledge and Kegan Paul: London, 1977), p. 3.
2. Fran Skinner, *Witchcraft for the Non-witch: 101 Questions Answered* (Private Publication, 1988).
3. Vivianne Crowley, *Wicca: The Old Religion in the New Age* (Aquarian Press; Wellingborough, 1989), p. 52.
4. Starhawk, *The Spiral Dance* (Harper and Row Publishers: San Francisco, 1989), p. 173.
5. J. S. La Fontaine, *Initiation* (Penguin Books: Harmondsworth, 1985), p. 78.
6. Crowley, op. cit., p. 52.
7. Starhawk, op. cit., p. 68.

8. David Burnett, *Unearthly Powers* (MARC: Eastbourne, 1988), p. 98.

9. Crowley, op. cit., p. 65.

10. Crowley, op. cit., p. 73.

11. Skinner, op. cit.

12. Crowley, op. cit., p. 78.

13. New Constitutions of the Odinshof (1989).

14. Crowley, op. cit., pp. 218–223.

15. Victor Turner, *The Forest of Symbols* (Cornell University Press: Ithaca, 1989).

16. Tanya Luhrmann, *Persuasions of the Witch's Craft* (Basil Blackwell: Oxford, 1989), p. 231.

17. Colin Turnbull, *The Human Cycle* (Paladin: London, 1985).

18. Nicola, *Pipes of P.A.N.*, No. 32 (Summer, 1989), p. 17.

19. Skinner, op. cit.

20. Nicola, op. cit., p. 15.

21. Skinner, op. cit.

22. Burnett, op. cit., p. 94.

11

Altered States of Consciousness

They had me lie down on the bamboo platform under the great thatched roof of the communal house. The village was silent, except for the chirping of crickets and the distant calls of a howler monkey deep in the jungle.

As I stared upward into the darkness, faint lines of light appeared. They grew stronger, more intricate, and burst into brilliant colours. Sound came from far away, a sound like a waterfall, which grew stronger and stronger.

Just a few minutes earlier I had been disappointed, sure that the Ayahuasca (drug) was not going to have any effect on me. Now the sound of rushing water flooded my brain. My jaw began to feel numb, and the numbness was moving up to my temples.

Overhead the faint lines became brighter, and gradually interlaced to form a canopy resembling a geometric mosaic of stained glass. The bright violet hues formed an ever-expanding roof above me. Within this celestial cavern, I heard the sound of water growing louder and I could see dim figures engaged in shadowy movements. As my eyes seemed to adjust to the gloom, the moving scene resolved itself into something resembling a huge fun house, a supernatural carnival of demons. In the centre, presiding over the activities, and looking directly at me, was a gigantic, grinning crocodilian head, from whose cavernous jaws gushed a torrential flood of water. Slowly the water rose, and so did the canopy above them, until the scene metamorphosed into a simple duality of blue sky above and sea below. All creatures had vanished.[1]

Within the British Isles, pagans can look to many historic sites that epitomize ancient myths veiled by the mists of time. The land itself seems to carry the very "roots" of Celtic and Germanic magic and religion. Here one can identify places where sacred rituals have been performed from before recorded history. With the expansion of the European peoples to the Americas and Australia, the migrants lost those historic roots. Perhaps this is why many groups in North America are looking back to the lands of their origin and following Celtic and Norse paganism. Others are looking to the traditional beliefs of the people who once roamed the lands that the Europeans have conquered and displaced. Could it be that these displaced people had a relationship with the land, which the proud European must discover? The keepers of the traditions of these indigenous societies were the shamans.

Shamanism is a visionary tradition that stretches back beyond recorded history. Until about 1980, shamanism was considered no more than an exotic rite performed by a few bizarre practitioners among some of the isolated tribal societies of the world. In the West, it was only the anthropologists who discussed the concepts and practices of the shaman. Terms such as *medicine man*, *sorcerer*, *magician*, *witch doctor*, and *shaman* were used with little definition. Deliberations revolved around the question of whether the participants were schizophrenic or addicted to drugs. Then, suddenly, there was a change.

Anthropologists such as Carlos Castaneda[2] and Michael Harner[3] not only observed the rituals of the shaman but began to practice them. The account recorded at the beginning of the chapter is the record of the first shamanistic journey of Michael Harner. Suddenly, frightening new worlds seemed to open before these anthropologists, bringing a host of new questions. Was this the way of the animal powers that Western people had long forgotten? Are these shamans, who have been despised for so long, in fact at the very forefront of human exploration of the magical path? It is therefore not surprising that shamanism has become a new and growing element within the current neo-pagan movement.

Shamanism among tribal societies

Shamanism is a word derived from the language of the Tungus people of Siberia and has been used of a wide variety of practitioners among primal societies.[4] Among the peoples of the circumpolar region of the Arctic, shamanism was the traditional religion. Similar beliefs and practices were found among the American Indians, although it is difficult in their case to distinguish between shamans and other technicians of sacred power like the priests, medicine men, and sorcerers. In Mexico and the Amazon forests, shamans use hallucinogenic drugs such as the peyote cactus and chewing tobacco to enable them to move into their spiritual journeys.

Shamans in Indonesia and Malaysia exhibit many familiar characteristics of all shamans, such as trance states and communication with animal spirits. Both Japan and Korea have a tradition of shamanism, but here one finds the refined and delicate actions characteristic of these societies. Here also the practitioners are usually women rather than men as found in most other shamanistic societies. Shamanism predates the coming of Buddhism in these countries as it does in Tibet where the ancient religion of Bon has a major shamanistic aspect.

Mircea Eliade's book, *Shamanism: Archaic Techniques of Ecstasy*, has influenced all researchers in shamanism since it was first published in 1951.[5] He showed that despite the obvious difference in mythologies, culture heroes, and deities, there is a remarkable consensus in the shamanistic cosmology. More than this he showed an appreciation for the worldview of the shaman which differed from that of previous Western observers.

The characteristics of the shaman may be briefly classified as follows:

1. A shaman is essentially the healer of the society.
2. He moves into a trance, which may be described as an ecstasy or altered state of consciousness.
3. He depends on the assistance of spirit guides that are usually animal spirits.

4. He is a spiritual warrior fighting against the spirits of sickness and evil magicians.
5. He has the ability to travel in spiritual worlds and to "see" spiritual beings (gods, demons, ghosts).

Although early anthropologists regarded the shaman as being characteristic of schizophrenia, Eliade and later Harner[6] argued that the issue lays not within tribal society but with the Western way of thinking. The Western worldview focused on the material nature of reality, discounting the mystical and spiritual tradition. Shamanism therefore appears irrational and totally illogical. However, when a person becomes a shaman, he or she is able to appreciate the other state of consciousness in which the shaman moves.

Why is shamanistic practice so common throughout the tribal peoples of the world? Michael Harner answers this question in the following way:

> I suggest that the answer is, simply, because it works. Over many thousands of years, through trial and error, people in ecological and cultural situations that were often extremely different, come nonetheless to the same conclusions as to the basic principles and methods of shamanistic power and healing.[7]

Harner would argue that it was just because these tribal societies had such a low level of technology that they had to utilize the abilities of the mind to its highest degree.

States of consciousness

The shaman's universe may simply be described as consisting of three levels. Human beings live on the earth, which is regarded as a middle zone between an upper and a lower world, associated with the sky and underworld respectively. The three zones are believed to be linked by a central vertical axis that passes upward and downward through "holes" in the cosmic vault. It is through these "holes" that the shaman is able to pass into different levels of existence.

The link between heaven and earth has many variants. Among the Evenk people of Siberia, a mighty river is considered to join the three levels of the cosmos. World trees are common ideas among the shaman in central and north Asian religions. The Yakuts of Siberia, for example, believe that a tree with eight branches rises from the "golden navel of the earth" and reaches up to the heaven. This cosmology is very similar to that of Yggdrasill, the sacred ash tree of Norse mythology, which was considered in an earlier chapter.

To perform his work, the shaman has to move between the different realities. Each reality may be coped with successfully only when one is in the appropriate state of consciousness. In the lower world, the shaman must be aware of the state of consciousness needed to deal with the spirits and powers that dwell there. Only the shaman who masters his actions in all realms will be able to combat the evil forces that afflict his people.

For this reason, both Castaneda and Harner have drawn a distinction between two states of consciousness. Castaneda calls them ordinary reality and nonordinary, but it is Harner's terms of shamanistic state of consciousness (SSC) and ordinary state of consciousness (OSC) that are becoming most widely used. The generally used definition of an altered state of consciousness is that given by Arnold Ludwig, who describes it as "any mental state(s) induced by various physiological, psychological, or pharmacological maneuvers or agents, which can be recognised subjectively by the individual himself (or by an observer of the individual) as representing a sufficient deviation in subjective experience or psychological functioning from certain general norms for that individual during alert, waking consciousness."[8] Although Ludwig's use of the word *alert* has been questioned, because shamans may be very alert during SSC, the expression "altered state of consciousness" seems the most applicable and has been appropriated by modern shamans.

The SSC differs from the trance characteristic of spirit possession and mediumship in that the shaman has total recall after he has returned to OSC. In other words, there is no amnesia and so the shaman is able to recount the events that have occurred along his spiritual journey. This fact accounts for the graphic pictures and events described by the shaman on his return to OSC.

Contemporary shamans consider the SSC as having a reality possibility even more valid than that of the OSC. This is because our materialistic culture has so influenced us that it has suppressed our experience of other levels of consciousness.

> A shaman can move out of the cultural trance of consensus reality to access the visionary realm and see deeper into the web of life and thus understand the flow of events in the ordinary world from a much different perspective. Ordinary people live in a state of "waking sleep" (said Gurdieff), deeply hypnotised by the apparent reality of the world-out-there. The shaman knows that is only a reflection of the real world, world-in-here.[9]

The steady beat of the drum is a common means by which SSC is achieved. The single beat of the drum contains a wide variety of sound frequencies that simultaneously transmit impulses along a variety of nerve endings to the brain. The result is a change in the rhythms of the brain that is little understood. However, during SSC it appears as though the shaman is still lightly connected to OSC because if the drumming is stopped he will come back rapidly to OSC.[10] The monotonous rhythm of the drum acts like a carrier wave, both to help the shaman enter SSC and to sustain him on his journey. Perhaps this is why many shamans speak of their drums as their "horse" or their "canoe."

In *Divine Horses*, Maya Deren,[11] a young American dancer visiting Haiti, describes the sensations produced in her by prolonged exposure to drum rhythms during a Voodoo rite she was attending. After a time she felt as though she was actually being taken over by the beat as it ceased to be outside her. It appeared to be within her as physical responses of foot tapping and clapping that became muscular spasms beyond her control. At the climax she lapsed into a trance. She was later told that she had spoken with the voice of the goddess of love, Erzulie.

Entrance into SSC may also be achieved through rattles and chanting. Chants tend to be relatively slow and monotonous, increasing in tempo as the shaman approaches SSC. With experience the shaman learns how to prepare himself so that he is quickly able to move into SSC and then accomplish his healing task.

Animal powers

In the shaman's world, for him to achieve his healing task he needs the assistance of a spirit guide. There are two essential types of spirit guides as far as the shaman is concerned. The first are those spirits that are substantially under the shaman's control and are willing to serve him in the role of "familiar spirits" (power animals). Second are those spirits who maintain a certain independence and are not automatically subject to the shaman. These are often regarded as minor deities or spirits of deceased shamans.

Traditional societies frequently feel a close association with various animal or plant species—a belief called totemism. Many shamans consider their familiar spirits to be animal spirits: bears, wolves, hares, eagles, bulls. The shaman, in possessing a particular animal spirit, is considered able to influence an entire species.[12] These helping spirits in animal form play an important role in the preliminaries of the shamanistic ritual. The Tungus shaman, who has a snake familiar, attempts to imitate the reptile's motions during the ritual. The Eskimo shamans seek to turn themselves into wolves, and the Lapp shamans become wolves, bears, or reindeer. Within the American rainforest, the spirit of the jaguar has grasped the imagination of the Indians.[13] "In appearance, this shamanistic imitation of the actions and voices of animals can pass as 'possession.'"[14]

Harner claims that everyone who has survived childhood's hazards and illnesses must, according to the shaman, be under the protection of their guardian spirit.[15] The tragedy, he claims, is that they are totally ignorant of the presence of that spirit. This awareness may be achieved by the shamanistic practice of "calling the beast." This involves the use of the continuous rhythm of the drum in a darkened room. As one slowly dances shaking a rattle, one is encouraged to move into SSC. The seeing of your animal spirit usually occurs as one moves into SSC, after which the dance shifts to a faster and faster rate. Then one stops dancing and mentally welcomes the animal to stay in one's body.

Harner makes a very bold claim to his students: "Remember, guardian spirits are always beneficial. They never harm their possessors. And you possess the guardian spirit; it never possesses you. In other words, the power animal is a purely beneficial spirit, no matter how fierce it may appear. It is a spirit to be exercised, not exorcised."[16] It seems strangely inconsistent that most shamanistic societies consider the shamanistic role as one to be avoided unless one is compelled. As the Eskimos would say, "No one chooses to be a shaman."

The concept of a primal shamanistic culture of all societies has been promoted by Joseph Campbell.[17] This has resulted in a growth of interest in shamanism from those within all the different pagan paths. Thus, Nicholas Mann in his study of Celtic beliefs, writes,

> The role of the Power Animals has always been to link the human species with the larger collective environment or ecosphere. We are all a part of each other. By dreaming of an animal, by performing a ritual, by retelling an ancestral creation myth, the Dreamer, the Shaman, the Bard is working with the essential unity of life, and can journey into the collective spheres of being through the mediating role of the animal.[18]

Mann would state that the animal symbols on the ancient Celtic standing stones arise from "inner journeying and initiatory knowledge."

The shamanism of Castaneda

If Mircea Eliade provided the academic framework for an understanding of shamanism, it was Carlos Castaneda who popularized the subject and made it accessible to the person in the street.

Carlos Castaneda is something of an elusive person. His real name was Carlos Arana (or Aranha). He seems to have come to the United States from either Lima, Sao Paulo, or Buenos Aires, and in 1959 acquired American citizenship. Castaneda had enrolled at the University of California (UCLA) to study anthropology, and in 1960 he began a study of the use of medicinal plants among the Yaqui Indians.

Castaneda claimed that he became a student of an Indian "brujo" (sorcerer) called Don Juan Matus. According to Castaneda, Don Juan considered the world "out there" to be no more than one of a number of worlds. In order to transform one's perception from ordinary to magical reality, an unlearning process has to occur. The apprentice must learn to rise above his worldview and join himself between the two universes of the real and the magical. Don Juan taught that by the use of hallucinogenic drugs such as mescalito (peyote) and humito (psilocybe mushrooms) one could more easily enter the other world (Harner's SSC).

Four of Castaneda's early books tell of his apprenticeship to the sorcerer: *The Teachings of Don Juan; A Separate Reality; Journey to Ixtlan;* and *Tales of Power. The Teachings of Don Juan,* published by the University of California Press, seems like a serious piece of anthropological research. However, from the beginning there were those who questioned some of Castaneda's writings.[19]

First, no one has ever met or even seen a photograph of Don Juan, and this includes Castaneda's academic committee. Don Juan does not fit the typical model of a Yaqui Indian, and sacred mushroom rites were unknown among the Yaqui. Second, although Castaneda claimed that the manuscripts were translated from Spanish field-notes, no such field-notes have ever been presented. Gordon Wasson raised some serious linguistic questions about such phrases as "I ran like the son of a bitch" and "Don't lose your marbles." Were there any shaman-Spanish equivalents to these American expressions?

De Mille is a former clinical psychologist who taught at UCLA, and since 1970 he has worked as a writer and editor.

He has raised serious doubts about the authenticity of Castaneda's accounts. He was incredulous of such accounts as that of the sewing of a lizard's eyelids recounted in Castaneda's *Journey*, especially when it was nearly dark and he had never seen anyone do it before. De Mille considered the incident to be no more than a rewrite of one recorded in *The Handbook of South American Indians* that describes the sewing of a toad's eye and mouth by a skilled Peruvian sorcerer.

The writings of Castaneda cannot be regarded as scholarly anthropological works. Even Harner has agreed that the later books became embellished as the popularity of the Don Juan saga grew. Castaneda has certainly benefited financially from the Don Juan series. Nevill Drury, who is highly supportive of the application of shamanism in the modern world, has had to conclude,

> So what emerges from the Carlos Castaneda debate is that Carlos himself is probably the actual visionary and many of the shamanistic perspectives have been implanted in the personage of the real, partially real, and unreal being known as Don Juan. In this sense it hardly matters to the person interested in states of consciousness and perception whether Don Juan is real or not since the fiction, if it is that, is authentic enough. It is nevertheless interesting that later Castaneda works, like his 1984 publication *The Fire From Within*, have been presented in some editions as "novels."[20]

The shamanism of Harner

If the works of Carlos Castaneda have very suspect academic criteria, Michael Harner has impeccable credentials as an anthropologist. He has been visiting professor at Columbia, Yale, and the University of California. He is now the founder and director of the Foundation for Shamanistic Studies in Connecticut. After the death of Mircea Eliade, Harner is probably the world's leading authority on shamanism. He has studied the shamans of a variety of North American Indians—Wintun, Pomo, Coast Salish, Sioux and Jivaro—and it was with the

Conibo Indians of the Peruvian Amazon that he experienced his initiatory vision.

Harner is not merely an academic, but he is a practicing shaman who leads many shamanistic workshops in North America. There are several emerging groups in Europe that follow the methods of Harner. Why is shamanism growing in the world today? Michael Harner has the following answer:

> An important reason shamanism has wide appeal today is that it is spiritual ecology. In this time of worldwide environmental crises, shamanism provides something largely lacking in the anthropocentric "great" religions: reverence for, and spiritual communication with, the other beings of the Earth and with the Planet itself. In shamanism, this is not simple Nature worship, but a two-way spiritual communication that resurrects the lost connections our human ancestors had with the awesome spiritual power and beauty of our garden Earth.[21]

Michael Harner teaches in his workshops how shamanism may bring healing. His favored technique is that of the "spirit canoe."[22] In this case, some ten to fifteen persons sit on the floor in a canoe configuration, facing the same direction. The person in need of healing lies in the center of the canoe. One of the group members sitting in the rear of the canoe begins to beat the drum. The drumming enables the participants to focus their energies on the purpose of healing. The shaman-healer then uses a rattle to define the sacred space and summon the healing spirits.

The shaman then enters the canoe and lies beside the sick person. The shaman and his helpers in the spirit-canoe now visualize the vessel passing down into an opening in the earth. As the drumming continues, the shaman moves into SSC to find a source of spiritual energy for his patient. He rides the drumbeat and visualizes a tunnel leading to the altered state of consciousness. Here he looks for an animal that, according to Harner, presents itself to view from four different directions. Once the animal has appeared, the shaman holds it to his chest, and imaginably returns to OSC. He then kneels beside the sick person and breathes the animal into the patient's head through his cupped hands. The shaman whispers to the client, "I have given you a hare," or, "I have given you a fox," depending on which creature has presented itself. The patient then rises to dance the newly received power-animal to the continuing beat of the drum. At the same time, other members of the group may have their own spiritual journey.

Could the shamanistic journey be no more than vivid imagination? Michael Harner has given the following reply:

> Imagination is a modern Western concept that is outside the realm of shamanism. "Imagination" already prejudges what is happening. I don't think it is imagination as we ordinarily understand it. I think we are entering something which, surprisingly, is universal—regardless of culture. Certainly people are influenced by their own history, their culture and individual history. But we are beginning to discover a map of the upper and lower world, regardless of culture. For the shaman, what one sees—that's real. What one reads out of a book is secondhand information. But just like the scientist, the shaman depends upon first-hand observation to decide what's real. If you can't trust what you see yourself, then what can you trust.[23]

Shamanism and channeling

Shamanism is certainly a growing influence within the total neopagan movement. SSC allows the possibility of discovering one's own archetypes, alongside the use of dreams, visualization and myth. Shamanism, it is claimed, brings one closer to an identity with nature in going back beyond the various tribal religions of the world to the oldest of all religions—the universal practice of shamanism. The trend is therefore to look to shamanistic practices among all traditional societies.

Shamanism is not only a religion, but as with all traditional religions, a means of total healing. Thus it is not merely concerned with individual needs, but reaches out to other hurting human beings. As such, shamanism is becoming a major dimension of holistic healing within the New Age movement.

The notion of altered states of consciousness (SSC), characteristic of shamanism, has close parallels to other concepts within the New Age movement, especially channeling. Channeling is essentially a modern form of spiritism in which the practitioner claims a link with some spiritual being who provides a source of knowledge.[24] Whereas shamanism has developed from an anthropological study of traditional societies, channeling has closer links with psychology. There are however many points of similarity.

First, both involve a form of trance. Dr. Kathryn Ridall, a professional psychologist and channeler, explains the role of trance in the following way. "Trance allows an individual to disconnect from the conscious personality with all of its habitual responses, reactions, and interpretations. Trance allows us to create the state of openness and receptivity we need to resonate with and channel another being."[25]

Second, both channeling and shamanism involve the use of spiritual beings to provide assistance in the process. There is, however, a difference; shamanism, as we have seen, tends to relate to animal spirits while channeling conceives of spirit guides in terms of human personalities.

Finally, both shamanism and channeling claim to provide a means of holistic therapy. "Channeling: linking to a source of higher knowledge to give guidance and insights into daily life. It is also useful for therapists to obtain deeper knowledge re their work and ways to develop it."[26] Similarly, Harner writes: "Shamanism goes far beyond a primarily self-concerned transcendence of ordinary reality. It is transcendence for a broader purpose, the helping of humankind."[27]

In Part 3 we have considered the means by which the powers are invoked. We have examined the basis of magical rituals as a means of obtaining one's desired objectives. We have considered the calendar rites and rites of passage characteristic of much of the neopagan movement. Finally, we have considered the psychological techniques by which some are seeking altered states of consciousness. It is now necessary to ask the question, who are the neopagans?

Notes

1. Michael Harner, *The Way of the Shaman* (Bantam Books: Toronto, 1986), p. 3.
2. Carlos Castaneda, *The Teachings of Don Juan: A Yaqui Way of Knowledge* (Pocket Books: New York, 1968).
3. Harner, op. cit.
4. David Burnett, *Unearthly Powers* (MARC: Eastbourne, 1988).
5. Mircea Eliade, *Shamanism: Archaic Techniques of Ecstasy* (Routledge and Kegan Paul: London, 1978).
6. Harner, op. cit., p. 62.
7. Ibid., p. 53.
8. Arnold Ludwig, "Altered States of Consciousness" in *Altered States of Consciousness,* ed. Charles T. Tart (Anchor/Doubleday: New York, 1972), pp. 11–24.
9. Information leaflet of the London-based Eagle's Wing Centre for Contemporary Shamanism (1990).
10. Harner, op. cit., p. 64.
11. Maya Deren, *Divine Horses: The Living Gods of Haiti* (Thames and Hudson: London, 1953).
12. Harner, op. cit., p. 74.
13. Nicholas J. Saunders, *People of the Jaguar* (Souvenir Press: London, 1989).
14. Eliade, op. cit., p. 93.
15. Harner, op. cit., p. 83.
16. Ibid., p. 88.
17. Joseph Campbell, *The Way of the Animal Powers* (Time Books: London, 1984).
18. Nicholas R. Mann, *The Celtic Power Symbols* (Triskele: Glastonbury, 1987), p. 23.
19. "Don Juan and the Sorcerer's Apprentice," *Time* magazine (March 5, 1973), pp. 30–35.
20. Nevill Drury, *The Elements of Shamanism* (Element Books: Shaftesbury, 1989), p. 87.
21. Michael Harner, *The Foundation for Shamanistic Studies: Newsletter,* Vol. 2, No. 4 (Spring, 1990), p. 1.

22. Harner (1986), op. cit., pp. 116–120.

23. Quoted in Drury, op. cit., p. 99.

24. Elliot Miller, *A Crash Course on the New Age Movement* (Monarch: Eastbourne, 1990), p. 142.

25. Kathryn Ridall, *Channeling: How to Reach Out to Your Spirit Guides* (Bantam Books: Toronto, 1988), p. 18.

26. Shelley Wilmans, Advertising leaflet for course on channeling (Autumn, 1990).

27. Harner (1986), op. cit., p. 179.

Part 4

◯)

THE NEW PAGANS

12

The People Called Pagans

The neopagan movement has only become visible in the United Kingdom since the repeal of the witchcraft law in 1951. It is in fact only part of a much wider series of new religious movements claiming to offer new religious worldviews and experiences. Various studies have been made concerning the nature and growth of New Religious Movements in Britain which Eileen Barker estimates to be between 1,500 and 2,000.[1] Recognizing the complexity of the task, we will now try to understand something of the dynamics of the neopagan movement and its adherents. How many people are actually involved in the neopagan movement? What paths do they follow? What type of persons are they? Why do they turn to paganism?

Counting members

A first question that always arises when discussing a new religious movement of whatever type is how many people belong to it? It is only natural that people want to know if it is a large and growing movement, or if it consists only of a dozen or so, meeting in a private house. The problem in providing any answer to this question is that of definition. What can one count?

Take, for example, the question of how many Christians there are in England. The answer depends on how one defines the word "Christian." One definition would be to say that a Christian is anyone who claims to be a Christian when asked in a typical street survey as carried out by one of the organizations for opinion polls. The question may be drafted: "Do you regard yourself to be a Christian, Muslim, Hindu, Sikh or other?" Such opinion polls reveal that 66% of the population in England would call themselves Christians. This would be the group that Peter Brierley calls "notional" Christians.

The MARC Survey of English churches of 1989 sought to use a different definition and counted the number of people who were attending any local congregation on Sunday, October 15, 1989. There will have been people who were not present on that day, possibly because they were on vacation, who would have been present on fifty other Sundays of the year. Likewise, there may have been people present who had never been in church for the last year or so. However, the survey gives a measure of the number of people present in church on an average Sunday. If one was to conduct a similar survey at one of the major Christian festivals, Christmas or Easter, there would be a greater number of people present.

Even among those who attend church, there will be different levels of commitment. There will be people who are actively involved in the congregation, including elders, deacons, and Sunday school teachers. Others are content merely to sit in the congregation and attend when it is convenient. There may even be those persons who have a very strong personal religious conviction, but for various reasons do not attend any church at all. One can therefore identify several levels of commitment to the established local congregations.

Christians may alternatively be defined, not by their attendance in the church rituals, but by their personal beliefs. This may require certain key issues to which the person is required to give intellectual assent. For example, "Do you believe that the virgin birth of Christ was a historic fact?" "Do you believe that Jesus Christ historically rose from the dead?" It shows that this is a far more complicated definition of who is a Christian, and identifies several streams based on belief.

Within the neopagan movement one can identify similar degrees of commitment. This means that the question "How many neopagans are there in Britain?" cannot be answered in a simple numerical way. One can possibly identify three levels of commitment similar to that within the church. The broadest level is that of people who at some time have "dabbled in" or "flirted with" one or another aspect of paganism. The second is that of those who have made a commitment to pagan beliefs and are currently practicing these beliefs on a more or less regular basis. Finally, there are those who are deeply committed to paganism and may be involved in a full-time capacity of one form or another.

The broadest definition is almost impossible to define as the fringe becomes so diffuse that it involves anyone who has had any involvement in any occult practice. It is perhaps the second level which is both the most useful and the easiest to define. These people actually practice their beliefs, and this provides a means by which the numbers can be estimated. Although there are a few pagan temples, only a small number of people are involved with them and this would not give any meaningful statistic even if it could be obtained.

"The Sorcerer's Apprentice" is the largest mail-order occult store in Britain. In 1989 it had "over 40,000 clients on file throughout the UK."[2] Chris Bray, the proprietor, claims to turn over between 800–1,000 items each week including books, magic robes, incense, etc. He employs ten people full-time.[3] "Mysteries," the largest shop for occult items in London, opened in 1982, and has seen trade double every six months with about 200 customers a day.

Another way by which the growth of the movement may be assessed is in the number of publications. The Aquarian Press is the largest publishing house committed to producing occult and mystical literature. It has so far published 10,000 copies of Marian Green's *Magic for the Aquarian Age*, reference to which was made in previous chapters. The initial print run of Aquarian publications is 3,000 copies. "The largest occult magazine, *Predictions*, has a monthly circulation of 35,000 but no doubt the large majority of its readers are not magicians. The editor of the magazine claims that she knows personally of over 200 magical groups."[4]

The introduction of computerized desktop publishing (DTP)

has made possible a new type of popular specialist magazine. DTP has stimulated the growth of pagan magazines, and many magazines even give information concerning the type of equipment used. Eighty different magazines were recorded in *The Directory of Occult Resources* 1990 *(DOOR)*. These magazines range from four photocopied pages to professionally printed magazines of the style of a high-quality church magazine. Although no actual print runs are recorded by the magazines, it is obvious from their mode of production that they would number from about 200 to possibly 2,000 copies. If one takes 500 as an average print run for each of the 80 different magazines, this would mean a total of 40,000 copies. Although some neopagans would obtain more than one title, each magazine may be read by a number of people.

In 1989, the Occult Census reported "a conservative estimated population of 250,000 Witches/Pagans throughout the UK and many more hundreds of thousands of people with a serious interest in Astrology, Alternative Healing Techniques and Psychic Powers."[5] These figures would appear to be somewhat inflated from the observation of the various resources that would indicate a lower figure of no more than 100,000, but having many fringe members. According to Tanya Luhrmann, Chris Bray, who was responsible for the Occult Census, says that there are far more "dabblers" these days but no more "serious occultists."[6]

The interest of the news media in occult, magic and witchcraft has certainly increased dramatically during the last few years. Occult fiction, both as books and videos, has become a major sales line. One result is that far more people are becoming aware of what is performed within such rituals, and consequently have a fringe interest. This has been stimulated by a complex series of beliefs and philosophies coming under the term New Age. Thus, it seems that the greatest growth has been within the fringe of the movement among interested observers rather than actual practitioners.

The number of full-time practitioners appears to be small, limited to those who run pagan/occult bookshops and mail-order pagan arts and crafts. The majority of committed practitioners support themselves through some form of secular employment, some being employed as computer programmers. This observation was first noticed by Margot Adler in the 1985 questionnaire of pagans in the United States. She remarks, "80 percent of the Pagan community actively used computers and that there was an important and striking relationship between the two."[7]

The character of the neopagans

A few attempts have been made to analyze the type of people who join marginal groups. Standard sociological texts have tended to discuss the growth of cults and sects in terms of "deprivation" theories.[8] Tanya Luhrmann regards this theory as "patently false in magic. These participants come from the middle class. . . ."[9] She describes the practitioners she had contact with in the London area as "the sort of person who takes the relatively dramatic step of initiating contact with magicians and then enjoys the practice well enough to continue with it, may well be imaginative, self-absorbed, reasonably intellectual, spiritually inclined, and emotionally intense."

The problem with all such studies is that one can only make personal contact with a relatively small number of practitioners. Luhrmann has made an excellent study of those of the magical path within the London area. However, a practicing witch from Wales writes concerning Luhrmann's analysis: "This is an overlong, wordy academic tome which is surprisingly gossipy about the incestuous London occult scene. . . . Unfortunately, based on a very small sample, it misrepresents its practitioners as dreamy, middle-class romantics."[10]

The conclusions of the 1989 Occult Survey would tend to support Luhrmann's comments about those who participate within the movement. Out of the 1,000 practicing occultists completing the survey, 10% were unemployed, 3% described themselves as unskilled workers, 21% had attended university, and 10% were students at the time of completing the questionnaire. The survey states: "The conclusions from these figures are many and varied. It seems that Occultists by and large have a higher level of educational ability and socio-economic grouping than the norm."[11] It must be added that, as with all surveys, it tends to be the more highly educated who are willing to complete such questionnaires, thus, giving a bias within the results.

The Occult Survey also made some interesting observations concerning the ages of those involved in the movement. The average age of those who completed the survey was thirty-two years, and about 70% of those persons were between twenty and forty years old.

> As the modern Occult Revival began in the Sixties it is natural to have a disproportionately younger population as the popularisation of occultism continues to grow. All the evidence points to a continuous interest and activity throughout the seven ages of mankind but statistics to categorically prove this assumption will not of course be available for several decades yet.[12]

Interest in neopaganism seems to begin in the early years. Sixty-seven percent of those completing the Occult Census indicated that they had first become interested in occultism before the age of eighteen years, 22% between eighteen and twenty-five, 6% between twenty-six and thirty-five. These figures are not too different from those that would be obtained from a survey of church members, asking them when they had first made a commitment to Christ. The figures show the importance of the teenage years in formulating religious commitment.

Those surveyed also showed a predominance of males, "62% as against 38%."[13] It is difficult to explain this feature, but it seems that men are more willing to complete such questionnaires. It also appears that women are more involved in the Wicca traditions rather than the magical. "Fifty percent of our sample considered themselves single whereas 37% considered themselves married. Thirteen percent considered themselves neither single nor married."[14] The low proportion of married couples is partly a result of the general youth of the sample, but it is difficult not to speculate that the movement particularly attracts the unmarried.

Why do people become pagans?

This is not a question which can be simply answered. The replies depend on who is asked and the perspective of the questioner. The following are some of the answers which I have been given:

1. Rebellion: Neopaganism provides a radical alternative to that which is available within secular society. The movement is essentially a counterculture movement breaking away from a materialistic, non-spiritual culture. They are disillusioned with science and its claim to possess all answers. Participants regard themselves as being at the forefront of a new social movement, but few seem to know where the movement is going. Many magazines discuss the subject of future developments in neopaganism.

2. Religious needs: The rebellion has often focused on an inherent need for spiritual, mystical, or magical experiences. Some have reacted from a strict legalistic Christian family background. Many feel that the established Christian church has failed both them as individuals and society as a whole.

3. Concern for ecology: The widespread concern for ecological issues is seen within neopaganism as we discussed within the context of Gaia, in chapter 5. This is further illustrated in the Occult Census with regard to the choice of political parties. These are ranked as follows:

   1st Greens
   2nd Liberals
   3rd Democrats
   4th Labour
   5th SDP
   6th Marxist
   7th Communists
   8th Conservatives

9th Trotskyites
10th Anarchists.[15]

"The nearest party to the ideals of most occultists is the Green Party. This embodies the caring and empathic link with nature and the planet which is at the heart of all occult systems."[16] However, a cautionary comment should be made that not all those who have connections with the Green Party have corresponding sympathies with the neopagan movement.

4. Spiritual aspect of feminism: This is another common motivation, especially among the Wiccan paths.

5. Family tradition: A few believe that such practices have continued in some branch of their family for generations. This is most common among the Wiccan covens.

6. Ritual participation: "Need for play," as it was called by one informant, illustrates an important feature of the movement. People want to participate in the enactment of the archetypal imagery which has become popular through the influence of Jungian psychology.

Another feature which must be considered is the failure of Christianity. We will return to this in chapter 14.

Neopagan paths and interests

We have mentioned the fact that within the neopagan movement there are many different paths. The whole movement allows dynamic religious creativity with the syncretism of ideas and practices. It is therefore difficult to make a simple assessment of how many people are involved in which path. The Occult Census sought to identify the participants' interest in sixteen major areas of the movement, and to give four levels of interest (see figure 12:1). An immediate difficulty is the lack of definition with regard to these terms.

Although one can criticize many aspects of the survey, it does provide one of the first insights into the movement, and as such reveals several interesting features.

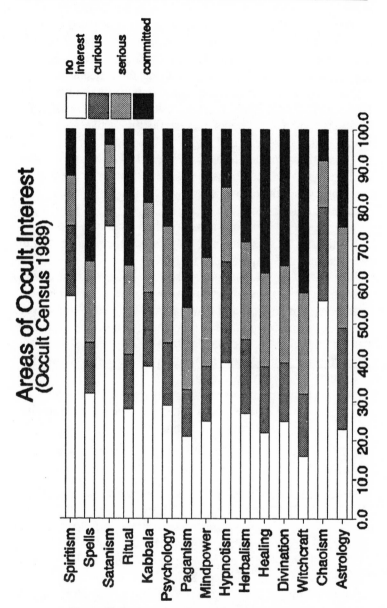

Figure 12:1 Areas of interest in neopagan activities according to the Occult Census, 1989.

The first point to note is that the aspect which polled the lowest level of interest was satanism. Three quarters of the sample said that they had no interest whatsoever. Second, witchcraft and paganism show themselves to be the areas of particular interest. As we have already mentioned, these tend to be the two most common traditions within the wider movement. Rituals and spells also poll a high level of interest, but this would be expected within both the Wiccan and magical paths.

Third, there appears to be little interest in spiritism and theosophy. Both of these philosophies were popular at the turn of the century, but they have not caught the imaginations of those involved in the modern movement.

Fourth, over a third of the sample had a committed interest in divination, but this was in no way universal as can be seen in the fact that 25% expressed no interest.

The Occult Census sought to provide statistical information concerning the movement. Copies have been sent to many researchers, universities, and newspapers. The aim of the survey was to inform those outside of the neopagan movement, and so halt the ongoing anti-occult campaign. The census does not seem to have achieved this aim, but it has certainly shown the complexity of the phenomenon.

As a counterculture movement it is generating not only its own traditions, but its own arts and crafts which are expressive of much of the life of the community.

Notes

1. Eileen Barker, *New Religious Movements: A Practical Introduction* (HMSO Books: London, 1989), p. 148.
2. *The Occult Census: Statistical Analysis and Results* (The Sorcerer's Apprentice Press: Leeds, 1989), p. 36.
3. Tanya Luhrmann, *Persuasions of the Witch's Craft* (Basil Blackwell: Oxford, 1989), p. 5.
4. Tanya Luhrmann, "Persuasive Ritual: The Role of the Imagination in Occult Witchcraft," *Archives de Science Social de Religion* (1985), 60 [1], pp. 151–170.

5. Occult Census, op. cit., p. 3.
6. Luhrmann (1989), op. cit., p. 6.
7. Margot Adler, *Drawing Down the Moon* (Beacon Press: Boston, 1986), p. 446.
8. H. Richard Niebuhr, *The Social Sources of Denominationalism* (Meridian Books: Cleveland, 1929).
9. Tanya Luhrmann (1989), op. cit., p. 99.
10. *The Cauldron,* No. 55 (Winter, 1990), p. 9.
11. Occult Census, op. cit., p. 15.
12. Ibid., p. 12.
13. Ibid., p. 12.
14. Ibid., p. 12.
15. Ibid., p. 22.
16. Ibid., p. 23.

13

Pagan Arts and Crafts

Art is an act of creation, designed to please the aesthetic senses. People are rarely content with a purely utilitarian approach to life. Pot and basket makers decorate their work with shapes and lines, colors and symmetry. Houses are designed and painted according to the owners' particular tastes. People even decorate their own bodies with earrings and various makeup to make themselves more attractive. Stories, proverbs, riddles, and songs are the oral art that is part of every culture. Art is an essential part of human creativity.

The neopagan movement has developed its own particular artistic expression. This is to be expected from a movement that places such emphasis on symbol and myth. By seeking to understand the nature of modern pagan art, one can gain more of an insight into the artists themselves as they express their individual feelings and ideas.

Affecting and reflecting culture

Anthropologist Alexander Alland defined art as "play with form producing some aesthetically successful transformation-representation."[1] By "form," Alland means the culturally appropriate use of material, space, and time. "Aesthetically successful" means that an emotional response is engendered in the artist, and hopefully the observer. It is the expression "transformation-representation" which is essential to Alland's definition. By this he means a symbol or metaphor that in the particular context conveys a specific meaning. If that symbol is cut away from the object or idea represented, it may be used within a different cultural context.

Alland in his definition tries to capture something of the universality of art among human beings and the cultures in which they live. This is a different approach from that common to Western civilization. Western society tends to make a critical distinction between good art and poor art, or rather "art" and "non-art." This was shown by the shock of many at the modern forms of art in the Tate Gallery, for example. What makes the "Mona Lisa" art, but the paint and studs on the leather jacket of a Hell's Angel non-art? Part of the answer is that in Western society there has emerged an "art establishment" of art critics, historians and teachers. These people define what is and is not art. In many cultures, however, there is no such distinction. But this does not mean that people do not make aesthetic judgments about what pleases them most.

While all societies have many forms of art, each has its own definition of what they regard as pleasing. Beauty is indeed in the eye of the beholder. The polyphonic music of the European is considered an atrocious discord by many tribal people. The neck rings worn by the Chin women of Burma as an adornment are viewed with horror by the fashionable North American teenager.[2]

Art has three major functions. First, it gives pleasure both in the production and appreciation. This is especially true in dances and songs when the group can join in social harmony and enjoyment.

Second, art offers a means of self-expression. The artist is able to declare his emotions and ideas. In this way he is like a prophet portraying his perspective of the world in terms of visual symbols. Art is embedded in culture and "will reflect or be controlled by culture to a greater or lesser degree, depending upon the nature of the relationship between art and other cultural areas."[3]

This leads to the third function, which is that of communication. Art forms function as a store house of meaning for a society. In preliterate societies they provide ways by which the children are educated in the traditions and worldview of their people. Art therefore acts as a guide to the worldview and beliefs of a people. These are not expressed in abstract ideas but as symbolic forms. By studying these forms one is able to understand something of the heart of a people. They provide symbolic demonstrations of the themes of society.

For example, Hindu paintings are a cacophony of humans, animals, and deities reflecting the illusory nature of the world with no distinction between the natural and the supernatural. Islamic art, in contrast, does not make use of any human or animal figures in case there is any hint of making the object equal with Allah and so committing the sin of shirk. There has therefore developed within Islam the use of intricate designs and calligraphy. Gothic cathedrals with their lofty roofs and stained-glass windows provide an image of the divine that is designed to touch the Christian's heart. The outer rays of the sun shine through the window to produce an inner illumination for the soul.

Changes in the worldview of a society can often be examined by studying its art forms. This can even be observed within complex societies where social groups express themselves in particular forms of dress and behavior. Art therefore provides a bridge in understanding the assumptions and beliefs of a people, and this is equally true with the neopagan movement.

The emphasis of the pagan movement on symbols and archetypes has stimulated rich and highly creative forms of art. Neopagans have turned to many ancient cultural traditions for their inspiration: the North American Indians, the Celts and Vikings of Europe, and the many traditions of the ancient Middle East. In addition, the artists have been able to draw on the perspective of modern scientific data, and even the imaginations of their own minds.

Before we turn to consider the nature of modern pagan art, a word of warning needs to be given to the newcomer to the movement. In the same way that the art of any other culture appears strange and meaningless at first, so that of the neo-pagan movement appears off-putting to the outsider. Yet a consideration of those aspects which cause one a sense of shock or unease can provide a bridge to an understanding of the very message being communicated by the artist.

The visual arts

The various art forms of modern technology provide a wide scope of expression for the neopagan artist. These can range from the computer art of the Mandelbrot set to hand-painted pictures of the beauty of nature.

The first thing that strikes the newcomer to neopagan magazines is the boldness of shapes and forms. Dramatic postures, sweeping lines, staring faces, stark shapes, and empty skulls dominate magazines and pictures. These imply a desire for a heightened sense of reality. The shapes and forms are symbolic of another, more real world that has a strange mystery and power unique to itself.

Second, one observes a mixing of animal, human, and spirit forms in a similar way to that found within Hindu art. Irish pixies are blended with geometrical forms with a beautiful symmetry. From out of the curving shapes of a tree, or hair, or water one comes to identify a face staring back at you. This is most often seen in the image of a planet within whom and part of whom is the figure of a female face of Gaia (see figure 13:1). Within the material forms the artist is pointing to a spiritual form that is real and with whom one may directly communicate.

Third, ancient artistic styles can be seen such as those of the Australian aborigines whose haunting simplicity has captured the attention of many modern artists. Neopagan art often takes up the shapes and styles of ethnic art which is becoming more widely displayed in Western museums whose imagery is used in modern fashion design.[4] A common feature among the Celtic tradition is the interlocking design characteristic of Celtic crosses (see figure 1:2).

*Figure 13:1 Modern pagan art often focuses upon "Gaia,"
and possesses a deep ecological awareness.*

Fourth, one can observe the fantasy images of the great myths of history. The Arthurian tradition displays figures of King Arthur, Merlin the magician and the knights of the Round Table. The Lady of the Grail may be shown as the figure of a woman dressed in a long flowing gown, her hair tumbling down her back in beautiful locks. In her hands she holds the sacred grail that in Arthurian tradition was the quest of Arthur's knights. The Merlin legends inspire many contemporary groups who dress in long robes thought to be characteristic of the Celtic magician. It is the followers of this tradition who are often seen taking part in summer solstice celebrations at Stonehenge.

A final category consists of the images drawn by past magicians and occultists. The images of the medieval mystics, astrologers and magicians are frequently reflected in the visual arts. The zodiacal signs are also common, as is the tree of life, and the Kabbalistic Rose and Cross. The drawings of Levi continue to be widely used, especially his depiction of the sabbatical goat allegedly worshiped by the medieval Templars. This drawing may be seen at various levels. The first is that of the slightly comic and yet horrifying devil of folklore. The head is that of the horned goat on whose forehead rests the pentagram. The masculine figure has well-developed breasts and wings, and sits cross-legged on the globe of the world. At the deepest level, Levi considered it to represent the Astral Light that is the immeasurable medium of occult phenomena.

As we mentioned earlier, Aleister Crowley derived much inspiration from the Golden Dawn and its leaders. Although he eventually broke with the order, he made great use of the Golden Dawn color system with its yellow, red, and purple colors. This system of color and shape has been adopted by many within the movement although they have made their own adaptations.

Oral art

Many magazines dedicated to the pagan path contain a section on poetic verse. The quality of the poems varies considerably, but they express much of the thought and feelings of the writers. The following poem reveals a great awareness of nature as the living, vital personage of Gaia.

> All stands poised;
> Between Light and Darkness,
> Between Summer and Winter,

Hung in the balance
As the twin arms of the scales
Level in equilibrium.

Now the tides spiral inward,
Fruit hangs heavy
With its ripening promise of lush juiciness;
Sharp, sweet and bitter,
Like the cold tang of early morning.

The goddess is going.
Scarlet, crimson, tan and yellow
banner the trees
in the final glorious splendour
Of her travelling mantle.
As she passes,
The leaves whirl and scatter in the rising wind.

Soft grey tendrils wreathe and cut;
The sweet, misty breath of the weakening Sun
Kisses the Earth goodbye.
Her tears decorate webbed gossamer
With myriads of sparkling diamonds;
Like the stars wheeling
in the night sky overhead
Farewell   Diana Wayland[5]

From the Arthurian traditions comes a poem of "Merlins
Enclosure."

We wait the return of The Merlin
The Age demands it,
The Stars foretell it.
The ancient stones of Dragon Bones
Whisper it.

In elder voices they say it,

> prepare they say
> in elder tongues
> Make ready and ready the day
> For when The Merlin returns.
>
> From strands more distant
> than we have yet travelled
> yet closer than nail to finger,
> he stirs from watching sleep.
> No iron can bind him
> no thought confine him
> on Dragon wings
> The Merlin comes.

Black humor is another aspect of oral art that is especially strong in Chaos magic. The aim is to use words and ideas which shock. The outsider can only feel revulsion at such crudeness designed simply to nauseate. There is no beauty, only hopelessness.

I had a dream last night . . . a beautiful azure butterfly fluttered into my room and I netted him and pondered for hours whether I should kill him with cut up laurel leaves on cotton wool and pin him; or wait for him to die a natural death of starvation under the netting and place him in a glass case; or to open the window and let him go. I should have pinned him, but this was the butterfly of my imagination and he played me a tune on a harp in the shanty town of my river-front in Ascuncion, Paraguay, where I stayed cooped up in a humid shed owned by a Nazi living tucked away under a slowly revolving fan in his bed behind mosquito netting. I killed this creature because he was not a butterfly but a cockroach.

I
STAMPED
ON HIM![6]

Crafts

Art is more than pictures and words; it includes many varieties of crafts. The neopagan movement has generated a new market of crafts and services. Many of their magazines have advertisements similar to the following:

> Mists of Antiquity—Books and Crafts: Incense, Temple Statues, New Age Music, Oils, Herbs, Woodcarvings, Slate Engraving, Runes, Tarot, Crystals, Altar pieces, Wands, Staffs, Jewellery, Hand-made candles, Commissions. "Let your tools be as individual as you are. . . ."

> Mystical Swords—Straight blades, slender, broad, leaf blades. Elaborately designed casts for the hilts, eg Goddess, God, mythic beasts. Woodcraft. Historical research for designs. Armour. . . .

> White Light Pentacle/sacred Spirit Products—Elegant Pentacles in 14K Gold & Sterling Silver, many set with crystals and gemstones. Ankhs & Horns of Isis pendants. Triple Goddess Rings & Earrings. Healing wands. Rune wheels & boxes. Incenses & Oils. Vulcanson metalworking. Magickal & fantasy ceramics. Incense burners. Altar patens, chalices & ritual tools. Power objects. And much more. . . .

Cloaks

Generally witches operate "sky-clad," while magicians wear a robe. This is usually a full-length cloak with a hood, or else worn with a hooded cloak. The design is usually very simple and can be easily manufactured by those least skilled in needlework. A cord or belt goes around the waist, and soft slippers or sandals are worn, if the practitioner prefers not to go barefoot. The general image is that of the old Celtic monk characterized by Merlin or even Friar Tuck.

Weapons

These, according to the purists, should be handmade by the practitioner himself or herself. In practice, the manufacture of a thirty-three-inch steel blade for the sword is not possible for most people. Therefore a wide variety of small craft groups have emerged to provide the necessary weapons. Many of these are handmade to the symbolism of the particular "myth" followed by the individual or group.

Incense and perfumes

The use of incense has been common in many religions and magical rituals from ancient times. Today, incense and perfumes are being used in the neopagan rituals to produce an atmosphere that is conducive for ritual work. Various organizations are experimenting to produce incenses which invoke a particular mood.

Ritual perfumed oils are used in a similar way, but act on the person instead of the atmosphere. They are applied to the bodies of the participants, and may be used as an everyday perfume. The strict Wiccan view would be that each incense should have its own complementary perfume, and there is a particular incense for the various rituals. For example, one producer writes in his catalog of:

High Priest Incense & Oil: Used by the Lord of the coven as a personal scent.

High Priestess Incense & Oil: Used by the lady as such.

Initiation Incense & Oil: Used in initiation rituals for new coven members.

Handfasting Incense & Oil: The Wiccan way of uniting Man & Woman.

Moonchildren: Can be used by Coven members to complement HPriest/ess incense & oil.

Eight Paths: A very regal incense used at high sabbats.

Merlin Incense & Oil: For the Wisdom of the Ancients.[7]

Art includes the creation of those forms that stimulate the human senses. The development of perfumes by the movement illustrates their desire to produce a heightened atmosphere—a sense of the mysterious and exotic. In ancient times perfumes were used to produce a sacred space, and this is frequently referred to in Wicca in its attempt to look back to the witches of earlier times.

Even so, one may still be surprised to find advertisements such as the following,

TRADITIONAL WITCHES FLYING OINTMENT.
Probably our best achievement. Our skills in the preparation of Herbs etc, for magickal purposes have come to the fore in this preparation. The use of an ointment to aid Astral Travel has been known for centuries & with reference to traditional recipes we have created a beautiful creamy wax ointment that has an aroma like no other, tested by ourselves so we know it works. This unique product costs £3.00 per Jar.[8]

Art and magic

For anthropologists, the study of art history provides great insight into the development of cultures over a period of time and the interaction between cultures. Within secular society the art form is seen as separate from the meaning it conveys within the culture. A vibrating of the air by the human throat, that which we call a word, is conceived as totally distinct from the meaning that it communicates to the hearers. If words are only vibrations, why do they cause pains and joys? If the form and meaning are so distinct, how can forms have such devastating effects? Perhaps secular society has lost an understanding of the symbolic, and therefore of the place of myth and ritual.

An art form is not totally separated from its meaning, but can take on and become the center of that meaning. As the anthropologist Paul Hiebert writes,

In some societies, the art symbol itself becomes the referent of the meaning. A mask used in a dance not only represents a spirit but is that spirit, and the wearer becomes possessed with it when he dons the mask. Dances become, not enactments of other aspects of life, but life itself.[9]

Here lies the meaning of ritual and magic within traditional societies. The carved image of the deity is more than a symbol of the god: it actually becomes the god as worshiped by the devotee, at least within the mind of the devotee. The ritual dance serves magical purposes intended to cause rain or attract game for those who partake. When the tribal priest takes on the mask of the local deity, he not only acts the role of the deity, but becomes the god. Thus, a study of the arts and crafts of the modern pagans must not be considered as some academic novelty, but a different perspective of the meaning of symbolism and arguably a source of power.

Notes

1. Alexander Alland, *The Artistic Animal* (Doubleday Anchor Books: New York, 1977), p. 39.
2. Victoria Ebin, *The Body Decorated* (Thames and Hudson: London, 1979), p. 12.
3. Alland, op. cit., p. 120.
4. M. McLeod and J. Mack, *Ethnic Sculpture* (British Museum: London, 1985).
5. Diana Wayland, *Touchwood* (Lughnasadh, 1989), p. 24.
6. Editor, *Kaos,* No. 11, p. 4.
7. *Wiccekraefte Catalogue* (Beltane, 1989).
8. Ibid.
9. Paul G. Hiebert, *Cultural Anthropology* (Lippincott Co.: Philadelphia, 1976), p. 399.

Part 5

◯)

THE
FUNDIES

14

Prejudice and Discrimination

Is there still persecution? Yes!!! How many times have you seen Black Magic or Witchcraft headlines in newspapers? Crimes under this title have nothing to do with the Craft of Wicca, but we still get the blame. The Witchcraft Act was repealed in 1951, but people are still afraid of losing their jobs, homes and children if others discover their religion. This persecution and public horror, is mainly due to the Christian Clergy's antagonism and ignorance.[1]

One major issue in the relationship between neopagans and others is that of prejudice and discrimination. The two terms are often used interchangeably in ordinary speech, but in fact they refer to two different, though related, phenomena. Prejudice is a "prejudged" attitude towards members of another group. These people are regarded with hostility simply because they belong to a particular group, and are therefore assumed to have undesirable qualities that are supposed to be characteristic of the group as a whole. "Discrimination," on the other hand, refers to action against other people because they are members of another group with an associated unwillingness to tolerate their behavior. In its extreme form this becomes persecution.

Stereotypes

Prejudice is always based on a rigid mental picture that is considered to summarize the characteristics of members of a particular group. These images are "stereotypes," and are an unavoidable feature of normal social life, especially in multicultural societies. Living in a complex world we need to make use of categories to simplify the vast amount of data connected with our particular surroundings. Each of us, for example, has a stereotype of what an Eskimo is like. The word "Eskimo" brings images of igloos, fur clothing, hunting with spears and dog-sleighs. The essence of prejudiced thinking, however, is that the stereotype is not checked against reality. It is not modified by experiences that contradict the rigid image. A television program on the Eskimos of Greenland may show them living in prefabricated housing with electricity and central heating. The men still go hunting, but they now use snowmobiles and hunt with guns. The stereotype does not match with the image presented on the documentary. When this occurs it is common for a prejudiced person simply to disregard the new information as "the exception that proves the rule" and not as grounds for questioning the original belief.

A stereotype is often summarized by some derogatory term that illustrates contempt for the outsiders. Hindus consider the cow to be a sacred animal, and speak with contempt of the Christians in India as "cow-eaters." Jews speak of Gentiles as "uncircumcised." The city dweller calls someone living on a farm a "country bumpkin." The reader will remember that the word "pagan" comes from the Latin word used by the Roman city dwellers of rural people. With regard to the neopagan movement, the very expressions "witch" and "pagan" are loaded with derogatory connotations from both history and modern fiction writers such as Dennis Wheatley. Fundamentalist Christians, on the other hand, may find it surprising that neopagans contemptuously label them as "fundies."

Margot Adler recognizes the danger of stereotypes:

> But words like witch and pagan do not rest easily in the mind or on the tongue. Pop journalists present a Neo-paganism composed of strange characters and weird rites or describe bored suburbanites dancing naked in a circle in their living rooms. More serious jour-

nalists see in it a dangerous trend towards the irrational. Psychologists dismiss it as a haven for neurotics who seek power in magical cults.[2]

The study of stereotypes can be helpful in segregating the truth from the imagined role. Christians tend to have two stereotypes of the neopagan movement, one essentially evil and the other rather foolish. We shall consider these stereotypes under the terms "witch" and "pagan." We will then seek to understand the pagan stereotype of the "fundies."

Witch

Ask a Christian to make a word association with the word "witch" and you will probably find that the following words are given: satanist, evil, black, harmful, immoral. Beyond the picture of the witch as an old woman wearing a pointed hat and riding a broomstick one can identify several important elements that are enclosed within the stereotype.

Deviant: We have already commented on the historic association of witches with devil worship. This illustrates the image of witches and pagans as those who have chosen evil rather than godly Christian ways. Deviance refers to the violations of what a society considers to be important patterns of behavior. Deviance is a relative matter, because the determination of who is deviant depends on who makes the definition. In a "Christianized society," such as Europe, it was the established church which set the norm.

Destructive: The assumed evil nature of a witch leads to the conclusion that they act in an anti-social manner. Stories such as cannibalism, sexual orgies, and plots to kill and maim are a common part of the image associated with the word "witch." Shakespeare's description of the witches' brew in *Macbeth* is horrific, but it does reflect popular ideas:

> Liver of blaspheming Jew,
> Gall of goat and slip of yew
> Silver'd in the moon's eclipse,

Norse of Turk and Tartar's lips,
Finger of birth-strangled babe,
Make the gruel thick and slab.

Witches are perceived as causing harm to all that is decent and orderly in society. Individuals, especially the weak and young, are liable to be afflicted by their evil practices.

Sexual perversion: "Witch" is often associated with hedonism and freedom from sexual restraint. Naked dancing, group sex and child sex are all part of the stereotype. This has been highlighted by the recent media reports concerning child abuse. Christians should not forget that stories of cannibalism and sexual orgies were levied at Christians in the Roman Empire. Such accusations have been made against minority groups throughout history.

Primitive: "Witch" is a word relating to historic times. It represents an era that was considered to have been left behind by modern society, an era which was primitive and ignorant. The revival of the use of the term has merely reinforced a sense of horror among Christians.

It must be noted that it is the modern pagan movement itself which has revived the use of the provocative term "witch." This, on the one hand, has encouraged discrimination against a movement considered deviant, while on the other it has drawn some people to the Wicca movement for that very reason. The movement appears particularly attractive to those who feel ostracized by society, or who are rebellious against it and are looking for an alternative lifestyle. For these reasons some would prefer to abandon the word "witch," but others would argue that the word can be rehabilitated.

Pagan

As mentioned previously, this term does not in general carry such negative connotations as that of "witch." There is almost a sense of incredulity among Christians concerning those who claim that they want to get back to the old religion.

Naive: Pagans are often pictured by Christians as a group of "odd" people who like to dress in archaic robes and perform rituals at sunrise at Stonehenge. They are generally regarded as harmless and naive.

Foolish: They are perceived as those who prance about barefooted and eat vegetarian dishes. This picture is merely reinforced by the national press, as in the following example:

> On the college lawns overlooking the hazy summer beauty of the Menai Straits, 40 men and women whose ages ranged from early twenties to late sixties walked barefoot in a large circle to the sound of the beating drum. They were performing the Medicine Wheel, a ritual ceremony of the North American Indians which represented life, Pat Hansen, from Denver, told them. Some tobacco—hastily purchased from the local shop because Ms. Hansen had forgotten to bring the sacred Indian herb, chinikanik—was burned to sanctify the ground. "Lift your hands to your heart and draw in the sacred smoke, blessing yourself with the Great Spirit. Make your connections with Mother Earth and her tranquillity," she exhorted them. Janet from Scotland, Myra from Cheshire, Andrew from Tasmania et al raised their arms and made their connections.[3]

Simple lifestyle: The Christian stereotype of the "pagan" has images of organically grown foods, use of herbs for healing, and even homemade clothes reminiscent of the hippies of the 1960s. Their "back-to-nature" philosophy makes them anti-pollution, anti-nuclear and anti-war. They are usually perceived as being against the established education system, preferring home-based teaching.

It needs to be stressed that the popular press does encourage these stereotypes in their reporting, and that they are not uniquely held by fundamentalist Christians. Turning now from the Christian's stereotypes of "witch" and "pagan" we need to examine the pagan's stereotype of the "fundie."

Fundies

The derogatory stereotype of the fundamentalist Christian held by those within the neopagan movement is made up of the following characteristics:

Bigoted: The adverse reaction to "fundies" held by most neopagans is primarily based on the strong attachment that Christians hold to a fixed body of religious teaching and practice. A quotation from a pagan magazine illustrates this point.

> The policy of all fundamentalists can be summarised like this, If you are not for us, then you must be against us . . . "heads" we win, "tails" you loose. . . . The lynch-pin of their line lies in the absolutely literal and "face value" truth of the words of the Bible without even the slightest deviation or allowance for interpretation.[4]

Fanatical: Their bigotry does not allow the fundies to tolerate any other beliefs. All other religions and traditions are disregarded as erroneous, evil, and heretical. The result is that they are fanatical in their beliefs in the same way that many Iranian muslims were during the height of the Islamic Revolution. The persecutions of today are merely seen as a revival of the witch-crazes of the Middle Ages, especially those led by Matthew Hopkins. It is not surprising therefore that a recent pagan apologetic was entitled *The Matthew Hopkins File*.[5]

Legalistic: The "fundies," according to the stereotype, advocate strict codes of behavior that are against most forms of pleasure, especially sexual enjoyment. Their basic law may be summarized as, "Thou shalt not."

Proselyters: "Fundies" are seen as eager to make converts by whatever means. Many practicing neopagans have been offended by the harsh attitude of some fundamentalist Christians in their attempts to convert them. Neopagans regard them as being ignorant of both the nature of the movement, and the reasons why they have joined the movement.

Persecutors: Neopagans fear persecution by "fundies." One

practicing pagan writes concerning fundies: "Their tactics include anything from fire-bombing homes to persuading councils that pagans are not fit parents and that their children should be taken into care." It is in part because of such activities that he asks that he remain anonymous.

Discrimination

The fear of persecution felt by many neopagans is illustrated by a letter circulated by a pagan family to several pagan magazines in 1990. It illustrates what many neopagans would regard as a modern witch-hunt against them. The letter was written by a pagan couple "so that pagans can be warned about just what can happen."

> Tonight, just after tea, we were subjected to a flying visit from the Social Services Department and the local C.I.D.! There had, it seems, been a complaint made to the N.S.P.C.C. that our little boy was being abused during certain "occult" rituals that we held involving people who cavorted about naked. "Devil Worship" was also mentioned! What a wonderful thing to accuse someone of!
>
> The Social Services were most concerned that my son Christopher (his name is not Christopher but Michael!) was in "moral danger." When we asked just what this term meant, we were told by the C.I.D. officer that it could actually mean just about anything you'd care to choose!
>
> We spent well over an hour trying to explain to the Social Services official and the police that this was completely untrue, but how do you prove that you're innocent? Yes, we are pagan. No, we don't have groups of naked people cavorting about. We work *alone*. Our child is the most precious thing we have, and we are more likely to "turn Christian" than ever consider abusing him. Then the house was searched—with our permission. Were we really going to refuse? Did we want to keep our son?[6]

This account illustrates some of the difficulties faced by the Social Services and the police regarding child abuse and ritual practices. In this particular case, there is a twist to the story concerning who reported the couple. "And just who would you imagine would do such a thing? A Christian fundamentalist group, perhaps? No, it was a 'fellow' Craft member."

Bias

Both neopagans and Christians must be aware of bias and extreme attitudes. As with all newsworthy material it tends to be sensational. For example, reports from Northern Ireland tell of the street in which the latest bomb blast has occurred, but nothing is said of the many streets in which there has been peace and harmony that day. Similarly, within Christian circles the most horrific occult stories are told, and as neopagans are now pointing out, such stories may often have little factual support. The pagan movement, to a great extent, is run by women who as wives and mothers are concerned for the sacred values of human life.

On the other hand, the neopagans must recognize that among their movement there are sexual deviants even though they may only be a few. By the very nature of the stereotype of "satanist," "witch," and "pagan" held by the person in the street, certain paths of such a diverse movement may attract people of deviant sexual persuasion. Alongside this, one must also recognize that there have been those within the established church who have been guilty of sexual and moral abuse.

Human rights

Neopagans would argue that they are merely practicing their own religion and should be allowed to do so without persecution.[7] In this they often refer to Article 18 of the Declaration of Human Rights which reads: "Everyone has the right to freedom of thought, conscience and religion. This right includes the freedom to change religion or belief, and freedom either alone or in company with others, in private or in public, to manifest religion or belief, in teaching practice, worship and observance."

How can a Christian complain of the persecution of Christians in a Muslim or communist country when he denies neopagans the possibility of practicing their beliefs? It would be hypocritical to deny a person of whatever religion the opportunity of practicing their beliefs, but it is obvious that society must impose certain restrictions for the well-being of the whole. Crowley's declaration, "Do what you like" cannot be left unqualified. Even he added the command "Love is the Law, Love under Will." Any and every stable society must impose certain moral restraints. This is easier in a mono-cultural society, but is also essential within a multi-cultural society.

The restraints imposed should include the following:

(a) The respect of individual rights. No person should be coerced by any means to do that which he or she does not wish to. This would immediately condemn child abuse.

(b) The respect for social order. There should be a responsible attitude to the patterns laid down by society for the safety and convenience of the vast majority. For example, I may like to drive down the center of the road, but it would be dangerous both to myself and to other road users. Anarchy is not an acceptable option for any stable society, and never has been.

(c) The respect for the beliefs of others. This does not mean that one must agree with their beliefs, but one should not seek to cause offense deliberately. This is the basic issue of the Salman Rushdie affair concerning the book *Satanic Verses*.

However, it should be remembered that neopaganism is not simply a religion, but involves magic. Fran Skinner, for example, in her book of 101 questions answered for non-witches writes:

What is the difference between "White" and "Black" Witches? These are common terms to denote those who use magic for the good of all (White) and those who use the energies for evil and self gain (Black). It must be said that those who cultivate evil for its own sake are not Wiccans, but either maniacs or criminals, and should be dealt with appropriately by the authorities.[8]

This raises a major moral issue, and highlights the complexity that faces the legal system within this country.

Apologetics

During the 1980s, the neopagan movement has been characterized by the growth of network, or contact groups. Some of these groups are seeking to answer the criticism of nonpagans by writing factual books and appearing on television and radio.

The Sorcerer's Apprentice, Britain's largest occult distributor, has instigated a "fighting fund" to answer libelous reporting. *The Occult Response to the Christian Response to the Occult,* or more briefly ORCRO, is a sixty-page magazine that is published about six times a year. ORCRO's stated policy is "to formulate a more coherent position as regards the many and several Christian groups who oppose Occultism in any shape or form."[9] Although written in a sarcastic and sometimes crude style, the magazine attempts to monitor what is being written and broadcast by Christians. It seeks to provide a defense against and refutal of inaccurate Christian comment.

Christians would not wish to institute the horrors that accompanied the witch-crazes of earlier centuries, but neither would they want innocent persons to be hurt and abused by those who are evil and corrupt. Christians must be careful to respond from fact rather than prejudice.

Confessions

One of the greatest influences on Christian attitudes is that caused by the confessions of witches, especially those who have become Christians. In response to these testimonies, pagan writers are quick to point out any errors or inconsistencies. Magazines, such as ORCRO, dissect every phrase that is written to show any inconsistency and error.

In Africa, witches have made confessions such as: "I have killed fifty people including my own brother." "I have taken the womb of another woman."[10] Often these events could not have occurred in the physical realm. What appears to have happened is that a woman has had a dream, or even an evil thought about a person, and soon afterwards that person has died or become barren. This has led anthropologists to regard witchcraft as illusory.

The question before us is whether the matters confessed actually did occur as described by the witch. This question is far from simple to answer for many reasons.

First, some persons recognized as being in need of psychological treatment have claimed the reality of things that have no physical verity. However, the act of confession has in itself been of therapeutic value. The anthropologist Geoffrey Parrinder in his book on witchcraft writes:

> Until the rise of the modern study of psychology one might well have been excused for refusing to credit the witches with the invention of the catalogues of their horrible deeds. But we now know so much more of the strange complexities of the human mind, that one would hesitate to assert that the confessions cannot have been invented. Some people like confessing, even what is impossible. Confession is said to be good for the soul. For every murder committed today there are several false confessions. What seemed in olden days to be unnatural desires now appear but too human.[11]

Second, the line between physical reality and illusion may not be as clear as we sometimes assume. For example, I was once involved in counseling an intelligent young lady who believed that at regular intervals some spiritual being would come and have sexual relations with her. She never saw the spirit, but was conscious of its presence, odor and sexual stimulation. No one had any external evidence for the occurrence of these events, but to the young woman they were real. On the one hand, they could be discussed in psychiatric terms, but on the other hand they could be understood in terms of Incubi and Succubi. Incubi were male spirits who were believed to prey on sleeping women, and Succubi the equivalent female spirits.

Confessions from the middle ages often give obscene details of debaucheries between demons and witches.[12]

This young lady was deeply aware of these experiences, and was revolted by them. To her they were more than dreams or fantasies. They were physical experiences, but an outside observer would not have found any evidence. This is precisely the problem that has perplexed the Social Services concerning ritual child abuse. In one case, "the main evidence was from a six-year old boy who had spoken of satanic practices. However, it had been found that he had watched horror films. His ten-year old sister is believed to have backed his claims, saying she saw the alleged abuse 'in her dreams.'"[13]

Third, there is the problem of leading questions. This is a similar issue to that found in the witch-crazes of the middle ages. "Hopkins was accused of putting this type of question: 'You have four Imps, have you not?' She answers affirmatively, Yes. . . . Are not their names so and so? Yes, saith she.'"[14] To be accurate, Hopkins denied that he used such a method, but he suggested that magistrates did not question the accused sufficiently about their confessions. The danger of leading questions is that they imprint themselves on the minds of young people and those of a highly gullible disposition. New features suddenly arise within the confession as it is retold based on the previous leading question. The confession may often be expressed in terms which the person believes that the hearers are wishing to hear.

Finally, it must be recognized however that some responsible people are convinced that events such as those which have been reported do in fact occur. A report in *The Independent* newspaper states:

A psychiatrist said that two patients had gradually disclosed details of a cult after speaking for months about killing babies and sexual abuse. "They have good recall. These are not suppressed memories." . . . Earlier this week a Harley Street psychologist said: "I am absolutely convinced that children have been killed during these rituals. I have heard it too many times for it not to be true. A lot of the babies are induced before they are born or are born at home and used within a short period."[15]

The Occult Census of 1989 indicates that the majority of those involved within the movement would refute evil practices, and only 14% had ever worked evil magic. The Census comments, "Although even 14% of evil magick is as unacceptable to many genuine occultists as it will be to members of the general population I doubt whether many people, occultists or no, can honestly claim never to have thought ill or sought revenge at some point in their lives."[16] There can be little doubt about the fact that there are those within the movement who physically practice satanic rituals. These people may constitute only a small fraction of the total, but they must be restrained.

The problem comes, as we have seen, in discerning what has occurred tangibly and what is more in the realm of the imagination. Christians must be aware of the various paths within the neopagan movement and not assume that all match their stereotypes of satanists and witches. Most "white" Wiccan groups are endeavoring to distance themselves from anything labeled as satanic. Care must be taken in accusations, or pagan families who love their children may be ravaged by ensuing legal action. On the other hand, failure to respond to clear evidence will result in children being damaged for life.

The failure of the Christian religion

Realizing that almost all modern pagans have come from a nominal Christian society, it seems logical to ask why this established religion has been rejected for one of the various paths in neopaganism. Where has Christianity failed? Why has the pagan been left with the stereotype of the "fundie"? Obviously, various answers would be given by neopagans depending on their personal background. The following are a few common criticisms:

1. Lack of spirituality

This first criticism may come as a surprise to many Christians. What is meant is that the Christian religion is essentially secular. Comments by leading churchmen denying the deity of Christ and questioning the teaching of the Bible have caused great disillusionment to those seeking a spiritual experience. However, more than this, the life-style of the average Christian appears to be that of a practicing deist. God, like the clockmaker, has finished His creation, set it in operation, and then left it alone. God has become a distant entity with no relevance to an individual's daily life.

It is a shame on the established church that this image has been portrayed. The Bible, on the other hand, speaks of a God who is concerned with the affairs of humanity. He wants to communicate with us through meditation and prayer. The Christian life is radically different from that of the secular materialist, and this should be evident.

2. Lack of any concern for the environment

From the time of Max Weber, Protestant Christianity has been associated, in the minds of many, with Capitalism and the exploitation of the natural world.[17] Certainly, a materialistic approach has caused much environmental degradation, pollution, and desertification. All data shows a rapidly worsening ecological situation. What has gone wrong? As we have seen already, this has led to a concern for Mother Earth—Gaia.

Christians appear to have been slow to respond to the ecological crises. The Bible, in contrast, presents a concept of harmony in the relationship of human beings with the rest of creation. Genesis 2:15 states that "the LORD God took the man and put him in the garden of Eden to tend and keep it." Christians should have an active concern for the ecology of the planet.

3. Lack of the experiential

Establishment Christianity is seen by neopagans as essentially cold, rational, and intellectual. The church is criticized as singularly cerebral and lacking any experiential participation. The congregation merely watch as the minister performs the ritual. In Wicca, there is no congregation; all participate in the ritual, all are "priests." In an age where one's feelings are of such a priority, many are finding new experiences within the neopagan traditions using ritual, symbolism, and psychic experiences.

A major theme of the Reformation was the "priesthood of all believers." This concept formulated Paul's teaching of the Church as being like a body (1 Corinthians). Each part has its own particular gifts which enable the total body to function. It is not surprising that today's growing churches are those which encourage participation and worship.

4. Lack of social awareness

Wars, famines, and poverty among great wealth appear to be poor advertisements for nearly 2,000 years of Christianity in Europe. Nominal Christians make up the greatest percentage of wealthy people on the planet—why are they not willing to share their affluence with those who are destitute? Where is the practical working out of the command of Jesus to the rich young man, "If you want to be perfect, go, sell what you have and give to the poor, and you will have treasure in heaven; and come, follow Me" (Mt. 19:21)?

5. Lack of understanding of gender issues

Christianity is perceived as a patriarchal religion dominated by a male priesthood. The church epitomizes a generally patriarchal society in which women are second-class citizens. The debate in the Church of England concerning the ordination of women is seen by many neopagans as an illustration of the whole issue. Those women happily involved with the church are considered to have been indoctrinated by the contemporary patriarchal society and fail to perceive their subordinate status.

Once again the Western cultural expression of Christianity hides the richness of the teaching of the Bible. The equality of all is fundamental teaching within the Christian church. As the apostle Paul writes, "There is neither Jew nor Greek, . . . slave nor free, . . . male nor female; for you are all one in Christ Jesus" (Gal. 3:28).

Christian lifestyle

One high priest of Wicca summarized his criticisms to me, "Christianity has been unresponsive to the needs of the twentieth century." Christians need to admit their failure to represent a valid, relevant form of Christianity for this age. As Hans Küng has written,

> *Christians* themselves are the strongest *argument against Christianity:* Christians who are not Christians. *Christians* themselves are the strongest *argument for Christianity:* Christians who live a Christian life.[18]

Christians must live out the reality of the life and teachings of Christ in the contemporary world. Talking to a Wicca priestess on this subject she suddenly surprised me by saying that if she had lived in the first century A.D. she would probably have been a Christian. The dynamic and reality of the growing church in the midst of persecution caught her imagination. Perhaps it is something of these characteristics which she now sees in Wicca that draws her to this religion.

The offense of the gospel

It would be misleading, however, to say that people are attracted to neopaganism simply because of the failings of the church which Christians could rectify. The reasons for people preferring paganism to Christianity may result from a rejection of certain Christian teachings. A high priestess of Wicca has expressed her views in the following way:

1. Pagans believe that Christian belief is wrong.

To Pagans, many of the basic ideas of the Bible are wrong. It is not that Christians have failed to provide a "valid, relevant form," ie the right packaging. Pagans do not accept the content. They would reject for example the unique divinity of Jesus, the resurrection of the body, the view that God/the Goddess made his/her will known on a once-and-for-all basis through one individual, the view that the various sorts of Christian Bible represent historical truth rather than metaphysical speculation, and the view that human beings are spiritually superior to the rest of the Goddess' creation. Pagans tend to be pantheists, polytheists or monists and consider monotheism irrational.

There are ideas in the Bible which are acceptable to Pagans, just as there are religious ideas in all sacred scriptures which would be acceptable. Pagans see all mysticism as leading to similar conclusions—the reality of a divine force or being, whose essential nature is love. The forms with which people choose to worship that divine being may be different, but they are all seen as imperfect expressions of humanity's impulse towards the divine.

2. Many aspects of Christian belief are morally repugnant to Pagans.

The idea of sin being atoned through human sacrifice, and the concept of a final judgement whereby some human beings are condemned to eternal torment and others to eternal bliss are unacceptable to Pagans. These ideas do not equate to our concept of a Goddess of love, who cares for and cherishes her children. Pagans also believe that monotheism will by its nature propagate persecution and intolerance of others.[19]

The strong polarity between neopagans and fundies has resulted in a total misunderstanding of each other's position. On the one hand, the fundie fails to appreciate that there are various paths within the neopagan movement, and most love their children and are responsible members of society. On the other hand, the neopagan has failed to realize the absolute holiness of the unique Creator God and the wonder of salvation in Christ Jesus alone. A true Christian perspective perceives neopagans as being in moral, spiritual, and physical danger. It is like a person casually handling a gun which they do not realize is loaded. Any responsible person would call out that there is danger—take care! To this the neopagan may ask: "Where is there any danger?" It is this subject we must now address.

Notes

1. Fran Skinner, *Witch-craft for the Non-witch: 101 Questions Answered* (Private Publication, 1989), p. 6.
2. Margot Adler, *Drawing Down the Moon* (Beacon Press: Boston, 1986), p. 5.
3. *The Independent* (Monday, July 23, 1990).
4. *Sirus* (May, 1990), p. 9.
5. Keith Morgan, *The Matthew Hopkins File* (Deosil Dance Pub.: Pwllheli, 1990).
6. *Sirus* (May, 1990), pp. 7–8.
7. Chris, "Pagan Persecution Now!", *The Deosil Dance*, No. 22 (1990), p. 28.
8. Skinner, op. cit., p. 11.
9. Editorial in *ORCRO Magazine* (May/June, 1990), p. 2.
10. David Burnett, *Unearthly Powers* (MARC: Eastbourne, 1988), p. 139.
11. Geoffrey Parrinder, *Witch-craft: European and African* (Faber and Faber: London, 1963), p. 112.
12. Ibid., pp. 67–69.
13. Jack O'Sullivan, "Release children in Satan case," *The Independent* (September 11, 1990).
14. Parrinder, op. cit., p. 80.
15. O'Sullivan, *The Independent* (August 8, 1990).
16. *The Occult Census* (Sorcerer's Apprentice: Leeds, 1989), p. 32.
17. Max Weber, *The Protestant Ethic and the Spirit of Capitalism* (George Allen and Unwin Ltd: London, 1952).
18. Hans Küng, *On Being a Christian* (Collins: London, 1979).
19. Personal correspondence with a leading member of the Pagan movement, dated March 3, 1991.

15

A Myth to Live By

A symptom of alienation in the modern world is the widespread sense of meaninglessness. Carl Jung recognized that many of his patients sought psychotherapy not for any clearly defined disorder but because they felt that life had no meaning. Jung had a positive view of religion unlike Freud, and he believed that accompanying the decline of Christian religion among the European peoples there is increasing evidence of a general psychic disorientation. Modern man has lost the religious foundations to his life. He is bereft in a material world, without a myth by which to live. He lacks what Jung called "the symbolic life." As Carl Jung writes,

> Man is in need of a symbolic life. . . . But we have no symbolic life. . . . Have you got a corner somewhere in your house where you perform the rites as you can see in India? Even the very simple houses there have at least a curtained corner where the members of the household can lead the symbolic life, where they can make their new vows or meditation. We don't have it. . . . We have no time, no place. . . . Only the symbolic life can express the need of the soul—the daily need of the soul, mind you! And because people have no such thing, they can never step out of this mill—this awful grinding, banal life in which they are "nothing but."[1]

The secular worldview has been impressive in the way that it has stimulated the developing modern technology which has enabled humanity to cope with their physical well-being. However, it has been an unprecedented failure in meeting man's mythical needs. It has given partial answers to the question of *how* I exist, but has not answered the deeper question of *why* I exist. As Joseph Campbell has deduced, myths, as revealed in the religions of the world, are the search for meaning and significance. As he says, "We need a myth to live by."[2]

Finding a myth to live by

In general, we have been conditioned to make a distinction between myth, story and Scripture as three different forms of text. This differentiation, however, is not recognized by Jung or Campbell and those who follow them within the neopagan movement. Caitlin Matthews writes in her book on the goddess, "For many people, a 'myth' is an untruth; for others it represents redundant scripture; stories are considered to be appropriate for children, the bedridden or the blind; while scripture is the prop and stay of the devout. Myth, story and scripture, however, are all forms of text to live by."[3]

In this context "myth" cannot therefore be equated to a fairy story, but as the beliefs held by a particular person or society. This was precisely the problem that I first faced in India. I thought that I could prove the superiority of the Christian message to the Hindu myths by offering proof that the events recorded in the Bible actually occurred in space and time. The Hindu gurus, on the other hand, were seemingly unimpressed. For them what mattered was not whether the story was historically verifiable or not, but whether it contained truth. We will therefore here use the term "myth" in its wider connotation as "a story that recounts purportedly historical events to explain how traditions, major doctrines, religions, and similar nuclear concepts arose."[4]

In answer to the question of how does one find one's myth, Jung and his followers point inwards. As Edward Edinger writes: "The ultimate goal of Jungian psychotherapy is to make the symbolic process conscious."[5] Myths are the archetypal images within us. When we dream it is as if we are fishing in our unconscious for some deep symbols. Thus, myths can emerge into the conscious mind as one dreams, and during the history of humanity these have been encapsulated into the myths and legends of the world religions.

The stories of Greek and Roman mythology are just a part of the rich symbolism that arises from the traditions of tribal societies. However, the attempt is not merely to recognize the old mythology. All myths are for their time and their particular people. The ancient myths must be reworked into a form relevant for the contemporary world. Thus, the stories of King Arthur and the Kingdom of Avalon found in the Arthurian tradition have been reworked to provide a relevance for the present world situation. Similarly, with regard to finding a myth of the goddess, Matthews writes:

> If we choose to work with ancient mythologies of the goddess, we must not live in our own ancestral past, whether or not we perceive this to be a golden matriarchy, or an egalitarian society in which men and women lived amicably together. We live in the twentieth century, and there has been rather a lot of water under the bridge since those days. Some people may not find it appropriate, for example, to invoke the goddess to make them fertile. In ancient times, children supported the tribal framework and such prayers were commonplace (and still useful for infertile couples). However, in a time when over-population and effective methods of birth-control has changed our social structure, where women are released from continuous child-bearing, other levels of fertility must also be sought after.[6]

Myths also arise from the human mind through visualization and imagination. Science fiction and fantasy stories press the reader toward a release of the archetypal symbolism into his consciousness. As I am caught up by the story, the emotions of joy, fear, or love penned by the writer become valid experiences for me. As with the writings of C. S. Lewis and Tolkien, the mythical worlds of which they wrote become places of new levels of consciousness for me. Those holding to such views would deduce that the inner experience of an altered state of consciousness is that which is true and real.

This immediately raises the question of the trustworthiness and credence of such reworked stories. Matthews answers the question most directly.

> There is truly only one criteria in such a choice: does it work for you? . . . Trust and confidence only come when our chosen myth has been tested and found to be supportive, but to start with, we must act according to a basic premise: we must behave "as if" the myth was trustworthy. These important words give us the faith to begin.[7]

There is one myth that is often disregarded by most neo-pagans without much consideration, and yet it is acknowledged as meaningful and valid to about one-third of the population of the world. It may therefore be called "the Great Myth," and it is that which relates to the person of Jesus Christ. The story of Jesus Christ is one that has brought admiration and recognition from all religious leaders who have ever heard the account. In whatever form the church has expressed the story throughout the centuries, the simple elegance of the Gospel narratives has a great appeal.

A myth must provide answers in three areas of life. The first is that a myth should have philosophical credence, second there should be practical application to daily life, and finally there must be power to be effectual. We will first consider the philosophical credibility of the "myth" of Christ.

The significance of the "myth" of Christ

What is it that makes the myth of Jesus so different from the mythology of other religions and visionaries?

Holistic

First, the myth is a total experience in that the events occurred within space and time. It does not exist merely as some Jungian archetype in the subconscious, but was acted out within human history. This means that the rational intellect can be used to study the myth as well as human intuition. The reality of the people of Israel is an undeniable fact of history, as is the growth of the Christian church. No book has been subject to such archaeological and scientific scrutiny as the Bible.

Those holding to a mythical worldview say that it is the personal, inner experience in an altered state of consciousness that is the definition of what is true and real. They argue, "If you can't trust your own personal experiences what can you trust." Thus, their dream world is just as much a reality as their experience of sitting in a chair reading this very book.

We must be careful not to deny such experiences as sources of knowledge. We may, for example, offer a friend a sample of some exotic dish we have cooked, and say, "Taste it and see how good it is." No scientific equipment would ever be able to provide one with the experience of tasting the new food. However, the advocates of this approach are in danger of making the altered conscious experience the highest definition of truth and reality. By affirming this inner reality, one ends in denying the ordinary daily experiences of life. Whatever myth we follow there is still the need for us to eat and drink, breathe and move. These are all acts that are part of the world we experience in a normal state of consciousness. A shaman in another state of consciousness (SSC), if hit by a London bus would die even though he is experiencing another reality in which there are no buses. The normal state of consciousness cannot be disregarded or negated. Whatever state of consciousness that you may experience, some time you will come back to the awareness of the world that is generally called "normal" or "ordinary." Any myth that is worth following must have a relevance to the ordinary state of consciousness (OSC).

This point is illustrated by the classic story of the invisible gardener by Anthony Flew and John Wisdom.

Once upon a time two explorers came upon a clearing in the jungle. In the clearing were growing many flowers and many weeds. One explorer says, "Some gardener must tend this plot." The other disagrees, "There is no gardener." So they pitch their tents and set a watch. No gardener is ever seen. "But perhaps he is an invisible gardener." So they set up a barbed-wire fence. They electrify it. They patrol with bloodhounds. . . . But no shrieks ever suggest that some intruder has received a shock. No movements of the wire betray an invisible climber. The bloodhounds never give cry. Yet still the Believer is not convinced. "But there is a gardener, invisible, intangible, insensible to electric shocks, a gardener who has no scent and makes no sound, a gardener who comes secretly to look after the garden which he loves." At last the Sceptic despairs, "But what remains of your original assertion? Just how does what you call an invisible, intangible, eternally elusive gardener differ from an imaginary gardener or even from no gardener at all?"[8]

If a myth lacks correlation to a rational understanding of human experiences as lived out in a shared understanding of space and time, then it loses its credence. It is of no value holding to a myth of King Arthur and the holy grail if there is no historical evidence. A myth to live by should have historical credibility.

Validity

It must be recognized that the previous argument is based upon the use of logic, whereas the real issue is a matter of basic assumptions. Jung would say that it is unimportant whether a myth is historically true or false, but whether the myth is in the psychology of the believer.

> Psychology is only concerned with the fact that there is such an idea, but it is not concerned with the question whether such an idea is true or false in any other sense. It is psychologically true inasmuch as it exists. Psychological existence is subjective insofar as an idea occurs only in one individual but it is objective insofar as it is established by a society.[9]

Altered states of consciousness, such as SSC, are experiences that cannot be measured or analyzed, and neither can they be communicated to those who have not had that experience. As Francis Schaeffer writes: "The built-in trouble with all these existential experiences is that the content of such an experience is not open to communication. Only the unknowing would demand, 'Please describe to me in normal categories what you have experienced.'"[10] By definition, the altered state of consciousness is beyond rational explanation to another human being. Thus, Jung's "psychological truth" is little different from illusion. Visualization is merely the exercise of imagination. The Jungian criterion for validity (or objective truth) is social acceptance, and this of course is relative. The myth held by a Wiccan coven only has relevance within that coven. The myth of the shaman similarly only has validity within that group.

Among all the various levels of consciousness, how can one know what is the "real" reality, and how can one deal with the contradictions between differing experiences of consciousness? Mark Cosgrove gives a fascinating example of this confusion, recorded in the science fiction story *The Yellow Pill*.

A psychotic "patient" and his "psychiatrist" have two separate experiences of reality. The "patient" thinks he is on board a spaceship and has killed some invading Venusian lizards, whereas his buddy, who imagines he is a psychiatrist, has just caught space madness and has tied the "patient" up. The "psychiatrist" believes he is a world-famous psychiatrist interviewing a homicidal maniac in a straitjacket who has just shot five people, claiming they were Venusian lizards. Neither man shows any signs of mental illness except from the other's view of reality. At the end of the story the "psychiatrist," doubting his own world, takes a yellow pill that helps increase perceptions of the real world. He then wakes up on a spaceship with dead Venusian lizards all around him.[11]

Accepting the mythical method of knowing by experience makes the ordinary state of consciousness (OSC) just as unreal as the SSC. How do you know that with the next yellow pill you won't wake up in a spaceship or a mental ward? You can never be sure.

The mythical thinker is dependent on circular reasoning as Matthews recognizes in addressing the question of the trustworthiness of a myth: "The question of authority is very much tied to our own self-image and confidence; if we don't believe in ourselves, we won't be able to believe in our personal myth. It is indeed a circular business!" In other words, experience creates your assumptions, and you interpret your experiences in the context of your assumptions. The search for meaning in myth therefore leads only to meaninglessness and futility.

The only escape from such a meaningless cycle is through grounds other than subjective experience. These must have a rational basis that can be examined within the ordinary state of consciousness (OSC). The myth that I follow must make sense within my rational perception of the universe which I experience with my senses. Christianity claims that God's self-disclosure was in the external universe and in the personality of a human being. This is why the historicity of the person of Jesus Christ is so significant as are the records of his teaching and life-style by first-hand witnesses in OSC.

The apostle Peter writes: "We did not follow cunningly devised fables when we made known to you the power and coming of our Lord Jesus Christ, but we were eyewitnesses of His majesty" (2 Pet. 1:16). Similarly, the apostle John writes to the young church: "That which was from the beginning, which we have heard, which we have seen with our eyes, which we have looked upon, and our hands have handled, concerning the Word of life. . . . that which we have seen and heard we declare to you, that you also may have fellowship with us" (1 Jn. 1:1, 3). There is no discontinuity in Christianity between facts and faith.

This does not mean that one can approach God solely on the basis of rational deduction. No matter how good one's argument, one can only lead a person to an abstract idea of "the First Cause." A myth must be discovered, and become part of one's experience. After His resurrection Jesus said to the doubting Thomas, "Reach your finger here, and look at My hands; and reach your hand *here,* and put *it* into My side. Do not be unbelieving, but believing" (Jn. 20:27). John continues his narrative, "Jesus did many other signs in the presence of His disciples, which are not written in this book; but these are written that you may believe that Jesus is the Christ, the Son of God, and that believing you may have life in His name" (Jn. 20:30–31).

It should however be recognized that the true basis of Christian faith is not the faith itself. Christian faith rests on content—which is the life and death of Christ as they occurred within history. As Francis Schaeffer has written: "My believing is not the basis for being saved—the basis is the work of Christ. Christian faith is turned outward to an objective person: 'Believe on the Lord Jesus, and thou shalt be saved.'"[12]

Practical application of "myth"

"A true hypothesis consistently accounts, not only for the external, empirical data, but also the internal data of human experience, such as intellectual honesty, justice and love."[13] A myth to live by must have existential viability.

An important feature of Christianity has been the way in which throughout history it has been traditional societies who have readily responded to the Christian message. The very people who were closest to the original ethnic myths were those who chose to become Christians. It is unfortunately true that there have been cases in which pagan societies have been converted by social, political or even military coercion. One example is the forcible conversion of the pagan Saxons of what is now northern Poland by Charlemagne. One could even question how much the remaining tribal societies of the twentieth century have been influenced in their conversion through the dominance of Western culture. Even so, the growth of Christianity among pagan people could not have occurred to such a degree without their genuine appreciation of the superiority of the gospel message to their traditional beliefs. When the Dani warriors of Irian Jaya became Christians, they eagerly took the message of Jesus Christ to their neighboring tribes. There was no coercion in this task, but a realization that they had come to know a great truth that had transformed their lives and which they wanted to share with others.

A similar case is shown in the mission of St. Patrick to the Celts of Ireland. As Constantine FitzGibbon writes of St. Patrick:

> His work must be clearly distinguished from that of modern missionaries. Unlike the Spanish priests in Central and South America, he was not brought to his mission by armed men, nor did he have the armed forces, and a powerful Christian administration, to rely upon or at least to render him the support of their mere existence. . . . St. Patrick had little of the former and, coming from a Europe in chaos, only the theory of civil administration. . . . St. Patrick met them with a pure, young, unsullied faith and with nothing more.[14]

The Christian religion took on much of the Celtic culture. The Druids soon appeared to have introduced Christianity into their schools before they became schools for monks. Almost immediately the Irish Christians began their missionary work.

Whatever the historical background of the story of King Arthur, by the time of the sixth century, the Celts in southwest England were already Christians. Those who are currently seeking to follow the Celtic path or the Arthurian tradition must ask themselves the question why the ancient Celts were willing to give up much of their beliefs for Christianity. Certainly, much of their ancient mythology continued in Celtic folklore, but Celtic society became distinctly Christian with a strong missionary emphasis.

Although the Saxons and Angles became Christian through the influence of missionaries sent out from the Roman Empire by the Pope, Rome was no longer a political threat to the British people at that time. Rome was no more than the remains of an aging superpower in the minds of the people of Britain. Even so, the Saxons and Angles accepted the Christian religion, and this can only be because what they discovered in this religion was far more meaningful and significant than their traditional beliefs.

Cultural relevance

Joseph Campbell reminds us that as our culture changes the traditional myths become increasingly irrelevant. "It is no good going back to the old-time religion."[15] It is for this very reason that Caitlin Matthews argues that a myth must be re-worked to be made relevant for the contemporary situation. But the problem faced by most tribal societies is that they are unable to adapt their mythology to the changing world situation. Their worldview is rigid, unable to adapt to change. This is why most people from shamanistic societies have turned away from their belief in the powers of the shaman. They have seen greater power in Western technology, and some have come to discover even greater power in the Christian gospel.

Pagan people have found in Christianity a "myth" that is adaptable and relevant to their situation. The simple elegance of the "Great Myth" offers the ability to transform human cultures without stripping the people of their traditional way of life. When Christianity came to the Celts, the Angles and the Saxons, it did not come as the imposition of some alien culture. It transformed the old culture, purifying the best and removing the worst. The richness of Celtic culture was not lost when the Celts became Christians, but caused it to flower as "Celtic Ireland's Golden Age."[16] Traditional symbols were used to express a new truth.

This ability of Christianity to adapt and transform human cultures has been an inherent characteristic of Christianity. It was on this very point that the apostle Paul argued in his letter to the Galatians. Jews are able to become Christians without denying their Jewish heritage, and likewise Gentiles can become Christians without denying their heritage and becoming Jews. Christianity has a dynamic that enables it to be relevant to any and every culture. The only danger is that once accepted, human institutions formulate the message in ways which are fixed and unbending. Thus over long periods of time the established expression of Christianity becomes increasingly culturally irrelevant and unintelligible to a contemporary generation. It is like the proverbial "generation gap." This is not the fault of the "myth," but of its human expression in the particular culture. Perhaps the church in Europe should apologize to this present generation for preferring to hold on to its long established traditions rather than making Christianity relevant to this age.

Ethical application

All human beings have sense of awareness of what is "right" and "wrong." Although neopagans tend to hold to some view of moral relativity, they too make a distinction between "white" and "black" magic. They understand what is meant when asked if they have performed an "evil spell." Everyone has certain moral criteria, but the question that must be addressed is on what principles are these based?

The Christian belief in a supreme creator provides the basis of absolute truth based on the nature of God Himself. This moral absolute has been revealed by God concerning human nature, purpose, and lifestyle. The coming of Christianity to pagan peoples has caused a radical change in their ethics. The ancient Christian Celts held to a strong sense of morality and holiness, which caused them to be shocked at the growing decadence of the established church of Rome. Similarly today, when tribal people become Christians, one often sees the end of intertribal warfare and cruelty, and an increase in mutual care.

However, having written this, I am conscious of the fact that it is often so-called Christian societies which have caused so much harm in the world. It is they who have the greatest number of armaments and wealth, and they who so often let other human beings die of starvation. A meaningful theory of ethics must not only point to a better way of living, but must also explain the corruption within society. The Bible calls it "sin," and reveals that it is part of the make-up of all people. Christians will testify to having been changed, and of their desire to live a more holy life, but they will also recognize their moral failings. They have within them the desire to be like Christ, the One they claim to follow.

Choosing a myth

We finally return to the question with which we began this chapter: How should we go about deciding which myths are worth believing in?

The starting point in deciding what is worthy of belief must be evidence. The levels of rigor demanded of the evidence will be different for different propositions: the less likely the proposition, the greater the degree of rigor required. But how do we assess likelihood?

Gary Jones, who himself has an interest in the occult, gives this useful illustration:

> For example, consider the three propositions:
> 1. Mozart lived from 1758 until 1791.
> 2. a proton is composed of quarks.
> 3. a brick, thrown into the sea, from a Chinese junk, will not sink.
>
> The Mozart proposition doesn't imply anything which would require a change to what I already believe about the world. I therefore have little difficulty in accepting it. The proton proposition, however, requires me to accept the existence of a whole new class of particles: the quarks. Therefore the proton proposition carries a greater burden of proof than the Mozart proposition. The evidence to support the existence of quarks seems compelling to me, so I am forced to revise my worldview. This revision is, however, quite easy: my everyday experiences are far removed from the world of sub-atomic particles.
>
> The brick proposition is very different. It implies that my belief in the universality of gravity and buoyancy, based on everyday experience, is wrong. This seems such a major revision to my world-

view that I require extremely good evidence to accept it. In the absence of such evidence, I reject the proposition.[17]

The Christian "myth" does not seek any preferential treatment to other "myths" as regards critical analysis. Pagan people throughout the world, who have never before had the opportunity of hearing of Christ, are now responding to the gospel. This demands that those looking for a "myth" to live by consider the life and teachings of Jesus Christ.

Notes

1. Edward F. Edinger, *Ego and Archetype* (Penguin Books: Harmondsworth, 1974), p. 109.
2. Joseph Campbell, *A Myth to Live By* (Souvenir Press: London, 1973).
3. Caitlin Matthews, *The Goddess* (Element Books: Shaftesbury, 1989), p. 17.
4. Charles Winick, *Dictionary of Anthropology* (Littlefield, Adams and Co.: New Jersey, 1977), p. 376.
5. Edinger, op. cit., p. 113
6. Matthews, op. cit., p. 18.
7. Ibid., p. 18.
8. Os Guiness, *The Dust of Death* (IVP: Leicester, 1973), pp. 340–41.
9. Carl Jung, *Psychology and Religion* (Yale University Press: New Haven, 1957), p. 3.
10. Francis Schaeffer, *The God Who Is There* (Hodder and Stoughton: London, 1969), p. 28.
11. Mark Cosgrove, *Psychology Gone Awry* (IVP: Leicester, 1979), pp. 105–6.
12. Schaeffer, op. cit., p. 133.
13. Gordon R. Lewis, "Criteria for Discerning of Spirits," in John Warwick Montgomery, *Demon Possession* (Bethany House: Minneapolis, 1976), p. 351.
14. Constantine FitzGibbon, *The Irish in Ireland* (David and Charles Publishers: Newton Abbot, 1983), p. 62.

15. Joseph Campbell, Television interview on BBC 2 (August 5, 1990).

16. FitzGibbon, op. cit., p. 5.

17. Gary Jones, "What to Believe?" *The Open Path*, Vol. 3, No. 1 (Spring, 1990), p. 25.

16

Authority and Power

But there was a certain man called Simon, who previously practiced sorcery in the city and astonished the people of Samaria, claiming that he was someone great, to whom they all gave heed, from the least to the greatest, saying, "This man is the great power of God." And they heeded him because he had astonished them with his sorceries for a long time. But when they believed Philip as he preached the things concerning the kingdom of God and the name of Jesus Christ, both men and women were baptized. Then Simon himself also believed; and when he was baptized he continued with Philip, and was amazed, seeing the miracles and signs which were done (Acts 8:9–13).

In choosing a myth to live by, one must ensure that it is a myth which has power to accomplish that which is needed. A myth may be intellectually satisfying, but unless it has the ability to affect my life and my world it is in effect only an illusion.

The modern world has grown out of the development of technology that utilizes the physical powers of this world. Massive machines have been constructed with the power to carve through the surface of the earth to build extensive highways and clear great tracts of tropical forests. Enough power has now been harnessed to allow humanity to fling a spaceship out of the Earth's orbit to the Moon and beyond. It is a power which has both helped and harmed. This is seen most clearly in the horror of nuclear weapons where unbelievable power is released with destructive force.

Throughout human history another level of power has been recognized by societies. It has been the healing power of the shaman, the ritual power of the magician, or the inherent spiritual forces within the witch. Like the physical power harnessed by modern society, these spiritual forces have been used to help and to harm. Within the neopagan movement many seek to understand and utilize this spiritual power which today's people find so intangible and yet immensely fascinating.

The Bible does not neglect the subject of spiritual power, although the Christianity of the European peoples has in recent centuries found the topic something of an embarrassment. Some theologians of a liberal persuasion have tried to explain the miracles of Jesus in terms of more tangible physical laws. Christians have turned towards modern medical science rather than utilizing the resources of the Spirit of God. Even so, many Christians are rediscovering the power and authority of which the Bible speaks. Western missionaries, on going to Africa, Asia or Latin America, often find that they have much to learn in this area from the national Christians. Young Christians coming out of traditional religions are much more aware of the nature of the spiritual realm than the secularized Western missionary. I am personally indebted to African Christians who have helped to open my own eyes to the power of the gospel in releasing people under the bondage of evil spirits. These tribal people know nothing of Jungian psychology, but they do know the reality and fear of the spirit world, and what the Christian gospel has to say in addressing them.

The worldview of spiritual powers

A worldview consists of the basic assumptions held by a people concerning the cosmos, humanity, wisdom, and morality. One of the curious features of a worldview is that we are not usually aware that we have such deep assumptions, and consider it to be the logical and natural way of understanding the world in which we live.[1] Western people have tended to follow a secular, materialistic worldview in which only that which can be seen and analyzed is regarded as having any real existence. This worldview may be illustrated by the simple diagram in figure 16:1. In this worldview, God, spirits, fairies, angels, and ghosts are classed in the category of "illusion." The Bible, on the other hand, presents a somewhat different model of reality, and this is most clearly illustrated in the teachings of Jesus Christ.

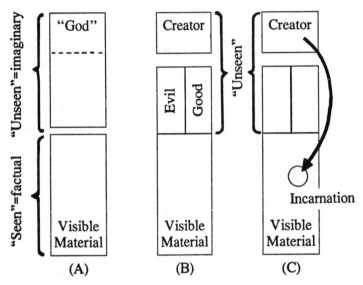

Figure 16:1 Comparison of Secular and Biblical Cosmology.

(a) Secular cosmology.
(b) Biblical cosmology, after the Fall.
(c) Biblical cosmology, with the incarnation of Jesus Christ the second Person of the Godhead.

God the Creator

Jesus had an unwavering assumption in the existence of God. God is eternal and distinct from that which He created. He is not an absentee landlord, but continues to be interested in all that goes on in His creation. God is sovereign over His creation with the power to destroy that which He has created, but instead He wills to accomplish His purposes for creation. In these purposes human beings play an important role as He is wanting them to enter into a meaningful relationship with Him. Jesus portrayed God as one who cares about human beings, but who refuses the evil that they do.

The unseen world

Jesus recognized the existence of a created world which spread beyond that of the physical world of which the materialist is so conscious. The spirit world was to Jesus as real as the physical world, and the spiritual and physical were not seen as two mutually exclusive realms. The two interpenetrated each other and influenced each other.

Jesus assumed the existence of spiritual beings eager to obey God and to serve Him. The Greek word used by the New Testament writers is *angelos* from which we obtain the word "angel" (Mt. 4:11; 13:39). Jesus was not simply expressing a superstitious belief of the Jews of His day. It was not His habit, indeed, He did not fail to correct popular opinion and traditions when they were wrong as in the case of His rebuke of the false ceremonialism of the Pharisees (Mt. 15:1–20).

The kingdom of Satan

Not only did Jesus believe in spiritual beings obedient to the creator, but He assumed the existence of those spirits in rebellion to God. The leader of this kingdom is Satan, often called in Greek *Diabolos* (the devil). Jesus always assumed that Satan was a person and not merely an evil force.

Jesus also accepted the power of Satan and the influence of his sovereignty. At the beginning of Christ's ministry He was tempted in the wilderness by Satan. "Again, the devil took Him up on an exceedingly high mountain, and showed Him all the kingdoms of the world and their glory. . . . 'All these things I will give You if You will fall down and worship me'" (Mt. 4:8–9). Jesus did not dispute the fact that Satan had the authority to do just this. "Jesus said to him, 'Away with you, Satan! For it is written, "You shall worship the LORD your God, and Him only you shall serve"'" (Mt. 4:10). There is no doubt that Jesus recognized the power of Satan. He spoke of him as being like "a strong man, fully armed" (Lk. 11:21), as "the ruler of this world" (Jn. 12:31; 14:30; 16:11), and the "ruler of the demons" (Mt. 12:24).

Not only does Jesus recognize the power of Satan and his angels, but He judges their character as evil and destructive. Jesus used various expressions of Satan. He is called "the evil one" (Mt. 6:13), "a murderer" and "a liar" (Jn. 8:44). He is powerful and cunning. He can cause physical illness as in the case of a woman who was bent double for eighteen years (Lk. 13:16), or the Gadarene man who was both a terror to himself and to others {Lk. 8:29).

Satan subtly seeks to tempt and trap human beings. The apostle Paul describes the work of Satan in the minds of unbelievers as causing blindness to the gospel: "But even if our gospel is veiled, it is veiled to those who are perishing, whose minds the god of this age has blinded, who do not believe, lest the light of the gospel of the glory of Christ, who is the image of God should shine on them" (2 Cor. 4:3, 4). The apostle Peter speaks of Satan as "your adversary the devil walks about like a roaring lion, seeking whom he may devour" (1 Pet. 5:8). Satan is not only an adversary of God, but of all humanity. Perhaps those following the satanic path especially need to give solemn thought as to whether their views and ideas of Satan are correct, or if they are actually being seduced into an evil trap.

Power confrontation

The worldview of Jesus Christ is one in which the kingdom of God is in perpetual conflict with the kingdom of Satan. He recognized a clear dichotomy between good and evil, God and Satan. This is a conflict of kingdom versus kingdom, power versus power.

The continuing message of Jesus was "the kingdom of God is at hand" (Mk. 1:15). The mission of Jesus was to enter the kingdom of Satan and win it back for the purposes of God. Charles Kraft says, "It is as if Jesus had parachuted into enemy territory, gathered followers, trained them, and then set them loose behind enemy lines with the intent of taking more and more territory from the other king."[2]

The kings of the ancient world would frequently invade the territory of neighboring peoples. If they were successful in their campaigns they would bring back some of the conquered people to their own land to be their servants. This is another relevant picture of Christ entering the kingdom of Satan and bringing back captives into the kingdom of God.

Jesus continually exercised his power and authority to oppose the kingdom of Satan. This is seen in His teaching and His healing.

> Then they went into Capernaum, and immediately on the Sabbath He entered the synagogue and taught. And they were astonished at His teaching, for He taught them as one having authority, and not as the scribes.
>
> Now there was a man in their synagogue with an unclean spirit. And he cried out, saying, "Let *us* alone! What have we to do with You, Jesus of Nazareth? Did You come to destroy us? I know who You are—the Holy One of God!"
>
> But Jesus rebuked him, saying, "Be quiet, and come out of him!"
>
> And when the unclean spirit had convulsed him and cried out with a loud voice, he came out of him. Then they were all amazed, so that they questioned among themselves, saying, "What is this? What new doctrine *is* this? For with authority He commands even the unclean spirits, and they obey Him" (Mark 1:21–27).

The Holy Spirit

The church has never found it easy to understand the nature of God, and has struggled in drafting a suitable model to describe His person. This is not surprising because if God is God then He is more than any human can comprehend, and all that any person can achieve is but an inadequate picture of an infinite deity. The model of the Trinity has often been used by the church to describe the one God in three persons. The persons of the Father and the Son have images that can be understood from normal human relations, but no such model is available for the Holy Spirit. He is, however, a person through whom the will of God is achieved.

When the Son became human He put aside the inherent powers of His divinity, and was subject to the same limited conditions as other people. Jesus did nothing supernatural until he was anointed by the Holy Spirit. "That word you know, which was proclaimed throughout all Judea, and began from Galilee after the baptism which John preached: how God anointed Jesus of Nazareth with the Holy Spirit and with power, who went about doing good and healing all who were oppressed by the devil, for God was with Him" (Acts 10:37–38).

Just as Jesus ministered in the power of the Holy Spirit, He calls His people to minister in the same manner. "So Jesus said to them again, 'Peace to you! As the Father has sent Me, I also send you.' . . . He breathed on *them*, and said to them, 'Receive the Holy Spirit'"(Jn. 20:21–22).

It is sad that the secularized worldview of most Western Christians has made it appear incredulous to them that they could know the same enabling power as Jesus Christ had known. Yet the teaching of Jesus makes this fact clear. The sorcerer Simon, with whose story we commenced this chapter, saw a greater power in the life of the missionary Philip than he ever knew in his own life. The Christians of the early church realized the power which was available to them. Charles Kraft recounts a significant conversation.

A friend of mine was chatting one day with a woman who had recently been converted to Christianity out of the occult. While in bondage to Satan, she had the gift of being able to "see" the amount of spiritual power different people carry with them. She told my friend that she had been able during that time to spot Christians "a mile off" because of the amount of power they carried! She remarked that she suspected that things might be quite different for a lot of Christians "if we only realise how much power we carry."[3]

Ministering in spiritual power

Jesus came not merely to defeat the kingdom of Satan, but to salvage from his domain a people who would minister in the same power that he knew and exercised. Even early on in His ministry, "when He had called His twelve disciples to Him, He gave them power over unclean spirits, to cast them out, and to heal all kinds of sickness and all kinds of disease" (Mt. 10:1). Later on He sent out seventy-two disciples and they "returned with joy, saying, 'Lord, even the demons are subject to us in Your name'"(Lk. 10:17).

Jesus conferred authority to the disciples. Authority needs to be distinguished from magic. Magic is the manipulation of spiritual powers by esoteric knowledge and rituals. Magic is therefore limited by the knowledge and skill of the practitioner as every magician knows. Authority, on the other hand, is that which is granted (by the one who rightly has that authority) to a person in submission to him. Authority is given to those under authority and does not depend on human skill or esoteric wisdom. Humility and meekness therefore describe the character of the person under authority, as it did with Jesus Christ who was submissive to God the Father.

The following illustration may be helpful in providing an explanation of "authority." The traffic is busy at the intersection of two roads, with cars and trucks vying with each other to cross over. Into the middle of the junction steps a policeman dressed in uniform. He raises his hand and the flow of traffic from one direction halts, and as he beckons to the other stream it moves. The policeman does not have the "power" to stop the oncoming vehicles, but he has that which is far better: he has been invested with the "authority" of the American people whose servant he is. The drivers recognize that authority and so obey.

The question may be raised as to whether Jesus has the right to grant such authority. This very issue was settled at Calvary. In His dying, Christ came under all the power of the kingdom of Satan and death. But Satan and hell could not hold Him because He had perfectly obeyed the will of the Father. As C. S. Lewis writes in the first of his Narnia stories, Aslan the lion yielded to the power of the witch in place of Edmond who had sinned and come under the witch's domain. Aslan died on the stone altar, but death could not hold him. As C. S. Lewis writes,

> "It means," said Aslan, "that though the Witch knew the Deep Magic, there is a magic deeper still which she did not know. Her knowledge goes back only to the dawn of time. But if she could have looked a little further back, into the stillness and the darkness before Time dawned, she would have read there a different incantation. She would have known that when a willing victim who had committed no treachery was killed in a traitor's stead, the Table would crack and Death itself would start working backwards."[4]

In this great parable, C. S. Lewis, who was a committed Christian, sought to express something of the wonder of what Christ accomplished through His death. This is the same wonder that lead the apostle Paul to pray for the Christians in Ephesus that they may know "what are the riches of the glory of His inheritance in the saints, and what *is* the exceeding greatness of His power toward us who believe, according to the working of His mighty power which He worked in Christ when He raised Him from the dead and seated *Him* at His right hand in the heavenly *places,* far above all principality and power and might and dominion, and every name that is named, not only in this age but also in that which is to come" (Eph. 1:18–21).

Recognizing that Christ has been given all authority in heaven and on earth (see Mt. 28:18), Christians need to learn to minister in that authority. People throughout the world are watching to see Christians put into practice that which their Bible teaches.

A means to an end

Throughout the ministry of Jesus, we never see Him using power and authority for His own use and glory. When He was hungry and tempted by Satan to turn stones into bread, He refused. When taken to a high tower and tempted to throw Himself off so that the angels would catch Him, He refused. Jesus never used His power to show off or to serve His own ends. "Jesus' use of spiritual power was always a means, never an end. He used God's power always to demonstrate God's love."[5]

This was the very issue that Simon the sorcerer failed to appreciate. "And when Simon saw that through the laying on of the apostles' hands the Holy Spirit was given, he offered them money, saying, 'Give me this power also, that anyone on whom I lay hands may receive the Holy Spirit.'

But Peter said to him, 'Your money perish with you, because you thought that the gift of God could be purchased with money!'" (Acts 8:18–20). Simon was still thinking in terms of magic rather than authority that comes only as a gift.

Authority is only given to be used in accordance with the will of the person who has ultimate authority. If the policeman on traffic control duty misuses his authority it will be removed from him. Jesus placed Himself totally under the authority of the Father, not as some mindless robot but in loving submission. Jesus could therefore say, "I always do those things that please Him" (Jn. 8:29). As the Christian lines his will up with that of the Father he is able to exercise the same authority. Jesus said, "And whatever you ask in My name, that I will do, that the Father may be glorified in the Son. If you ask anything in My name, I will do *it*" (Jn. 14:13–14). The Christian ministers through exercising authority which has already been given for use in achieving the purposes of God.

Power encounter

As the kingdom of God has grown within the world, it has continually been resisted by the kingdom of Satan in its rebellion to the will of God. The Bible expresses this conflict in terms of war, and a Christian is automatically enlisted into the army of Jesus Christ. However, Christians must be careful to understand the nature of this war.

First, it is not against other human beings, but against rebellious spiritual powers. "For we do not wrestle against flesh and blood, but against principalities, against powers, against the rulers of the darkness of this age, against spiritual *hosts* of wickedness in the heavenly *places*" (Eph. 6:12). God loves humanity and wants to redeem all that is possible within the bounds of their personal wickedness.

While refuting spiritual powers, we can ask for God's blessing on the people involved. For example, a Christian visitor to Rome had his pocket picked by a group of gypsy children and his wallet was taken. Amidst his feelings of anger, into his mind suddenly came the words, "Bless those who curse you, and pray for those who spitefully use you" (Lk. 6:28). He started to pray that God would bless those children. Suddenly the smallest of the children appeared, thrust his wallet into his hand, and quickly vanished into the crowd. He was amazed to find that nothing had been taken from the wallet. The Christian response to curses should be one of praying for the curser and asking that God would bless them.

Second, armor and weapons have been given to Christians who are commanded to "take up the whole armor of God" (Eph. 6:13). It may be useful to compare the Christian armor, described in Ephesians 6, with that mentioned earlier as used by many magicians.

Illustration	*Application*
Belt	Truth
Breastplate	Righteousness
Shoes	Readiness to take the gospel in a spirit of peace
Shield	Faith
Helmet	Salvation
Sword	Word of God

The Christian battle must not be carried out in anger and vindictiveness, but out of compassion for our fellow human beings and in an attitude of persevering prayer. The crucifixion of Christ on a human level appeared to be Christ's ultimate defeat, whereas it was to prove to be His great victory. Paradoxically, it is in weakness that the power of God is revealed within the life of the Christian.

Third, those coming out of the domain of Satan must clearly separate themselves from their old ways. This is not a matter of adopting middle-class Western morals, but of separation from the implements of evil. Spiritual power can reside in cultural forms such as words and objects, as every magician realizes. These must be dealt with if the person is to be free.

Of the magicians in Ephesus who became Christians, we read, "Also, many of those who had practiced magic brought their books together and burned *them* in the sight of all. And they counted up the value of them, and it totaled fifty thousand *pieces* of silver" (Acts 19:19). These scrolls were special talismans for safety in travel, and for these the magicians of Ephesus were famous throughout the Roman world.

In the old mansion house in which I now have an apartment, the son of one of my colleagues used to wake screaming at night. He had not done this before; he seemed a normal happy child. It was only since he had come to sleep in this particular room that the problem had occurred. Although the parents made this a matter of prayer, something still seemed wrong. Finally a search was made, and up in the roof above that bedroom spiritualist literature was found. It appears that long before this Christian family had moved into the accommodation the property had been occupied by someone who was a practicing spiritist. The literature was burned, and a group of Christians met to pray in the room to cleanse it from all that was evil. The boy never again woke with nightmares, and an atmosphere of peace filled the room.

Following this event, groups of Christians were organized to move throughout the house, almost like some military operation, praying in every room. During the twenty years since then many visitors have come to the old mansion house, and left commenting on the peaceful atmosphere that they have known there.

The magician and the witch know exactly what is being spoken of here. They know the spiritual powers that can be associated with the implements of magical ritual. They know the powers which can be released through the drawing of the circle by the wand. They also know that they cannot merely just change their minds about these activities like a person deciding not to go to a fitness club again. There has to be a distinct break. The old must be finished with, and this often requires what amounts to a rite of separation. The Ephesian magicians publicly burnt their talisman. In Africa, many tribal people come willingly to burn their fetish, idol or juju. No missionary can do this for them. They must do it with their own hands so that they can see that now that they are Christians the power of God resides in them as much as in any foreign missionary. Just as we saw earlier that many paths within the neopagan movement have rites of initiation, there needs to be a rite of separation for those who wish to be freed.

As the Christian church grows, there has always been an encounter with those forces rebellious to God. The neopagans are correct when they say that churches were built on the sites of pagan temples along ley lines. One neopagan writes: "When St. Patrick was bombing around Eire ridding the land of serpents it was not snakes he was killing . . . it was the Leys—the channels of Serpent (Dragon) energy."[6] Perhaps this writer needs to remember that this was not some alien army who invaded the Irish Celts, but a tiny band of Christians who shared the Christian message. It was the Celtic people themselves who chose to leave their traditional beliefs, and demonstrated their commitment by building churches on the very sites where they used to worship other deities. Something far superior and more powerful had come into their lives and they proved it by destroying the old for which they no longer had any use.

Exercising Christian authority

In what areas should the Christian exercise spiritual authority?

First, the area of physical healing. This tends to be the most spectacular, and so liable to misinterpretation and misunderstanding. My own personal experience has been little, but there are several cases. One occasion was on a visit to Korea. After I had finished preaching in the church, a middle-aged lady was brought to the front of the church in the wheelchair to which she had been confined for many years. "She wants you to pray for her healing," said my interpreter. I remember being filled with a sense of my own impotence. Once again I felt the tension between my own Christian experience and that which I believed was the clear teaching of the Bible. I called the elders of the church to the front as the congregation prayed fervently. I simply placed a little olive oil on her forehead in accordance with what the early church seemed to have done (Jas. 5:14). We prayed. After a few minutes the lady was able to get out of the wheelchair and she walked out of the church. She still needed someone to steady her because her legs felt weak, but she no longer needed the wheelchair.

The second area is that which many call inner healing. It is difficult to find a word that is adequate to describe what is implied here. Some have called it the healing of the emotions or memories. Carl Jung may consider it as the healing of the psyche. By "inner," what is meant is the non-physical part of a person. This cannot be entirely distinguished from the physical as it relates to the wholeness and well-being of the total person.

Broken relationships, unhappy childhoods, social, and sexual abuse are unfortunately common within contemporary society. Anger, resentment, bitterness, fear, and painful memories can continue to take their toll on the adult. Sometimes the person is unaware of the real issues, while in other cases they are aware. In some instances, there are deep psychological problems which need careful and experienced counseling, but in many cases the power of God may minister graciously to His hurting children.

The third area is the harmful effect of spiritual beings on an individual. As Michael Harner has written: "The altered state of consciousness component of the SSC includes varying degrees of trance."[7] At the lightest state the person is in control of his or her actions and has total recall of all that has occurred. At the next deeper level, the shaman may still have recall, but some animal power has taken over the control of his body. Finally, at the deepest level the person has neither recall nor any control over his or her actions. These two deeper states have often been called "possession" by many Christians, although the more accurate translation of the Greek word used in the New Testament would be "demonization."

The testimony of some who have become Christians from certain pagan paths is that they have experienced strong, if not violent, reaction from spiritual beings. The very spirits who they thought were eager to do their bidding actually held them in bondage. It required the exercise of the authority of Jesus Christ to release them from the power of these spirits, and the subsequent filling of the Holy Spirit.

Some common characteristics of demonization are as follows:

1. Sudden marked personality changes including change of voice.
2. Chronic and unexplainable fears.
3. Inexplicable depression and sadness.
4. Strong convulsions that are often destructive.
5. Perverted and degrading sexual desires.
6. Physical sickness, including epileptic convulsions.
7. Intense hatred of others and self.
8. Preternatural strength and anaesthesia to pain.
9. Irrational experiences.
10. Strong compulsion to flee from any Christian influence.

Jesus clearly assumed the authenticity of spirits and dealt with them as objective realities. One of the many examples recorded in the New Testament is that of the father who brought his tormented son to Jesus. "And as he was still coming, the demon threw him down and convulsed *him*. Then Jesus rebuked the unclean spirit, healed the child, and gave him back to his father. And they were all amazed at the majesty of God" (Lk. 9:42–43).

Finally, many new Christians become conscious of a sense of guilt and failure for all that has occurred in the past. Women who have suffered the abuse of rape often feel spoiled and defiled. God does not want to redeem His people only to leave them with an impossible burden of guilt; He wants them to know the reality of forgiveness, to know that they are like a new creation acceptable to God. "If we confess our sins, He is faithful and just to forgive us *our* sins and to cleanse us from all unrighteousness" (1 Jn. 1:9).

Jesus has given His people the authority to minister forgiveness. "If you forgive the sins of any, they are forgiven them; if you retain the *sins* of any, they are retained" (Jn. 20:23). Those who have come out of the neopagan movement have often felt the awfulness of some of the things in which they have participated. Can God forgive such atrocious acts? The resounding statement of the Bible is "yes," if only the person is willing to recognize the awfulness of sin.

For example, even some of the leaders of Nazi Germany who took part in some of the worst of the Holocaust, and some of whom participated in the neopaganism of the Nazi state, came to know Jesus Christ as their personal savior before their execution following the Nazi war trials. It does not matter whether one is Hindu, Buddhist, Muslim, Pagan or Christian by profession, there is only one way to know peace with God and that is through faith in the person and work of Jesus Christ.

The great secret that no guardian or power spirit will ever tell is that they know that their doom is certain. Jesus Christ is victor. "It is done! I am the Alpha and the Omega, the Beginning and the End. I will give of the fountain of the water of life freely to him who thirsts. He who overcomes shall inherit all things, and I shall be his God and he shall be My son" (Rev. 21:6).

Notes

1. David Burnett, *Clash of Worlds* (Monarch: Eastbourne, 1990).

2. Charles Kraft, *Christianity with Power* (Marshall-Pickering: London, 1990), p. 109.

3. Ibid., p. 125.

4. C. S. Lewis, *The Lion, the Witch and the Wardrobe* (Penguin Books: Harmondsworth, 1950), p. 148.

5. Kraft, op. cit., p. 123.

6. John Walbridge, *Moonshine* (Spring Equinox, 1990), p. 2.

7. Michael Harner, *The Way of the Shaman* (Bantam Books: Toronto, 1986), p. 62.

Postscript
to Neopagan Readers

I have written this book as an outsider who, being familiar with the traditional religions of other societies, has attempted to understand the growth of interest in the pagan tradition in Britain. I have tried to understand the rituals which are part of the various paths, and the philosophy behind these.

As a student of anthropology, I have tried to keep an academic detachment while seeking to appreciate the effect which anthropology itself has had upon the growth of the movement. I have sympathetically endeavored to understand the neopagan worldview and therefore the logic which is behind your beliefs and practices. Even so, I know that you will always consider me as an outsider. I hope, however, you will consider me to be a person who has listened to your voice and read your words, and has not merely reacted to some stereotype.

I feel as though I have sensed something of your emotions and that which drives you to look for answers in the pagan way. I am conscious also of the hurt that many of you have known from establishment Christianity, and for that I apologize. However, I would point you to the person who lies at the very heart of the church—Jesus Christ. As I have tried to understand what you believe, would you not spend a little time considering the person of Jesus Christ in whom I believe?

Please put aside the half-remembered stories from childhood and read for yourself a Gospel such as that according to Luke in the Holy Bible. If you would like to correspond with me, write to me in care of the publisher. I will do my best to respond.

I would like to close with an ancient Celtic blessing.

> Deep peace of the Running Wave to you.
> Deep peace of the Flowing Air to you.
> Deep peace of the Quiet Earth to you.
> Deep peace of the Shining Stars to you.
> Deep peace of the Son of Peace to you.

David Burnett

Appendix:

List of current pagan magazines in UK

Ace of Rods	Pagan contact magazine
Arachne	Feminist spirituality
Arwald	English Odinist Hof, Saxon-Norse Asatru faith
Ash	Earth mysteries and paganism
Awen	Keltic pagan poetry
Cauldron	Pagan journal of the old religion
Children of Sekhmet	Paganism and magic for Leo wiccans
Circle network news	Pagan and Craft newspaper
Dalriada	Pagan Celtic of Western Isles Gaelic tradition
Deosil Dance	Free-thinking pagan religions today
Downplay	Paganism, Magick, Wicca
Evohe	Pagan magical newsletter
Fenrir	Odinism & Chaos Magick
Forsight	UFO Psychic Phenomena Occult Mysticism
Gates of Annwn	Pagan contact magazine dedicated to the Old Religion
Gnosis	Journal of the Western Esoteric Tradition
Green Circle	Magic witchcraft and esoteric traditions
Greenleaf	Pagan ecology, alternative life-style
Hobgoblin	Alternative arts magazine (New 1990)
Inner Keltia	Keltic pagan religion and culture

Insight	Occult, Magick, Wicca
Isian News	Fellowship of Isis (Eire)
Kindred Spirits Quarterly	All pagans and lovers of Mother Earth.
L'Etoile	Official magazine of French wicca
Lamp of Thoth	Controversial serious occultism
Ley Hunters	Ley lines
Medicine Ways	Shamanism
Mercian Mysteries	New Earth Mysteries magazine for Midlands
Meyn Mamvro	Pagan-oriented Earth mysteries
Moonbow	Sheffield University Pagan Society
Moonshine	Shamanistic paganism
Moonstone	Pagan poetry and prose
New Celtic Review, The	Celtic festivals, philosophy, druids
New Dimensions	Kabbala, Mythology, Psychology, Gematria, New Age.
New Moon	Scottish celtic, Scottish Norse, Dionesia subjects
Northern Earth Mysteries	Journal of alignments, Earth currents, dowsing, stone circles, standings
O Fortuna!	Spiritual, Magick and ecological progress
Odalstone	Saxon-Norse heathen
Odinn	Pagan Northern Tradition, Odinism & Runes
Open Path	Open University Occult Society
ORCRO Magazine	The Occult Response to the Christian Response to the Occult
Pagan Animal Rights	
Pagan Funerals Trust	
Pagan News	Pagan news of Magick & Occult
Pagana	US Mensa
Panegyria	Pagan happenings in the Pacific North-West
Pentacle	New Age magazine for occultists in Wales.
Pipes of Pan	Pagans against nukes

Quest	Magick, Paganism, Wicca, Occult
Raven	Ancient magical knowledge
Round Merlin's Table	Western Mystery Tradition
Scot-ic Pagan	Old Religion, Paganism, Witchcraft, mythology, poetry in the celtic
Shaman's Drum	Eco-pagan, exploring pathways of shamanism and art.
Silver Wheels	Magazine aimed at uniting good pagan people.
Sirius	Occult, Gods & goddesses
Source	Journal of the Holy Wells preservation society
Spiral Magazine	Star-magick, Shamanism Paganism Wicca Nature spirit and occult fiction
Star of the West	Pagan and politics witchcraft humour
Starcraft	Devas, Channeling, New Age Shamanism
Starfire	New Aeon, Thelema, Tantra, Qabalah
Starlight	
Sut Anubis	Paganism, Wicca, Occult
The Bard	Celtic paganism
Touchwood	Paganism
Tribal Messenger	Magazine of festivals and events
Unicorn	Pagan news and views
Vigil	Journal of Wicca & Earth religion
Wiccan Gate Newsletter	Wiccan Pagan Ecology Folklore Animal Rights
Wiccan Rede	Craft
Wiccan Way	Craft
Wiccan, The	Newsletter of the Pagan Federation
Witching Well	Pagan newsletters of the Old Ways
Wood and Water	Ecopaganism, Goddess oriented

Index